Clyde Built

Clyde Built

*Blockade Runners, Cruisers and Armoured Rams
of the American Civil War*

Eric J. Graham

BIRLINN

First published in 2006 by
Birlinn Limited
West Newington House
10 Newington Road
Edinburgh EH9 1QS

www.birlinn.co.uk

Hardback
ISBN10: 1 84158 424 X
ISBN13: 978 1 84158 424 9

Paperback
ISBN10: 1 84158 584 X
ISBN13: 978 1 84158 584 0

British Library Cataloguing-in-Publication Data
A catalogue record for this book is available from the British Library

Typeset by Iolaire Typesetting, Newtonmore
Printed and bound by Antony Rowe Ltd, Chippenham

Contents

Foreword   vii

Acknowledgements   ix

List of Illustrations and Maps   xi

Introduction   1

Chapter 1: The Blockade   9

Chapter 2: The Clyde and the War at Sea 1861   27

Chapter 3: The Boom Years 1862–4   42

Chapter 4: The Clyde's Private Runners   71

Chapter 5: The Search for Speed   101

Chapter 6: The Search for Cruisers and Rams   123

Chapter 7: The Legacy   158

Appendix 1: Jules Verne in Glasgow   173

Appendix 2: The Black American Community
                    in Glasgow   174

Appendix 3: Letter from Blockade-running
                    Captain W. Russell to Thomas S. Begbie   176

Appendix 4: Sample of a Blockade Cargo Sale Notice   179

Appendix 5: Technical Notes and Measurements   181

Appendix 6: List of Vessels by Builder   185

Appendix 7: Who's Who in Blockade Running   216

Appendix 8: A Guide to Sources   221

Selected Bibliography   225

Index   229

Foreword

This is a remarkable book which uncovers the secret history of Scotland's key role during the American Civil War in blockade-running to the Confederate States. Outnumbered and outgunned, the Confederacy had a desperate need for arms from overseas and, at the same time, some means to sell cotton from southern plantations in European markets to obtain invaluable foreign currency to prosecute the war effort. There was only one problem. The Federal Government had immensely greater naval resources and so sought to bankrupt the enemy by encircling Confederate ports, imposing a rigorous blockade and starving the forces of the South of key resources. One reason why this strategy did not work in the short-run was the successful blockade-busting tactics of the Confederacy.

Now, in Eric Graham's meticulously researched book, the full story is told for the first time of how Clyde-built steamers were central to breaking the cordons of Union warships around the ports of the South. Using hitherto unexplored press sources and private archives, Graham has written a book which is at once a sound history of Scottish blockade-running and at the same time an exciting tale of adventure on the high seas, brimming with colourful episodes and extraordinary characters. The stakes were high – certainly the impounding of the ship and, for officers and crew, the possibility of trial as pirates. But the profits to be made by those willing to gamble on such a venture were also huge. At the height of the American Civil War it was estimated even two return trips could pay for the building and fitting-out of a blockade runner. After that, it was all clear profit.

Graham provides a boldly revisionist account of Scotland's role in the great conflict across the Atlantic. Ostensibly the nation was vehemently anti-slavery and so publicly supported Abraham Lincoln's crusade to abolish this moral evil. But business was business and, as this book reveals in convincing detail, many respectable Scottish merchants and shipbuilders were at the heart of a clandestine trade which brought great benefit to the Confederate cause. In 1864 at least twenty-seven Clydeside yards, employing around 25,000 men, were building blockade-runners as they tried to keep up with the insatiable demand from the southern American states. In that year alone, fifty runners were launched on the river, and the South became dependent on them for basic commodities, including food supplies. In addition, as many as 3,000 Scots served on these vessels while vital need for both higher speed and greater fuel efficiency pushed the Clydeside engineers to produce ever more efficient boilers. This was the economic context within which John Elder developed highly innovative 'compound engine' which served to consolidate Scotland's hegemony in global shipbuilding for many years to come.

Eric Graham's study is, therefore, Scottish history at its best. Written with both verve and panache it will attract a wide readership as an accomplished work of historical detection. But the book is much more than that. Graham's researches have also provided new perspectives on Scotland and the American Civil War, the history of Clyde shipbuilding and the shadowy nature of commercial relationships during a great transatlantic conflict. It deserves the highest praise.

T. M. Devine, OBE, DLitt, FRSE, HonMRIA, FBA
Sir William Fraser Chair of Scottish History and Palaeography
University of Edinburgh

Acknowledgements

My gratitude goes out to a small circle of like-minded associates – Tom Barclay, Michael Dun, David Hamilton and Graham Hopner – whose help and suggestions were, at times, inspirational. David's selfless contribution of his notes from the Greenock newspapers and general advice on technical aspects have, in particular, been greatly appreciated.

Sections of this book were greatly enriched by the help of genealogists – Martin Collyer, Sheila Duffy, Norman Leslie and John McCreadie – to whom I extend my appreciation.

I wish to thank the staff of the Information Section of Dumbarton Library for their active assistance with the Dumbarton newspapers and Denny records. Likewise, the staff of the Glasgow University Archive Services must be commended for their exceptional help with access to the Begbie and Scott letters – if only all custodians were so enlightened!

My wife, Jan, as always, has been key – providing support, acting as a sounding board and as a reviewer for all of this.

Eric J. Graham
Edinburgh, 2006

List of Illustrations and Maps

1 John Bull inviting Cousin Jonathan to sign the Declaration of Paris, *Punch* 1856
2 American View of the European response to the blockade, *Harper's Weekly* 1861
3 Chasing a blockade runner, *Harper's Weekly* 1861
4 Johnny Bull feeding the serpent, *Harper's Weekly* 1861
5 The British view of the Civil War, *Punch* 1862
6 British view of the *Trent* Incident, *Punch* 1862
7 John Bull's store of contraband, *Harper's Weekly* 1862
8 Palmerston and Napoleon confer on intervention, *Punch* 1862
9 British view of Lincoln's Emancipation of Slavery Proclamation, *Punch* 1862
10 American view of British duplicity, *Harper's Weekly* 1863
11 Lord Palmerston passing President Davis, *Punch* 1864
12 The question of neutrality, *Punch* 1864
13 Capture of Fort Fisher, January 1865
14 Britannia and Columbia – first move towards a settlement, *Punch* 1871
15 The inflated 'Alabama' claims, *Punch* 1871
16 The launch of Jules Verne's *Dolphin* – 1876 edition
17 The *Giraffe* undergoing conversion in the Meadowside Dock, Glasgow 1862
18 Model of the pre-war-*Alliance* (1856)
19 The *Alliance* as the *New Zealand*, *Australian Illustrated News* 1865
20 The blockade runner *Princess Royal* as a Federal armed blockader
21 A model of the *Evelyn*
22 Blockade runner entering Nassau, *Harper's Weekly* 1863
23 Run cotton bales at Nassau
24 John N. Maffitt onboard the blockade runner *Lilian*, *London Illustrated News* 1864
25 The crippled blockade-runner *Lilian*, preparing to surrender on 24 August 1864

26 Share certificate of the Universal Trading Company (Glasgow University Archives)
27 Drawing of the *Fingal* at Greenock
28 The *Fingal* undergoing conversion to the CSS *Atlanta*, 1862
29 The capture of the CCS *Atlanta* by the USS *Weehawken*, 1863
30 The USS *Atlanta*
31 Pre-war paddle steamers at the Woodyard, Dumbarton
32 The CSS *Shenandoah*
33 The CSS *Shenandoah* receiving guests at Melbourne
34 The *Pampero* laying in the Clyde, *London Illustrated News* 1865
35 Scottish Law Officers ponder the *Pampero* Affair
36 Plan of the North's *Ram*
37 North's Ram as the HDMS *Danmark*
38 US Secretary of the Navy Gideon Welles (ESME Library)
39 CS Secretary of the Navy Stephen Mallory (ESME Library)
40 US Secretary William Seward (ESME Library)
41 US Minister Charles Adams (ESME Library)
42 Prime Minister Lord Palmerston (ESME Library)
43 Foreign Secretary Lord Russell (ESME Library)
44 James D. Bulloch CSN (ESME Library)
45 John Wilkinson CSN, blockade runner (ESME Library)
46 John N. Maffitt, captain of the Confederate *Florida* (ESME Library)
47 Captain David Leslie and his family on the steps of his 'Bermuda' villa, Dunoon (Leslie Family Collection)
48 John Scott of Greenock (West Dunbartonshire Libraries)
49 Peter Denny of Dumbarton (West Dunbartonshire Libraries)
50 Jules Verne (ESME Library)

Maps

1 The American Eastern Seaboard and Gulf of Mexico   xiii
2 The Approaches to Charleston   xiv
3 The Approaches to Wilmington   xv
4 The River Clyde and Firth of Clyde   xvi
5 The Clyde Shipyards   xvii

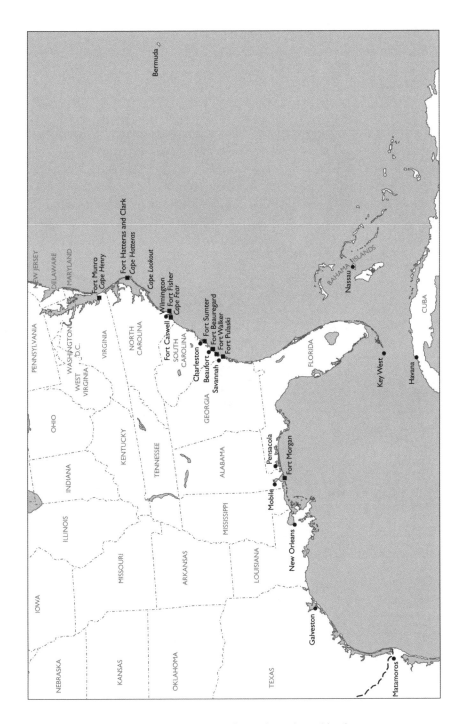

The American Eastern Seaboard and Gulf of Mexico

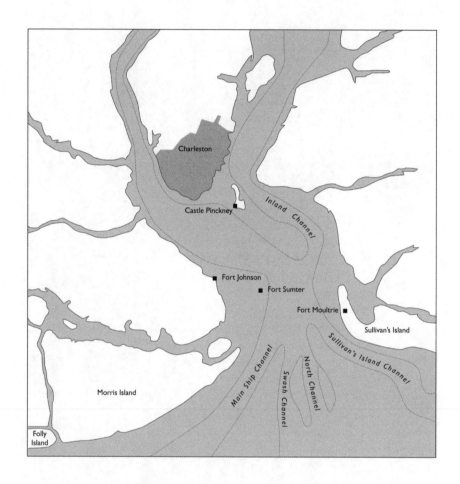

The Approaches to Charleston

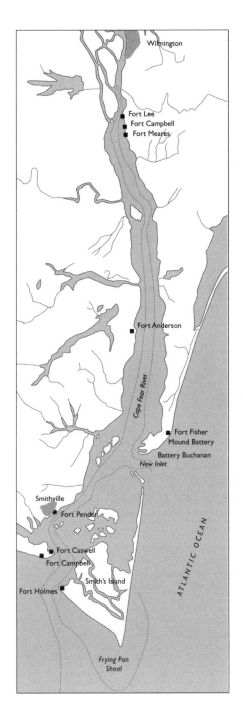

The Approaches to Wilmington

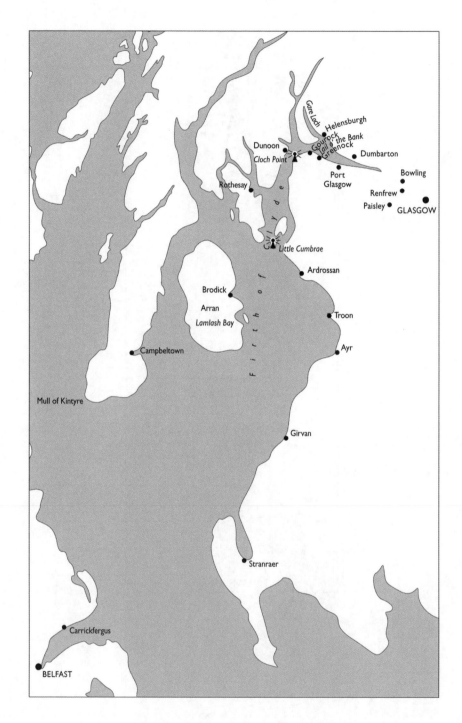

The River Clyde and Firth of Clyde

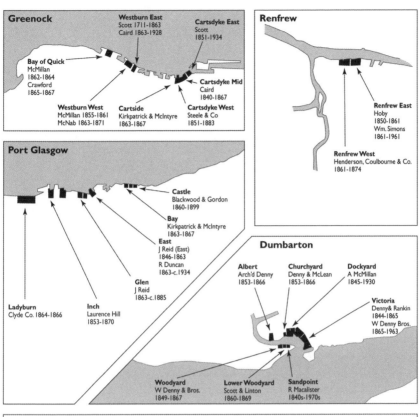

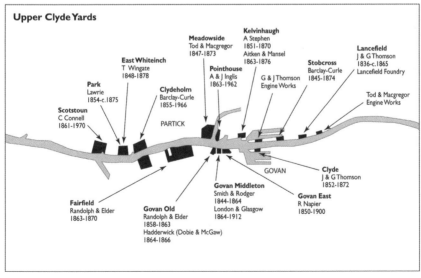

The Clyde Shipyards

Introduction

Set amidst the tumult of the American Civil War (1861–5), Margaret Mitchell's romantic epic, *Gone with the Wind*, has the suave pragmatic businessman Rhett Butler as the principal male character. It would be fair to say that many cinemagoers, mesmerised by so many dramatic sunsets, left their seats with only a vague recollection as to how the lavishly spending Rhett came by his money. He was the mastermind behind a complex 'blockade-running' operation.

This was the extremely lucrative business of running arms and luxuries in – and cotton out – from the beleaguered Southern ports in fast steamers. There were extraordinary profits to be made for those willing to gamble on such a venture – at the height of the war it was reckoned that two return trips paid for the vessel.

At sea, this evolved into a highly dangerous game of 'hare and hounds', played out on quarter or moonless nights by sleek steamers, blacked out and painted off-white or battleship grey. Having made the three-day ocean crossing from Bermuda or Nassau they sought to hug the calmer inshore line away from the influence and rough currents of the Gulf Stream. The 'game' was then to sneak up to one of the channels of the few Confederate-held ports during the night. If discovered, they would rely on their greater speed to charge through the inner lines of blockading Federal gunboats to gain the protection of a Confederate coastal battery. If the stakes for the men who ran the blockade were high, then so too were the rewards. The most successful captains received $5,000 in gold per run and the chief engineers half that amount.

Blockade running, despite being the key to the Confederate war effort, remains an interesting historical aside, traditionally overshadowed by the dramatic exploits of the few ironclads the Confederates managed to launch and by the sea raiders they slipped out of British shipyards.

The few books that have appeared on the exploits of the unarmed blockade runners have been written mainly by American academics, and hence from the American perspective. Most acknowledge in passing that the Clyde, as the producer of the fastest steamers in the world, was a prime supplier of these vessels. Recently, scholarly books and articles have gone to great lengths to catalogue exhaustively the three hundred odd individual steamers and the thousands of runs they made through the blockade. Much detail regarding their builders, owners and hull dimensions has been compiled in these publications from the records of Federal prize courts, American consular archives and Confederate Customs books.

From these lists it is quite evident that more than a third of the steamers that ran the blockade were 'CB' – Clyde-built. This statement is readily verifiable from the contemporary Clydeside newspapers. Indeed, the Glasgow newspaper *Morning Journal* published a full list in the closing stages of the war (14 January 1865) with the caveat:

There may be some little inaccuracy or incompleteness, but this was unavoidable due to the nature of the trade, publicity in many instances being rather avoided than courted, and many of the vessels having changed hands and names on arriving at the South. The table, however, will generally be found correct.

In stark contrast, the few modern short articles that have appeared in Scotland on this subject are the work of a small band of dedicated steamer enthusiasts. Published in such commendable specialist journals as the *Clyde River Steamer Club* magazine, their interest has been restricted to relating the pedigree and incredible war exploits of a few noted Clyde steamers.

It follows that very few Scots or Americans are fully aware of the extent of the Clyde's involvement in the Confederate cause. Far beyond merely being the location where many of their vessels were built, the Clyde is also the source of many of the runners' crews – certainly a high proportion of their captains and engineers. The Scots involvement is inextricably linked with, and a near perfect mirror image of, the much better known Merseyside experience.

Where the action storyline has been told previously, the focus has been, quite understandably, on the events which took place along the American seaboard. The human interest invariably centres on the dare-doing of a handful of determined naval officers who served as the captains of the few Confederate government-owned runners. These young men drove their steamers through hails of shells flying the

Confederate flag – in true Southern cavalier fashion – to deliver vital arms, munitions and war supplies from the warehouse islands of the Bahamas, Bermuda and Cuba.

A few wrote vivid personal accounts which were published in the aftermath of the war. Their thrilling, often romanticised, tales of racing through the darkness on their Clyde-built steeds, turpentine-soaked cotton blazing in the boilers, safety valves tied down, a loaded revolver on the lap (should the nerve of the Scots engineer fail), adds that sense of high adventure to their exploits. In most accounts they readily admit to succumbing to the intoxicating mixture of flirting with mortal danger during a hot pursuit at sea and a swaggering life onshore after a successful run. As the Scots Captain William Watson reflected on his 'retirement' from the running business: 'privation, danger and anxiety – on the whole a rather enjoyable occupation, with something of the zest of yacht-racing – a kind of exciting sport of the higher order'.

Occasionally, they mention the extraordinary profits made by the real 'Rhett Butlers', such as the formidable George A. Trenholm of Charleston. These men ran in everything from Austrian field howitzers and British Enfield rifles to vintage French champagne and Glasgow-bought ladies' corsets. Arguably, their businesses, when combined with the covert procurement operations in Europe, represented the most effective organisations within the Confederacy's otherwise ram-shackle war effort.

Unlike the heroic Confederate commanders, the Scots who served on the runners – perhaps as many as 3,000 – were careful to conceal their involvement on returning home. Those who had been captured and spent a short time in a Federal jail, took particular care not to let their past exploits be known. They knew they stood first in line to be prosecuted as mercenaries under the British Foreign Enlistment Act (1819).

Safeguarding their anonymity was the fact that none returned to the Clyde on the steamers they took out to the blockade. As often as not, their charges lay wrecked in the approaches to Charleston, Wilming-ton, Mobile or Galveston. Those not sunk or captured by the time the Confederacy collapsed were put up for sale at knock-down prices at the crowded quays of Havana and Nassau.

With the exception of Watson, the few Scots who did recount their exploits in print did so under pseudonyms – such as the Aberdeen-shire-born 'Mack' – and changed or blanked the name of their vessels to reduce further the risk of being identified later. Those who had served as captains had the most pressing reason to take the greatest care. At the height of the war, the Federal consuls residing in St George (Bermuda) and Nassau (Bahamas) had employed artists to sketch the most successful captains and their vessels. Indeed, the most persistent 'offenders' were branded 'pirates' by the Federal government and faced severe penalties if caught.

At the time these drawings were copied and distributed to the blockader commanders as an aid to ready identification. This caused the less foolhardy of the 'pirate' captains to try and pass themselves off as passengers when their vessels were stopped and boarded on the high seas. After the war, it was assumed by those involved in running that these drawings would eventually be handed over to the British government so that they might be prosecuted for breaching British neutrality.

For similar reasons, piecing together the murky world of the Clyde shipbuilders' dealings with the network of covert Confederate agents and private speculators who frequented their yards and vied for the newest vessels is a detective story in its own right. The evidence fully justifies the claims made at the time by the US consuls in Glasgow that there was a widespread conspiracy to supply the South with blockade runners and warships.

Adding confusion to the story of the Scots involvement in blockade running is the propensity of contemporary commentators, on both sides of the 'pond', to refer to all things 'British' as 'English'. In this manner, a Clyde-built steamer arriving at Bermuda from the Clyde and manned by a predominantly locally raised crew would be reported as a new arrival from 'England'. This irritating convention persists to the present day and still raises the hackles of even the most accommodating Scot.

The aim of this book is to illuminate the contribution of the Clyde, in all its manifestations, to this tragic war – one that claimed more American lives than the sum of all wars since.

If there are new 'heroes' in this book, it is the Clyde steamers and their transatlantic crews (the average crew size for a blockade runner was forty-five men) on one side, and the local Clydeside Emancipation Societies that dogged the shipbuilders and the government, on the other. They are heroes who, it must be said, were often pawns in a dark diplomatic game played between British and American foreign secretaries and their combatant ambassadors and consuls. Their incessant rowing over Britain's 'narrow' interpretation of neutrality is a major theme throughout. It was this interpretation that allowed 'free trade' Britain to maintain its 'laissez-faire' attitude towards the thinly disguised blockade-busting business activities of the Clyde shipbuilders and owners during the war.

This attitude was maintained until very late in the war – as long as all pretence of peaceful trading was kept up – namely, that the steamer was unarmed, sailed from the Clyde for a declared neutral destination, was under the command of a British master and flew the Union Jack. A month or so later the same vessel would be discovered under the illumination of rocket flares, haring through the lines of blockaders under a Southern commander with the Confederate flag streaming from the jack.

The new information at the core of this book is gleaned from local Clydeside Customs accounts, newspapers and business records. When collated, they bring out from the shadows those Confederate agents and private speculators who initially outwitted the officers of the British government and the hired detectives working for the resident US consul in Glasgow.

Much new light is shed on this area from the extensive correspondence of 'London-Scottish' Thomas Stirling Begbie, Britain's very own 'Rhett Butler', to his shipbuilding partner John Scott of Greenock. His letters (over a thousand in number over the period 1855–66) were found in a chest in the clock tower of Scott's Cartsdyke Dockyard in 1986. The bulk of them cover the war years and trace the fortunes of his personal dealings in blockade running. They abound with great technical detail of his runners, interspersed with very personal and spontaneous views of political and military events as they unfold.

Begbie was a major player from the very beginning. At the height of the war he set up two private joint-stock companies, the 'Albion Trading Company' and the 'Universal trading Company', which sent out fleets of steamers to the blockade. Both firms were described as 'principally of Glasgow' and attracted speculators from the Clydeside business elite, including the future lord provost of Glasgow.

Begbie's manic 'wheeling and dealing' is but one facet of this grim tale of intrigue and deception on Clydeside. Whilst he went about his blockade-running business, Confederate agents covertly ordered large ocean-going vessels for conversion to armed cruisers and a great armoured ram. The latter was twice the size of the more famous 'Laird's rams' built on the Mersey.

The cruisers were to be sent out around the world to raid the shipping of the Union. The intention was to draw away the best US warships from the blockade. The rams were intended to arrive off

Wilmington and Charleston and sink the blockading fleets, destroy the Union's naval dockyards, bombard Washington and go on to liberate New Orleans. Had the Confederates been successful in their plans, the blockade would have been breached and the entire course of the war (and perhaps even the final outcome) dramatically changed.

Scotland has a separate legal system from that of England. It is therefore in the records of the Scottish High Courts of Judiciary and Exchequer that the story of the battle to impound the warships built on the Clyde is to be found.

The other great struggle during the war was for the 'hearts and minds' of the workforce of the Clyde shipyards and of the cotton mills of west-coast Scotland. This aspect of the conflict is rarely, if ever, mentioned. This book seeks to rectify this omission by relating the vital role played by the local Emancipation Societies in mobilising the campaign to expose and halt the cruiser and ram building programmes in the Clyde.

Support of the abolitionist cause and President Lincoln's war with the slave-owning secessionists often involved personal acts of sacrifice. Whistleblowing by shipyard workers incurred instant dismissal and blacklisting. Likewise, the unshakeable moral stand taken by the mill workers, many made destitute by the 'cotton famine', is a truly humbling story. This show of solidarity and moral fortitude profoundly influenced Scottish middle-class opinion at the time as to whether or not the masses should be given the vote.

This book concludes with the legacy of the war. The fate of the thoroughbred 'CB' runners which survived the war has been traced where possible. Around twenty of those captured were acquired by the Federal navy and sent out as 'poachers-turned-gamekeepers' to the blockading squadrons. After the war they continued to perform illustrious naval service under the Stars and Stripes.

Those that avoided capture or wrecking were sold around the world at the end of the war. Some ended their days in places as far-flung as Chile and New Zealand. The last known survivor was the *Little Ada*, launched in 1861 by William Simons & Company of Renfrew, which finally succumbed to ice off Great Captain's Island, Connecticut in 1940. Such durability stands as a fitting testimony to the magnificent engineering skills of the Clyde shipbuilders from three-quarters of a century earlier.

Indeed, the great advances made in marine technology provided the launch pad for the 'Golden Age' of the Clyde Steamer. The speeds achieved by the custom-built blockade runners towards the end of the war were never exceeded until the introduction of the steam turbine in the early twentieth century. Similarly, the blockade runners set new standards in the field of marine endurance. Towards the end of the war, the pressing need was to complete a round running trip (over 1,000 miles) on a single bunkering of coal. The challenge was to reduce coal consumption without incurring a loss in speed. This pushed the Clyde engineers to develop much more efficient boilers that produced higher steam pressures and engines that optimised the energy extracted and converted into forward motion. John Elder's ground-breaking 'compound marine engine' was developed during the war. It paved the way for the Clyde's domination of the world's shipbuilding industry that lasted well into the twentieth century.

New business opportunities were also created by this conflict. Plotting the post-war fortunes of the major Clydeside players illustrates the ease with which they converted their ill-gotten gains from the blockade into highly respectable business pursuits. Neither they nor their captains were ever prosecuted under the Foreign Enlistment Act. Most enjoyed the fruits of their labours, without the slightest hint of social stigma for their actions. This cannot be said of their Confederate partners, many of whom were imprisoned or lived in exile after the destruction of 'Dixie'.

On the diplomatic front, the most lasting legacy was the restoration of good relations between Britain and the reunited America. Seven years after the war ended, the two nations reached a historical agreement to let the International Tribunal of Arbitration sitting in Geneva settle their outstanding grievances. There the American delegation pressed for reparations. The crux of their case was that Palmerston and his cabinet had displayed a gross lack of 'due diligence' in policing the neutrality of their subjects during the war. One specific charge, for 'indirect' damages, was that they had abjectly failed to stop the departure of British-built blockade runners and refused to order their governors in Bermuda and the Bahamas to close their ports to the running trade. Had they done so, General Robert E. Lee's armies in Virginia would probably have crumbled for a dire want of arms and munitions after their crushing defeat at Gettysburg (June 1863). Had they not been resupplied by the runners, the Confederacy would have been forced to accept that the war was unwinnable and so come to terms. This would have shortened the bloodletting by nearly two years.

The claim for 'indirect' damages at Geneva was, therefore, for the entire cost of the war damage since that battle. This was over and above settlement for the 'direct' damage done to their merchant fleets by the Confederate armed raiders that were not prevented from leaving the Mersey and the Clyde. William Gladstone, then Chancellor of the Exchequer, calculated that these two claims amounted to a staggering £8 billion. The Clyde's share in the liability, by a very crude reckoning based on numbers of runners and cruisers it supplied, would have been around one-third.

As it transpired, common sense prevailed. The Americans dropped the 'indirect' claim and Britain accepted liability for $15.5 million in damages as final settlement of the 'direct' claim. So ended a century of mistrust and rivalry between the two nations that laid the foundations for the cordial relations that exist to this day.

Chapter 1

The Blockade

Jules Verne's story *The Blockade Runners* is a moral tale of the fidelity of a daughter seeking her father in the midst of the American Civil War. The novel opens on a bleak winter's day, 3 December 1862, just over a year since the outbreak of this terrible conflict. The scene is that of an immense crowd milling round Meadowside Dock, where the River Kelvin joins the River Clyde and just a short walk from Glasgow's city centre.

The object of their attention was the newly completed *Dolphin*, which stood on the slipway of Tod & McGregor's shipyard. She was a large twin screw steamer built for Playfair & Company of Glasgow. To great applause and loud huzzahs this elegant shallow-draught vessel, constructed from a composite of iron and wood, obligingly slipped stern-first into the murky waters of the River Clyde. There she halted in mid-channel, caught by her restraining chains.

The reason for such a turnout of Glasgow's rank and file was not her size. Indeed, most of the spectators who had trekked to the dock would have been well used to witnessing the launching of much larger ships. Clydeside was then the busiest steam shipbuilding area in the world. Their presence in such great numbers was due to the well-founded rumour that she was purpose-built to run the blockade of the Confederate ports of war-ravaged America.

Verne presented it as public knowledge that she was to be fitted with two 'state of the art' 500-horsepower engines from Robert Napier's world-famous Lancefield Foundry, which was situated a short distance upriver from the Meadowside Dock. These mighty high-pressure steam engines were capable of pushing her through the water at a sustained thirteen knots. At such a speed she could – with the aid of a dark night, a high tide and a good measure of luck – run through the lines of lumbering Federal ships blockading the ports of the South.

In Verne's story, the two active partners in this 'peculiar trade' (as Edinburgh's *Scotsman* newspaper dubbed blockade running in the real world) had hatched their money-spinning scheme six months earlier in the Tontine Coffee House, situated under the arches of the Glasgow Town Hall. Captain James Playfair first discussed the prospect of a high-risk venture with his uncle, Vincent Playfair, founder and senior partner of the firm. He did so as they pored over the most recent war reports in the *New York Tribune*, the *New York Herald*, the *Richmond Inquirer* and the *American Review*. These newspapers had recently been imported by the New York steam packets via Queenstown (Cork).

Their news on the Civil War was over a fortnight old, as the transatlantic telegraph cable laid by the *Great Eastern* before the war had mysteriously gone dead after carrying only one message. Even so, there was no reason to change their view that the armies of the Confederacy were more than holding their own. It was, however, far from being a one-sided list of Southern victories. Back in April, New Orleans, the greatest conduit for the all-important cotton exports and European imports, had succumbed to a Federal amphibious force led by the audacious Flag Officer David Glasgow Farragut.

The Confederate ports on the Atlantic seaboard were, however, still accessible as their approaches were well protected by great coastal fortresses that were assumed to be unassailable from the sea. The conclusion reached by the Playfairs, lounging in the comfort of the Glasgow coffee house, was that this horrendous fratricidal conflict would be a long, bloody and costly one.

While this was a terrible prospect for those engaged in the severely depressed cotton textile industry of west-coast Scotland, it offered the potential for glittering rewards for those prepared – like the fictional James Playfair – to exploit the windfalls of war. He aimed to emulate the British-flagged steamer *Bermuda* which had, only three months before, run the blockade directly from West Hartlepool in the Mersey into Savannah, Georgia and back. In so doing she had reaped a fortune for her owners, Fraser, Trenholm & Company of Liverpool.

Verne's character Playfair reckoned that to join in this highly lucrative and growing trade, his firm needed only to acquire a new fast shallow-draught steamer with which to run in a cargo of vital munitions and war supplies. He would then use her speed to race her out again, through the blockading fleets, with a cargo of desperately needed cotton for the 25,000 idle looms in the mills of Glasgow and its hinterland.

The profit margin of this private venture was potentially enormous. The thirty-year-old captain reckoned that 'there are two millions of pounds to be gained in less than a month' if he made for Charleston, the most beleaguered of the Southern ports. He regaled his nervous uncle

with the scene of the quays at Charleston choked with cotton bales – all
to be had for a pittance. In addition, the Confederate military commander, General Beauregard, was certain to pay a 'golden price' for his cargo
of munitions, clothing, blankets and medicines for his bedraggled army.
Indeed, one successful round trip would pay for the *Dolphin* – and more.

He pressed his uncle that this was a business opportunity not to be
missed, as the situation might soon change. The British newspapers
were then confidently predicting that Lord Palmerston's government
would, along with that of Emperor Napoleon III's of France, soon
bow to public sentiment and recognise the Confederate States of
America as an independent nation. If this was to happen it was
thought that British and French ironclads would soon break the
blockade in the name of 'freedom of trade' with the fledging nation
– after which the opportunity to make a super-profit would be lost.

James assured his uncle that all Playfair & Company had to risk
was 'a ship and a cargo . . . a crew and a captain'. Should the venture
fail, there would be no comeback on the company from the British
government – as long as things were 'kept quiet'. If the captain was
captured, as long as he had not offered armed resistance, he and his
crew would have to endure a short spell in a Federal jail before the
British Consulate secured their release as non-combatants.

By the time of the *Dolphin*'s departure from the Clyde, at the
beginning of January 1863, the conflict had been in progress for
twenty-one months. During the seven months it took to build, launch
and dispatch her, the military situation had changed considerably – and
not in the direction that her owners had first anticipated. Despite great
provocation early in the war, there had been no move to break the
blockade by British or French naval forces. Indeed, it was now increasingly unlikely that such a turn of events would ever occur. The early
victories of the Confederate armies had since been checked and largely
negated, primarily due to a lack of war supplies of every description.
Federal naval forces, under Flag Officer Samuel Du Pont, had stormed
the isolated island forts guarding Port Royal Sound (South Carolina),
Pamlico Sound (North Carolina) and Fort Pulaski at the entrance to the
Savannah River (Georgia). Their acquisition by the North, following
ferocious naval bombardments, effectively closed the approaches to
these seaports to all but the most foolhardy of Confederate sympathisers.
The addition of these forts to those already held in Florida (Pensacola
Bay and Key West) created a chain of secure repair shops, wharves and
coal bunkers along the length of the Confederate coastline for the two
Federal blockading squadrons on the Atlantic seaboard.

Charleston and Wilmington were the last great Atlantic-facing Confederate ports still approachable. Their mighty coastal defences and complex channels made it impossible for the blockading squadrons to close them fully. They were, however, now just three hours' steaming away from a Federal naval base. The blockade could no longer be called a 'paper blockade', as the South's supporters in the British House of Commons had sought to label it since the outbreak of the war.

The latest American newspaper reports reaching Glasgow assumed that the forts guarding the Confederate ports in the Gulf of Mexico – Mobile and Galveston – were next on the list for capture by Farragut, the legendary Federal Naval Commander. Mobile (Alabama) was reckoned to be his immediate target, as this was last port of any depth in the Gulf which also had a railway link (albeit tenuous) to the Confederate armies fighting in the North. Galveston (Texas) was a remote outpost in the scheme of things and it was thought that this would be a lower priority – to be dealt with in due course.

All of this, ironically, played into the fictitious James Playfair's hands. The more chronic the supply situation became for the South, the higher the prices and the greater the fortune to be made by those bold enough to run the blockade.

The Playfairs were somewhat late in entering this fast-moving business. To meet the escalating demand for fast shallow-draught runners that could run over the estuary sandbars and shoals of the Southern ports, the Clyde had already been stripped of most of the prime deep-water steamers. Many were acquired by agents working for companies operating on behalf of the individual States or by the few centralised government departments of the Confederacy. By mid-1862 they too were facing stiff competition from private speculators in the United Kingdom anxious to cash in on the plight of the Southern States.

Thirty Clyde steamers had already crossed the Atlantic by the time the *Dolphin* left the Broomielaw in January 1863. These were the cream of the deep-water screw 'channel class' Irish Sea and Isle of Man ferries and larger side-paddle 'river class' steamers. They typically went via Madeira or Tenerife, after which they headed for the British islands of Bermuda or the Bahamas. These islands were, along with the port of Havana in Cuba, the offshore warehouses for this profit-driven and, at times, reckless trade.

During the year that followed (1863), a similar number of Clyde steamers left to join them. By December of that year, the *Scotsman* declared with some trepidation 'that there will soon be scarcely a swift steamer left in the Clyde'. In the last full year of the conflict (1864), as the building programme swung into high gear in the Clyde, over fifty steamers set out across the Atlantic flying the British flag. By early February 1865, as the Confederacy teetered on the verge of collapse, the *Scotsman* reflected that ninety-nine Clyde steamers had crossed to serve as runners, with a further eleven on their way out.

The final tally will probably never be settled, such was the degree of name changing and 'cover-up' surrounding 'the trade'. Perhaps as many as 150 steamers were involved; certainly 115 can clearly be identified. A handful are known to have been lost in transit. Their loss was not unexpected, as the smallest were just over sixty tons (registered) and had never before sailed outside the confines of the Firth of Clyde.

Only the month before, the Glasgow newspaper the *Morning Journal* had crowed the merits of 'CB' (Clyde-built):

> To say a vessel is 'CB' is a guarantee far superior to the 'A1' of Lloyd's. Such has been the confidence in 'CB' that after almost all our crack river and deep sea steamers had been purchased up, at prices exceeding by half their original cost, London, Liverpool, Ireland, and the Isle of Man were ransacked for Clyde-built vessels.

The article's sense of pride was, however, tempered by the grim reports that at least seventy of them had been destroyed or captured, leaving only twenty-nine still running the blockade.

Such articles were commonplace during the war. All were, however, careful to not to specify the purchasers or name the captains employed or mention their ultimate destination beyond St George in Bermuda or Nassau in the Bahamas. This cynical game of 'nod and wink' was played out the length of Clydeside, all to the great profit of the master shipbuilders. It was not a small rogue element in an otherwise law-abiding industry. The outraged US consuls in Glasgow reckoned that twenty-seven yards situated along the twenty-six miles of the River Clyde were involved in building a blockade runner or an armed raider for the Confederacy during the war years. Certainly all the major yards were involved.

The diplomatic stage for this unique and highly charged contest at sea had been set five years earlier, in 1856. In the immediate aftermath of the Crimean War, the 'plenipotentiary ambassadors' of the great maritime nations gathered at the Congress of Paris. Their common aim was to eradicate the contradictions in the 'Law of Nations' which 'in time of war has long been the subject of deplorable disputes that jeopardised international relations'.

The outcome was the 'Declaration of Paris' (16 April) which set out the four new basic rules to be followed in the event of a future international maritime conflict. These rules were remarkably free of convoluted legal jargon and deceptively simple:

1. Privateering is and remains abolished.
2. The neutral flag covers enemy's goods, with the exception of contraband of war.
3. Neutral goods, with the exception of contraband of war, are not liable to capture under an enemy's flag.
4. Blockades, in order to be binding, must be effective – that is to say, maintained by a force sufficient to prevent access to the coast of the enemy.

Led by Britain and France, all the major European maritime powers attending the Congress signed the Declaration. They did so in the conviction that they were witnessing the dawn of a new era in international relations – 'that the maxims which they now proclaim cannot but be received with gratitude by the whole world'. With missionary zeal the Declaration proclaimed that:

The Governments of the undersigned Plenipotentiaries engage to bring the present declaration to the knowledge of the States which have not taken part in the Congress of Paris, and to invite them to accede.

The United States of America was their prime target, but when approached refused.

This key event usually receives a short mention in the American view of the conduct of the Civil War at sea. It does, however, explain the European stance on the blockade and, hence, the role of the men on the Clyde who supplied the vessels that sought to break it. It also provided the legal framework for the massive claim for damages lodged against Britain by the victorious US government in the aftermath of the war.

At the time of the Congress of Paris, America's aloofness from the rest of the maritime community was largely determined by her rejection of the first new rule – the abolition of privateering. This ancient institution had been aptly described by the great Scots jurist Lord Stair, back in 1681, as 'the main privat interest in publick War'. In the old order, a sovereign state had, in times of war, the right to issue privateering commissions, known as 'Letters of Marque and Reprisal'. These permitted her citizens to fit out a private armed warship to seize, as lawful prize, the merchant vessels and goods of an enemy. The last vessels to be condemned by a British Prize Court in this way had been Russian traders taken in the Baltic during the Crimean War and sent into Leith.

The American President Pierce considered that the interests of America – with the second-largest merchant fleet in the world and an eye for acquiring portions of Spanish colonial Central America and the Caribbean – were not well served by this change. With only a minuscule navy compared to the great European powers, he was simply not prepared to surrender this cheap and instant option to wreak retribution on an aggressor or reduce a rival's marine.

This divergence of opinion between America and Europe was symptomatic of the general climate of mutual suspicion that had been mounting ever since the conclusion of the short-lived 'War of 1812' with Britain. The presence of US naval vessels in the Mediterranean and Caribbean and the rivalry of her merchant sailing marine for the seaborne trade of the world were eyed with grave concern in the corridors of Whitehall and only served to maintain the tension. Likewise, the other three new maxims (giving neutrals the right to carry an enemy's trade unmolested and defining what constituted a blockade of an enemy's ports) were viewed by the USA as rules made up to suit the great European naval powers with their grand fleets.

It took only a matter of days from the outbreak of hostilities in the American Civil War for this issue to come to the fore. The opening shots were fired on 12 April 1861. Their target was the beleaguered Federal garrison holed up in Fort Sumter situated in the middle of Charleston Harbour. On 15 April, Abraham Lincoln in Washington exercised his presidential executive powers to call up an army of 75,000 men to serve for ninety days to crush the rebel 'combinations too powerful to be suppressed by the ordinary course of judicial proceedings'.

Two days later the leader of the newly-born Confederacy responded:

Now, therefore, I, Jefferson Davis, President of the Confederate States of America, do issue this, my proclamation. Inviting all those who may desire, by service in private armed vessels on the high seas, to aid this government in resisting so wanton and wicked an aggression.

By issuing 'Letters of Marque and Reprisal' to Southern privateering companies, Davis sought to exploit the Federal Navy's great weakness in numbers. This forced the North to disperse its small naval fleet around the world to defend its massive and highly vulnerable merchant marine of unarmed sailing ships. Davis had little to fear in the way of retaliation in kind, as the slave-owning states had never owned a foreign-going fleet of any consequence. Traditionally their exports and imports trade had been carried by Northerners or foreign-flagged vessels.

But Lincoln was not to be distracted in his prime war aim. This was to crush the rebellion quickly in the agrarian South while it had very little in the way of an indigenous armaments industry. To ensure that they did not arm themselves from the arsenals of Europe, he issued a 'Declaration of Blockade' (19 April) of the entire three thousand miles of coastline of the seceding Southern states – from South Carolina to Texas. Eight days later, this edict was extended to include the ports of North Carolina and Virginia, adding a further five hundred miles of coast. The final mileage of coast to be patrolled was greater than the entire seaboard of Western Europe – from North Cape (Norway) to Cape Trafalgar (Spain).

His choice of the term 'blockade', rather than 'closure', sprung the trap laid five years earlier. The Law of Nations, as defined by the Declaration of Paris, only recognised a sea blockade as that imposed by one sovereign state against the ports of another. From the European viewpoint, Lincoln's choice of word had tacitly bestowed the status of nationhood on the seceding states.

Lincoln was fully aware of the international consequences and repercussions of his decision. Indeed, he did so against the express advice of Gideon Welles, his Secretary of the Navy Department. Lincoln's intention was to retrieve the situation by immediately acceding to the Declaration of Paris, thereby isolating the Confederate privateers as 'pirates' in the eyes of the international community. Britain appeared to fall in line with his view as it declared (1 June) that any privateer entering a British port 'under the flag of an unrecognised Power [would] be dealt with as Pirates'.

Lincoln's blockade of the Southern ports was a different matter. The British Foreign Secretary, Lord John Russell, fobbed off questions in the House of Commons as to the legality of this interference in free trade, as 'lamentable reports' that raised 'very serious questions in International Law'. To expedite matters, Lincoln instructed his Secretary of State, the pugnacious William Seward, to put in motion the process to accede to the Declaration of Paris. America was now to be seen as prepared to embrace the new order of maritime warfare at the earliest opportunity. On 24 April, Seward dispatched two new ambassadors, to London (Charles F. Adams) and to Paris (William L. Dayton), with an offer to sign, providing that the privateering ban was binding on both belligerents.

News of Lincoln's Proclamation and the instigation of a naval blockade preceded their arrival. Adams landed in Liverpool on the same day that Britain had declared its neutrality (13 May). The Queen's Proclamation, issued from the White Lodge, Richmond Park, referred to the South 'as the states styling themselves the Confederate States of America'. This, in turn, invoked the long-standing Foreign Enlistment Act of 1819 that expressly forbade any subject of the queen from enlisting, equipping or delivering ships of war to either side.

Up until then, Lord Russell had withstood the assaults in the House of Commons from supporters of both camps. He concluded the debate with the firm statement: 'We must have not been involved in any way in that contest by any act or giving any advice in the matter, and, for God's sake, let us, if possible, keep out of it!'

Five days after the die had been cast, Russell cordially received the resolute Adams (the son and grandson of two American presidents) in audience on 18 May. Adams considered the British Declaration of Neutrality 'premature' (a diplomatic way of saying against the North's interests). He reasoned with Russell that, while it did not formally recognise the independence of the Southern states, it did confer the status of 'belligerent' on them. As such they could be accorded a diplomatic status apart from the United States of America, just as Greece had been granted (1824) during its successful War of Independence from the Turkish Empire.

Matters were needlessly exacerbated when Dayton in Paris took it upon himself to attempt to re-negotiate the terms of the Declaration of Paris by reverting to the old American position recently abandoned by Lincoln. Alarmed by this development, Russell wrote to Lord Palmerston that he thought a 'trap had been laid'. Given the nature of the personalities involved, the talks were doomed to fail. Such was the acrimony and culture of blame, that there was no recovery of cordial diplomatic relations between London and Washington during the war. London was careful, however, not to offer any further diplomatic offence. The British consul in Charleston, the openly pro-Confederate John Bench, was expressly forbidden to visit Richmond, the seat of the Confederate government, or meet with President Davis.

Undeterred by the turn of events in Europe, Lincoln's administration declared Davis's privateering commissions illegal under international law. As such, their crews were to be tried and hanged as 'pirates' when caught. This was inevitably put to the test when the death sentence was passed on the crew of the *Savannah*, a captured Confederate privateer. Davis immediately retaliated with a threat to execute captured Federal officers if this sentence was carried out. In this particular piece of brinkmanship, Lincoln backed off and the captured crewmen were subsequently accorded the status of 'prisoners of war'.

It did, however, set out the iron rule for the blockade runners. Should they offer armed resistance to capture – so much as a single pistol shot – they immediately lost their status as neutrals challenging a blockade. In such an event any British subjects found serving on that runner were instantly labelled stateless 'pirates' and could be hanged under international law. On the other hand, if they chose to run under the flag of the rebels, then the crew was accorded the status of 'belligerents'. If captured they were 'prisoners of war' and likely to be detained for the duration of the war – with all the horrors which that entailed.

It was, therefore, a prime objective of all non-combatant blockade-running captains to run away as fast as possible when shot at and to surrender immediately if cornered at sea. Whilst the vessel and cargo would be lost to a prize court, the hope was that he and his crew would be released in a matter of weeks and expelled as undesirable non-combatants.

In addition to the danger of conferring status on the South, the other challenge presented to the North by the Declaration of Paris was that the blockade had to be 'effective' to be recognised as valid and respected by the navies and merchant marines of Europe. The great fear was that the blockade would be found wanting in substance after a short period of time. If this proved to be the case, then the Declaration clearly stated that vessels sailing under the flag of a neutral state were free to trade unmolested to and from the ports of either adversary as long as they were carrying non-contraband goods. In practical terms, this meant that they needed to produce a naval screen of such strength and deployment to make it impossible for a neutral to approach or leave any of the ports of the Confederacy without being stopped and challenged. It fell to the energetic US Naval Secretary, Gideon Welles, to put in place a procurement programme for sufficient naval vessels to institute a blockade of such depth and rigour as to command international compliance.

At the outbreak of the war, however, the Federal Navy's claim to be enforcing an effective blockade was the subject of widespread ridicule in the European press, nowhere more so than in the letters published in the pro-South London *Times*. This stance was taken up by Edinburgh's *Scotsman*, the *Glasgow Herald* and the local Clydeside papers – and with good cause.

At the time Lincoln's Proclamation was printed in these papers (2 May 1861) the Federal navy had just forty-two vessels in commission, with around the same number in reserve. The few modern steamers it had in service were scattered around the world flying the flag. Furthermore, its officer ranks were seriously depleted by the exodus of hundreds of Southern-born naval officers who resigned their commissions. Most of these returned home to offer their services to the Secretary of the Navy, Stephen Mallory, of the fledging Confederate States of America.

Mallory had no delusions about the disastrous impact that an effective Federal blockade would have on the Confederate war effort. He lost no time in dispatching 'incognito' a few hand-picked officers to Britain to set up a covert procurement operation in Europe. The two prime movers were Major Caleb Huse CSA and Commander James Dunwoody Bulloch CSN. Both were highly resourceful and very determined men.

Time was of the essence. By the end of four months Welles had forty-seven new naval hulls under construction at the Union shipyards. The first, the sloop-of-war USS *Tuscarora*, was launched at Philadelphia on 22 August 1861. Welles boasted that 'her keel was growing in the forests three months ago'. At the same time his agents were scouring the docks, buying up any commercial steamer suitable for conversion to an armed blockader. In the interim, the blockade could still be run with impunity.

By the time Verne's *Dolphin* steamed out of the Clyde, seventeen months after the launch of the *Tuscarora*, this situation had dramatically changed. The massive Federal shipbuilding and conversion programme was churning out 'Ninety Day' gunboats (so called because they were built in three months) and ironclads. In his second annual war report to President Lincoln, in December 1862, Welles could boast that

> We have at this time afloat or progressing to rapid completion a naval force consisting of 427 vessels . . . armed in the aggregate with 1,577 guns, and of the capacity of 240,028 tons . . . the number of persons employed on board our naval vessels, including receiving ships and recruits, is about 28,000; and there are not less than 12,000 mechanics and labourers employed at the different navy yards and naval stations.

How this massive escalation in naval power was to be sustained was explained by Gustavus V. Fox, his Assistant Secretary: 'I believe there is no work shop in the country capable of making steam machinery or iron plates and hulls that is not in full blast with Naval orders.' Ominously, he went on to predict: 'Before another year we shall be prepared to defend ourselves with reasonable hopes of success against a foreign enemy, and in two years we can take the offensive with vessels that will be superior to any England is now building.'

Such barely concealed threats to British naval supremacy were openly repeated abroad. Back in May, the American ambassador to the Russian court at St Petersburg had spared no effort to instruct a wider audience in a lesson in realpolitik. He pointed out that the population of the seven seceded states was just over two million, while the soon-to-be-reunited America was a world power in the making. Her population would top 100 million citizens in the not too distant future. He raised the provocative question: 'What if Ireland, Scotland or Wales shall attempt to secede from the beneficent government of the United Kingdom?' He helped his audience to the inescapable conclusion 'that England is a natural ally [of the USA]'. All such bellicose speeches and diplomatic notes were duly reported in the Scottish newspapers. Their reports weighed heavily with public opinion, often accompanied by editorials that highlighted the arrogance and menace behind them.

The British diplomatic stance on the blockade was confused from the outset. Towards the end of November 1861, when the Federal ship-building programme had yet to deliver, Lord Lyon, the British ambassador to Washington, wrote to Lord Russell from New York that he was still puzzled as to how to respond: 'I suppose the ships that run it successfully are more numerous than those which are intercepted. On the other hand it is very far from being a paper blockade. A great many vessels are captured; it is a most serious interruption to trade.' Even as he wrote, the Federal navy was claiming to have 'hermetically sealed' the entire Atlantic and the Gulf seaboards of the seceded states, from Hampton Roads in Virginia to the Rio Grande in Texas.

At this time what passed for the Confederate Navy consisted of two armed raiders and a motley collection of river gunboats and foreign steamers. The pride of the navy was salvaged old wooden Union warships and large steamers crudely converted to serve as ironclads. The best were iron-plated but most were simply sheathed with strips of railway track. Their marine engines were, as often as not, imported from the Clyde.

The Southern states had started a war wholly lacking an industrial base from which to sustain a prolonged conflict or with which to build a navy to rival that of the North. The only iron and engineering works capable of delivering plate and marine engines was the Tredagar Works at Richmond. Everything was gambled on a series of quick land victories and the unshakeable belief that Britain and France would soon be sucked into the war. Their grand navies would soon break the blockade in their desperate need to reopen the flow of cotton to Europe.

This so-called 'King Cotton' policy prompted a widespread and self-imposed embargo on exporting cotton from the South (unofficially approved of by President Davis) during the opening months of the war, in order to increase the pressure on demand and hasten the day. What cotton was allowed to leave had to be shipped through designated 'ports of entry'.

This was a disastrous policy. It lost the South the funds with which to equip its armies with the best of European armaments at a time when the Federal blockading squadrons had yet to materialise off its main ports. In September 1861, Davis faced up to the folly. The *Scotsman* immediately reported the abandonment of the 'Ports of Entry' scheme and the opening of all Confederate ports to the blockade runners. Around the same time the authorities of Spanish Cuba permitted Havana to become a haven for those running into the Gulf ports, principally Mobile and Galveston.

The Confederate Congress was reluctant to assume a central control of the running trade and actively promoted the formation of private blockade-running companies. The root of this ingrained attitude lay in the piecemeal way the Confederacy was formed. South Carolina was first to secede from the Union in December 1860. Over the next seven weeks, six more Southern states adopted the provisional constitution that created the Confederacy, whose elected president, Jefferson Davis, was inaugurated in February 1861. The fall of Fort Sumter two months later prompted four more states to secede from the Union.

All did so under a common cause: to defend their agrarian slave-owning society from the dictat of a centralised Federal government dominated by the more populous and industrialised Northern states. This resulted in a fierce defence of the individual sovereignty of each state. It followed that the various armies of the Confederacy were raised, controlled and supplied largely by their own state assemblies. The Bureau of Ordnance was one of the few central departments authorised to buy cannon and their munitions and to secure fast steamers for the common good.

The North's first response to the escalation in blockade running was to sink old sailing whalers, laden with stones, in the main channels leading into Charleston. In Europe this 'stone fleet' was seen as a blatant act of commercial vandalism which would deter free trade to this key port long after the war was concluded. Seward struggled to manage the situation by promising that they would be removed immediately after the war. In the event, nature was not to be defied. It took only a few months for the strong currents to cut new channels and break up the wrecks.

President Davis, dissatisfied with the poor performance of his emissaries in Europe, dispatched two former US senators, the veteran politicians James Mason of Virginia and John Slidell of Louisiana, to convince the British and the French that they should formally recognise the Confederacy and break the blockade. Washington considered their chances of success very high. In this case the war would be all but lost for the North.

On 12 October, under the cover of night and a rain squall, the two ambassadors ran the blockade at Charleston on the small steamer *Theodora*. Those manning the blockade were caught off-guard as they assumed that their breakout would be on the larger, lightly armed privateer *Nashville* that was also in Charleston harbour. The *Theodora* arrived at Havana with the Confederate flag flying, to the delight of thousands of local spectators. Most of the local population held pro-South sympathies, to the extent that one group of ladies made a new flag for the steamer before it departed for Nassau. She left without Mason and Slidell and their entourage as they had already booked passage on the British mail steamer *Trent* bound for Southampton.

Their departure on the *Trent* (7 November) was known to the US consul at Havana and he duly passed on this information to Captain Charles Wilkes of the visiting frigate USS *San Jacinto*. Wilkes, who had been cruising for illegal slavers, took it upon himself (it would seem) to overhaul the *Trent* in the Old Bahamas Channel, 300 miles east of Havana. In open international waters, he fired two shots across the British steamer's bow to make her hove-to. He then sent across an armed boarding party which, ignoring the vehement protests of the British captain, forcibly took off the Confederate party, after which the *Trent* was allowed to proceed on her voyage.

To the Europeans this act was an outrageous breach of international maritime law as set out by the Declaration of Paris. The insult to the British flag was deemed intolerable and immediately brought an ultimatum from the British government. Lord Russell, the Foreign Secretary, demanded that the two men be released, along with a full apology for the interception of the *Trent* from the Washington administration.

War was but a whisker away as the press-driven hysteria mounted on both sides of the Atlantic. In Scotland, the news of this wanton act of illegal search and seizure on the high seas broke on 28 November. The shockwave hit instantly, as one nervous American visiting Edinburgh reported at the time: 'I have never seen so intense a feeling of indignation exhibited in all my life. It pervades all classes and may make itself heard above the wiser theories of the cabinet officers.' The US First Secretary in London, Benjamin Moran, concluded that Wilkes' actions had done 'more for the Southerners than ten victories, for it touches John Bull's honour and the honour of his flag'. Thomas Begbie wrote from London to his shipbuilding partner John Scott of Greenock that he thought France would 'cheerfully' follow Britain if it came to a war, for 'although it isn't their flag which is insulted, they want the cotton desperately'.

The pro-South *Scotsman* declared that if this incident was indeed executed with Washington approval, then the US Federal government was plainly determined to provoke a war with Britain. None of the regional newspapers, normally sympathetic to the North, broke rank with this view. British honour and the freedom of the high seas were at stake.

In Britain utter disbelief turned into sheer fury at the arrogance behind this incident. Public outrage was fuelled by a contrived tale of a plucky mail agent on the *Trent* who shielded Slidell's young daughter from the bayonets of Wilkes' boarding parties with his body, uttering the defiant words: 'Back, you poltroons!' The *London Mercury* thundered that by 'his swagger and ferocity' Wilkes made an 'ideal Yankee'!

The sudden death of Prince Albert removed a moderating hand that had been curbing Palmerston's natural urge to issue unacceptable ultimatums to Washington. It did, however, sober up public opinion. Begbie summed it up: 'I have never seen such a gloomy feeling today . . . it has completely knocked out of joint all American politics.'

On 21 November 1861 the *Scotsman* reported the arrival of two heavily armed Federal naval steamers in British waters in pursuit of the Confederate privateers *Nashville* and *Sumter*. The general assumption was that they would not restrict themselves to this mission. If Wilkes was anything to go by, their commanders could be expected to extend their writ to include the stopping and searching of British incoming packets for Confederate agents and dispatches and seizing outgoing freighters for carrying war contraband off the British coast.

Most of the press concluded that the anglophobic Secretary Seward was intent on war with Britain. This would provide America with the excuse to seize Canada in compensation for losing the seceding states. This was certainly the view of the British cabinet, which reacted by immediately dispatching 11,000 troops to Canada. Orders were also given to stop all exports of saltpetre (the prime ingredient in gunpowder) to either side in the conflict.

In America, Wilkes was lionised by the newspapers, commended by the House of Representatives (who awarded him a gold medal) and was given the 'emphatic approval' of Navy Secretary Welles, along with a promotion. Had the British government and press known at the time of this officially backed wave of gloating over Britain, an armed conflict would probably have been inevitable.

Fortunately for both nations, by the time the reports of Wilkes' heroic reception had reached Britain by steam packet, the wave of war delirium had passed – to be replaced by a more considered view. Lincoln's comment that holding Mason and Slidell would prove to be a 'white elephant' was prophetic. In the eyes of the world Wilkes had acted illegally. If his prisoners were indeed 'contraband of war' (a most dubious interpretation of international law) then he should also have brought the *Trent* back with them to Boston to be tried in an American prize court for carrying contraband.

By mid-December 1861, the war fever had cooled considerably. Begbie commented: 'The opinion gathers strength that there will be no war and Mason and Slidell will be given up. It appears to me they underrate altogether the Yankee feelings.' He was not wrong. Mason and Slidell were released on 1 January 1862, leaving a bitter taste on both sides of the Atlantic. On 25 January Du Pont railed at what he saw as a Federal backdown:

> I hope now that our politicians will begin to learn, that something more is necessary to be 'a great universal Yankee Nation etc.' than politics and party. We should have armies and navies and have those appurtenances which enable a nation to defend itself and not be compelled to submit to humiliation . . . thirty ships like the *Wabash* would have spared us this without firing a gun.

In late February 1862, in the aftermath of the '*Trent* affair', the British government relaxed its opposition to selling war goods to the Confederacy. This was justified as playing even-handed with the two belligerents as there had never been a ban on supplying the North with arms and munitions.

As Nassau and Bermuda opened up for business, the British government felt the full force of the Washington administration's backlash. Seward instructed Adams at the London Legation to have his local consuls gather evidence, with the help of a team of hired detectives, of the mounting and blatant breaches of the British Foreign Enlistment Act of 1819. Over the coming months Adams repeatedly and forcefully assailed Lord Russell with conclusive proof of a highly organised and widespread conspiracy in the principal shipbuilding areas to supply blockade runners and warships for the Confederacy. All this activity was undertaken behind a tissue-thin guise of 'laissez-faire' trading.

In the exchange of stern diplomatic notes between Lord Russell and Secretary Seward that year, Russell tacitly acknowledged the increasing role of British vessels and crews in running the blockade. He thought it unlikely that the British Foreign Enlistment Act would deter them, for 'if money were to be made by it, [they would] send supplies to Hell, at the risk of burning their sails!'

From such a pragmatic viewpoint, it is understandable why he took the narrowest of interpretations as to what constituted a breach of neutrality. So long as they left Britain unarmed, flying the British flag and declared for a neutral port, it was 'not in our power to prevent such practices'. He made it clear to Adams that whatever these 'adventurers' got up to away from British shores, they did so at their own risk. For many British merchants, particularly Begbie's circle in London and Clydeside, this was the green light to move into the private blockade-running business.

Across the 'pond', Admiral Du Pont and his advisers chose to interpret Russell's step back from policing his own subjects as their signal to instigate a more aggressive intervention regime at sea. Federal cruisers were henceforth ordered to stop and board suspicious vessels anywhere along the Atlantic seaboard and the Caribbean – not just those found approaching the blockaded Confederate coast. The master's papers and cargo were to be checked and the hull searched for anything that might incriminate the master and owners or reveal the nature and ultimate destination of the cargo. This was a complete reversal of America's long-cherished defence of the freedom of navigation on the high seas and the very principle over which she had gone to war with Britain back in 1812.

Begbie viewed these developments with the gravest concern. Flying the British flag could no longer be taken as a guarantee of immunity from being stopped and boarded on the high seas. He wrote to his business partner John Scott of Greenock that he was disgusted by Russell's lack of backbone: 'Having told the Admiralty that we have a right to sell contraband of war to the Confederates and to deliver aboard at our colony, I wish he would, therefore, like a man, support the Majesty of the Law and confine the Yankee's attention to their legal concerns, viz., at the Blockade Ports – but it's hopeless!'

The first prize taken on the high seas under the new Federal initiative was the British-flagged *Bermuda*, detained by the USS

Mercedita on 27 April 1862. She was intercepted on her second passage between British islands of Bermuda and the Bahamas carrying a massive arms shipment, mainly on George Trenholm of Charleston's account. These included monster Whitworth and Blakely muzzle-loading rifled cannons capable of firing armour-piercing shells with great accuracy and range. Also found on board – not on the US Treasury's list of contraband, but no less necessary to sustain the new state in its conflict – were ten tons of telegraph electrical wire and six printing presses, together with five million postage stamps bearing the heads of Jefferson Davis and John C. Calhoun.

Taken at the time of her boarding was her captain's log book. This gave clear evidence of her previous run into Savannah, together with cargo manifests stating who had owned most of the war contraband on board. It was a great propaganda windfall for the North. Ambassador Adams' son, a reporter on the *New York Times*, lost no time in exposing the role of Fraser, Trenholm & Company of Liverpool in procuring arms for the South.

With such conclusive proof, it was a simple matter to have both the vessel and cargo condemned as war contraband in the New York Admiralty Prize Court – without risking another '*Trent* affair' diplomatic storm with the European maritime powers. This prize case set the legal precedent that Washington was to use, time and again, to justify the interception of British-flagged blockade runners in international waters and hundreds of miles from a Confederate port.

A year later, Du Pont revived the old concept of 'continuous voyage' to allow also the seizure of a cargo of contraband in transit to one of the warehouse islands. On 3 February 1863 the *Springbok*, chartered by Begbie, who also owned part of the cargo, was overhauled 150 miles east of Nassau. When boarded, her documentation was found to be in order on her legal passage from London to Nassau. She was, nevertheless, condemned when it was discovered that she was carrying a chest containing tens of thousands of uniform buttons stamped 'CSA' and 'CSN'. It was great blow for Begbie: 'This won't be put up with I fancy, but it complicates one's matters very disgustingly.'

This was the last major change to the 'rules' of the blockade-running game that was to be played out with increasing intensity for over another year. The saving grace for the crews involved was that their Federal pursuers were so intent on earning prize money that they rarely used excessive force to secure a valuable runner. The loss of life was kept to a minimum.

Chapter 2

The Clyde and the War at Sea 1861

The isolation of the Confederate States from the rest of the world began in earnest in November 1861 when the 'Blockade Strategy Board', chaired by Flag Captain Samuel Du Pont, launched its long-awaited offensive. A Federal naval fleet under his command arrived off Port Royal Sound, South Carolina, where it bombarded the Confederate-held forts Walker and Beauregard. This was quickly followed up by an unopposed landing of 12,000 soldiers who took vacant possession and seized the neighbouring islands. Du Pont wrote of his triumph: 'It is not my temper to rejoice over fallen foes, but this must be a gloomy night in Charleston.'

It was indeed a massive setback for the South. A sombre Major-General Robert E. Lee wrote from his headquarters to the Confederate Secretary of War of the magnitude of the loss of Port Royal:

> The enemy having complete possession of the water and inland navigation, commands all the islands on the coast and threatens both Savannah and Charleston, and can come in his boats, within four miles of this place . . . We have no guns that can resist their batteries, and have no resources but to prepare to meet them in the field.

At the end of that month the *Greenock Advertiser* reported on an incident in the River Clyde that brought the Civil War in America close to home for the first time. It appeared under the title 'The Confederate Flag':

> On Thursday the ship *Washington* of Glasgow, Captain J. [Joseph, not Jefferson] Davis, lying at the Wooden Wharf, Victoria Harbour, hoisted the Confederate flag at her foremast head. The colours of the flag are red and white and red horizontal, with a blue square containing seven stars in the corner. The display of this ensign

excited the wrath of a Yankee ship for New York, which passed down the river in tow in the afternoon. The captain hailed the *Washington*, and ordered the flag to be hauled down that he might 'spit' upon it, and on this request being received with derisive laughter, he said he would soon be alongside to take it down. He has not yet appeared to fulfil his threat.

Three days later the same newspaper carried an item in its 'shipping intelligence' column: 'The *Fingal* steamer from this port has reached Savannah with a most valuable cargo of war materials for the Confederates. This furnishes another instance of the mock character of the blockade.' That edition also carried a fuller report entitled 'ss Fingal':

A telegram received here yesterday states that this screw steamer, which sailed from the Clyde on the 10th of October, has run the blockade and reached the port of Savannah with her warlike cargo. From the difficulty of reconciling dates, it was surmised that the recent report of her capture off the coast of Florida was incorrect, and this proves to have been the case. Her cargo consisted of 11,341 rifles, 60 pistols, 24,100 lbs of gunpowder, 409,000 cartridges, 550,000 percussion caps, 500 sabres, a quantity of wrought leather belts, 4 cannon, 1 ½ tons of lead shot, 7 tons of shell, 220 swords, a quantity of wearing apparel, and 9,982 yards of blankets – the total value being £50,000.

This was the first public acknowledgement of the Clyde's deep complicity with those running the blockade to the Confederacy.

The procurement of the *Fingal* was typical of things to come. In June of that year, this fine iron-built 'channel class' screw steamer completed her sea trials on the Gareloch in the Upper Firth of Clyde. Her new owners, David Hutchison & Company, then accepted her certificate from her builders, James and George Thomson of Finnieston and Govan, Glasgow.

Nine days later she sailed out on her designated route between the Broomielaw (central Glasgow) and Stornoway (Isle of Lewis). This was one of the most arduous passenger routes in Western Europe. As she was too large for the Crinan Canal, her passage to the Outer Hebrides required her to clear the Firth of Clyde via the North Channel which separates Scotland from Northern Ireland. She then ran the length of the wild Atlantic-facing West Coast from the Mull of

Kintyre, through the treacherous Minches, to Stornoway in the Outer Hebrides.

She was snow-rigged and had a retractable propeller for cruising long distances under sail. Her carrying capacity (650 tons) was typical of a Clyde 'channel class' steamer. She was fast for her day. Powered by two 120-horsepower engines, her top speed was thirteen knots under a full head of steam.

These attributes were not lost on the Confederate navy agent, Commander James D. Bulloch, when he first visited the Clyde that July. His covert mission was to search for a suitable vessel to run the blockade with the largest single consignment of arms of the war. Dogged by Federal-hired detectives in Liverpool, he had travelled north by rail to the Clyde to escape their surveillance. Bulloch was an expert on shipping, having previously served in the US navy, and before that as a commercial sea captain. In his professional judgement, the *Fingal* was the fast sea-going vessel he was looking for.

She was only a month old when he first inspected her. He was, however, not able to acquire her immediately. He had to wait while the necessary funds were transferred from the Confederate Navy Department to Fraser, Trenholm & Company of Liverpool, the Confederates' principal financial agents in Europe. And so it was not until September that they arranged her purchase, at a cost of £17,500 – the first foreign vessel to be acquired by the Confederacy. On her return to the Broomielaw from her tenth passage to Stornoway (14 September) her master, John McCallum, was told that she was to be handed over to her new owners. In the Port of Glasgow 'Shipping Register' the change of ownership was duly entered as 'Sold to foreigners'.

Bulloch's name does not appear in the business transaction. His secretary John Low (a lieutenant in the CSN) fronted the purchase for him. Low arrived in Greenock having criss-crossed Scotland by railway to shake off the Federal agents who were following him. It would appear to have been a rushed transaction. As Bulloch noted in his memoirs, she was delivered 'complete with six dozen toddy glasses, with ladles to match. Each glass had the capacity of about a half-pint and they were hard and thick and heavy enough to serve for grapeshot, in case of need.'

Bulloch's interest in the *Fingal* had not gone unnoticed. The US consul resident in Glasgow, John S. Prettyman, had been alerted to his visits to the Clyde in the weeks before by Henry Sanford, the Head of the Federal Secret Service in Europe. Sanford was based in Belgium and had hired a rather unscrupulous private detective agency, headed by Ignatius Pollaky, to tail Bulloch, whom he dubbed 'the most dangerous man' the Confederacy had in Europe. The Liverpool US consul, Thomas H. Dudley, was the paymaster for Pollaky's detective agency and described them to Seward as 'not . . . very estimable men, but . . . the only persons we can get to engage in this business, which I am sure you will agree with me, is not a very pleasant one'.

Pollaky's detective in Greenock was Edward Brennan. Brennan's mission was to check the local hotels for Bulloch's return and to keep the *Fingal* under close surveillance. Brennan was also instructed to gather incriminating evidence as to her secret mission by 'all proper means', including theft, bribery and the interception of mail and telegrams. Brennan did his work with great diligence. He acquired a copy of her cargo invoices, interrogated dockers, quizzed Customs officers and chatted to her crew when they were ashore. He sketched her outline, labelling her identifying features, and made a note of a 'tongue-in-cheek' threat made by a local dockworker. This was to send a warning letter to the US Secretary of State as to the *Fingal*'s mission. All of this Consul Prettyman forwarded to Adams at the US Legation in London.

Some time shortly before she was due to sail, Bulloch had been warned by an informant inside the British Foreign Office that his interest in the *Fingal* was being investigated. He decided, therefore, not to risk bringing her round to the Thames to load her with the arms and munitions. These had been acquired abroad and from the Enfield Rifle Company by Major Huse and arranged by the pro-South London firm of Isaac, Campbell & Company. Instead, Bulloch chartered the London steamer *Colletis* to carry the whole consignment to the more remote port of Greenock. Shipping this cargo by sea, rather than by rail, was a clever move as the Greenock and Glasgow railway stations were being watched by Brennan and his men.

The *Colletis* left the Thames (29 September), triggering a spate of reports to Benjamin Moran, Adams' First Secretary at the US Legation. By the time of her arrival in the Firth of Clyde, the *Fingal* had been moved from the quayside to ride to her anchors on the 'Tail o' the Bank', an offshore anchorage at the mouth of the Clyde estuary. That night, and in great haste, the armaments were transferred. Bulloch was absent, as he had decided that his appearance in Scotland could easily compromise the whole operation at this most critical stage. It was left to Low, who had since assumed the role of second in command, to supervise the transhipment.

The vigilant Brennan observed the whole clandestine operation from the shore. He telegraphed his report to Moran that morning (7 October). Adams immediately stormed Lord Russell's office with Brennan's new evidence of this impending and flagrant breach of British neutrality. At the same time Adam had Moran dispatch Brennan's reports, including the sketch of the *Fingal* and the docker's jest, to Secretary Seward in Washington. It was accompanied by his latest intelligence: 'Her cargo is no doubt far more valuable than appears . . . from the invoices of ammunitions I sent you and consists of such articles as are now greatly needed by the Confederacy, so say their agents here.' This despatch reached Seward on 28 October. He promptly had the drawing copied and distributed to the blockader commanders with the direct order to apprehend her. By then the heavily loaded *Fingal* had vanished into the expanse of the mid-Atlantic.

She slipped away from the 'Tail o' the Bank' anchorage in foul weather on Thursday 11 October. She sailed under the British flag and a Scots master, John Anderson, who took his orders from Low. On board were two other Confederate agents who were returning home. Her departure and full cargo manifest were duly posted in the *Clyde Bill of Entry and Shipping List* the following day.

That Saturday, the local *Greenock Telegraph* broke the story under the heading: 'Shipment of Arms':

> The ss *Fingal*, has shipped this week a large number of boxes, containing from seven to eight thousand rifles: and she is said to have taken on board, at the tail of the Bank, before sailing a large quantity of ammunition from a lighter. These shipments were brought from London in a screw steamer, and the cargo will be worth about £50,000. The destination of the *Fingal* is ostensibly Madeira and the West Coast of Africa, though it is surmised that these munitions will find their way directly or indirectly to the Southern States of America.

The fact that this report was neither a headline story nor was taken up by the other Scottish newspapers would suggest that this covert Confederate operation had been all too transparent to the Clydesiders for some time and was not that sensational in news terms.

The *Fingal*'s rendezvous with Bulloch and his party at Holyhead (Anglesey) was delayed by bad weather and was not without incident. Four days after leaving the Clyde, the iron-hulled *Fingal* rounded the

Holyhead breakwater, just before daybreak. In the gloom she ran down the *Siccardi*, riding without lights. This wooden brig was loaded with Welsh coal and sank quickly in fifteen fathoms.

On shore Bulloch and Colonel Edward Anderson CSA were stirred from their lodgings and informed of the incident that was certain to involve the *Fingal* in an official inquiry. To avoid her detention by the local Customs officers, Bulloch and his party hastily scrambled aboard from a hired dinghy at first light. He ordered her master to put to sea immediately. He left behind a letter to Fraser, Trenholm & Company to resolve matters with the Austrian owners of the *Siccardi*, which they duly did. Bulloch carried on him a copy of the set of signals that Huse had sent in advance to Savannah 'secreted by removing the wrapper of a well-made cigar and carefully replacing, after rolling the paper containing the signals upon its body'.

In his memoirs, Bulloch described how he later found out, in a mid-Atlantic gale, that the *Fingal*'s freshwater tanks were almost empty. This he put down to the negligence of her Scottish master, whom he described as a man 'who acted according to his lights, which were dim'. Without condensing (desalination) apparatus on board, he was forced to put into the isolated island of Terceira in the Azores to water. The detour proved highly rewarding, as this place immediately struck Bulloch as an ideal rendezvous for the armed raiders he was planning to have built in Britain. The first of these, the *Oreto*, was already on the stocks in William Miller's dockyard in Liverpool.

When the *Fingal* and her crew finally arrived at St George's, Bermuda (2 November), they found the armed Confederate privateer *Nashville* waiting for them. Her captain, Robert Pegram CSN, had orders to deliver dispatches and a Savannah pilot to Bulloch. During the five days the *Fingal* was in port, the US consul on this British possession worked tirelessly to obstruct her coaling. He also tried to incite the Scots crew to desert while they were ashore by telling them the real purpose of their cruise – to run the blockade.

It is plain from Bulloch's account that his crew, recruited back in Greenock for a round passage to Nassau in the Bahamas, had their suspicions from the outset. Indeed, during the crossing, he had posted Low to keep an eye on the 'Jacks'. Once at sea again, the critical moment arrived when the subterfuge had to be discarded as the *Fingal*'s course was altered from Nassau to Bulloch's home port of Savannah. He summoned the men to the fore deck where he revealed his identity and that of his companions. His aim, he declared, was to run the blockade as a neutral – flying the British flag and without firing a shot.

He made it clear, however, that should they be confronted by a blockader, he intended to use her bill of sale, which was in his pocket, to relieve his Scots master of his command – as was the owner's right. He would then assume personal command, raise the Confederate flag and fight his way through. He promised his men that if they did not wish to sail with him, he would honour their terms of contract and carry them on to Nassau. There he would pay off the unwilling and find new men to fill their berths. For those who chose to stay and run the blockade with him, he reminded them of the risk of long-term imprisonment in a Federal jail, if caught after a fight. He concluded by reassuring them that the *Fingal* was more than a match for the cheaply built and lightly armed Federal steamers then on blockade duty. His memoirs do not state what cash incentive he offered, but it can be assumed that it was considerable.

The key figure in this struggle for allegiance was the highly skilled Chief Engineer McNair. Bulloch, who was himself of Scottish lineage (from Banff), seems to have had the measure of this man, whom he described as 'a silent, steady, reliable Scot, immovable and impassive as the Grampian Hills'. The crew followed McNair's lead when asked if they were willing to sail on and fight, if necessary. In his account Bulloch claimed that they answered 'Yes!', to a man.

The matter having been settled, the *Fingal* was set on a direct course for Savannah. During the passage, two of the four and a half inch Blakely field cannons were raised from the hold and mounted at the forward gangway ports. Two small 'boat guns' were also mounted on the quarterdeck to repel boarders. As the made-up cartridges for both these rifled cannons were beyond reach in the hold, barrels of gunpowder and bales of flannel were broached to make up new ones. The 'ladies' saloon' was converted into a shell magazine and armoury and stashed with rifles and revolvers. While still out in international waters and beyond observation, Colonel Anderson put the gun crews, a number of whom were old Royal Navy hands, through their drill.

In the engine room, the recently won over McNair had been at work setting aside a few tons of the best-shaped and cleanest coal. He asked and got permission to put out the fires in one boiler so that the scrapers could be run through the flues. With that done, he reckoned the deeply laden *Fingal* could sprint at eleven knots for a few hours, if need be.

All was ready by 11 November when they steamed up to the coast and then turned north to run parallel with the Wassaw Sound. The pilot was looking for a small inlet that connects, by way of the coastal inland waterways, to the Savannah River seventeen miles further north. Bulloch describes the *Fingal* creeping up to the coast in a thick fog, her engines throttled back, the crew in silent running order and with lights extinguished. The only chink of light showing was that from the binnacle so that the helmsman could see the compass.

It is a classic tale of blockade running, all the more so for being understated, devoid of bravado and with a touch of black comedy – the cockerel, taken on board at Bermuda and stowed on deck in the hencoop, started screeching at the top of his voice, threatening to expose their presence. The poor bird was finally throttled by a crewman after a couple of innocent hens had suffered the same fate in the panic to find the culprit.

Unable to find the narrow channel into the Wassaw Sound and with the fog lifting, the pilot decided to risk all and run up the coast at full speed to reach the main channel of the Savannah River where it joined the open sea. As fate would have it, the Federal steamers assigned to blockade the river were further up the coast supporting the joint army–navy assault on the forts guarding Port Royal Sound. And so the *Fingal*'s approach and entry into the river passed unchallenged.

Once she had crossed the bar, Bulloch fired a shot and ran up the Confederate flag on the foremast to alert the defenders in the massive brick Fort Pulaski that guarded the river mouth, to his arrival. After making the pre-arranged signals, courtesies were exchanged. The pilot then put her on a course up the narrow navigable channel through the extensive estuary shoals. He had to squeeze her past the underwater obstructions of two wooden vessels sunk in the fairway opposite the fort to keep out the Federal steamers. The deeply laden *Fingal* managed to avoid ensnaring the wrecks, but in doing so ran aground on a mussel bank. While she was stuck there, Colonel Anderson, a native and twice mayor of Savannah, rowed ashore and telegraphed for help.

After much effort and time, she was pulled off unscathed by a river paddle steamer which had been commandeered by the local naval officer as his flagship. Once clear of the bank, the *Fingal* made her way up to the quays of Savannah under her own steam with the greatest single delivery of armaments of the war. She arrived on the afternoon of 12 November, just over a month since leaving Greenock.

Two months later the *Greenock Telegraph* regaled its readers with an extract from a Savannah newspaper that described the 'Arrival at Savannah of *Fingal*':

This morning, about 8 o'clock, telegrams were received, announcing that a steel-clad steamer had arrived outside the bar, with arms ammunition, blankets, &c., for the Government. Later intelligence confirmed the fact, and as the news spread, groups collected about the corners, discussing the (at this time) unlooked for arrival. The most intense joy seemed to be manifested by all, as an eminent divine observed, 'surely God has blessed us in bringing us such needed articles at this time.' About half-past 2 o'clock p.m., the booming of cannon announced the arrival of the vessel, and instantly a rush was made for the wharves.

The steamer came gradually and gracefully up the stream, and at four o'clock anchored off the Exchange. Cheer after cheer went up from the gratified people, and as Captain E.C. Anderson – through whose instrumentality she had been purchased and brought here – stepped from the boat to the wharf, three times three and a 'tiger' were given him.

Also waiting at the quayside was Bulloch's friend, Captain John N. Maffitt. He was the man Bulloch had in mind to command one of the cruisers he was having built in Britain.

Bulloch telegraphed his arrival to Secretary Mallory and was immediately ordered to attend him at Richmond. On his journey north on the single-tracked antiquated railway system he was taken aback by the poorly clad soldiers being rushed to the fronts in Virginia and the West. Most did not have a blanket and were carrying old flintlocks and sporting shotguns; a few had percussion cap muskets; none had modern rifled muskets or bayonets. It was plain to him that in this unplanned war, the South was caught destitute of the trappings of modern warfare – everything from tents and uniforms to canister shot and field cannon.

Just how ill-equipped the average infantryman in the Confederate army was at the being of the war can be gleaned from a report published in the *Edinburgh Review* in 1859, recalling the firing of a smooth-bore musket with black powder:

The soldier was told, in firing at a man at 600 yards, to fire 130 feet above him: in other words, if you wished to hit the church door, aim at the weathercock; but, considering the lateral deviation, the chances were certainly 2 to 1 that you would miss the church altogether.

In the battlefield, having missed his man, the infantryman was left with the bayonet (if he had one) as his best defence against a charging rank. Conversely, charging over the same distance against defenders with modern rifles, with their flattened trajectory and greater accuracy, was to accept high casualties.

Given this dire state of affairs, the *Fingal*'s cargo of rifles was dispatched to the front lines as a matter of great urgency. Of the War Department's 7,500 '1859 patent' long Enfield rifles, half were rushed to Johnston's hard-pressed army defending Louisiana. Arguably more crucial were the 17,000 pounds of modern gunpowder, which allowed Beauregard's cannon to extract what was left of the Confederate army from the bloodbath of Shiloh fought on the banks of the Tennessee River that April. With its cargo discharged and dispersed, the two large Blakely cannons mounted on the Fingal's foredeck were dismounted and carted off to Fort Pulaski.

Bringing the *Fingal* to Savannah was a desperately needed propaganda victory for the Confederate cause. Her unopposed entry was broadcast to Europe as clear proof that the blockade was 'ineffective'. It was also a personal triumph for Bulloch, undoubtedly one of the most competent and far-sighted officers of the infant Confederate Navy. His daring plan proved what could be done if the government organised its own blockade-running operations.

He was, however, dismayed to find political infighting and pettiness between his leaders on his return to Richmond. His scheme to repeat the *Fingal*'s success by acquiring a fleet of government-owned runners fell on deaf ears. The individual states that formed the Confederacy clung doggedly to their independence. It had been their decision to raise and supply their own armies. None immediately saw the need to acquire their own blockade runners, as the Navy Department had done. They preferred instead to let the profiteering 'Rhett Butlers' manage the blockade running for them.

Secretary Mallory decided to send Bulloch and the *Fingal* back to Britain with a paying cargo of cotton and rosin (turpentine). She was also to carry officers selected as commanders for the new raiders being built on the Mersey and the Clyde. To this end John Fraser & Company of Charleston (the founding trading house of Fraser, Trenholm & Company of Liverpool) were instructed to buy cotton from the interior and have it delivered to Savannah.

By the time Bulloch returned to Savannah (23 November) the local military situation had dramatically changed. The Federal blockaders were back on station off the river mouth, having completed their mission to take the forts in Port Royal Sound. Their reappearance left the passage through the Wassaw Inlet as the only possible escape route by which to reach the sea without being sunk or captured. Gunboats cruising off the mouth of the Savannah River had already shelled Fort Pulaski by firing over Tybee Island, a distance of about a mile. The lighthouse on the island was in Federal hands and it could be only a matter of days before heavy calibre cannon were dragged across the island and into a firing position on the river bank opposite the fort.

Bulloch desperately pleaded that the procurement of cotton from the interior, given that the dilapidated railway system was chronically overloaded, should be abandoned through lack of time. To save precious days, he begged that the *Fingal* should be loaded with what could be bought on the spot in the Savannah area and got out to sea while she could. This advice was ignored.

It was not until 25 December that the *Fingal* finally crept down the river on a spring tide with 150 barrels of rosin and 400 bales of cotton. Bulloch informed Mallory that he intended to run her out as a neutral under the British flag and unarmed, 'as it is important to preserve her original character as an English ship . . . If, on our arrival in England, the Confederate Government has been acknowledged, the flag can be changed.' The opportunity to escape had long since passed. All exits from the Wassaw Sound were now patrolled by Du Pont's armed steamers that 'corked up Savannah like a bottle'. After a nerve-racking night, hiding off Thunderbolt Battery, Bulloch abandoned the attempt as futile and returned to Savannah City. He reported to Mallory that he had witnessed the gathering of five large federal warships off the river mouth. He correctly concluded that this was a precursor to a major offensive against Fort Pulaski.

With the *Fingal* blockaded in the river, Bulloch asked to be relieved of her command and allowed to return to Britain by other means. His priority was to oversee the construction of the two large cruisers being built at Liverpool and Dumbarton. His request was granted and the command of the *Fingal* was passed to Lieutenant George T. Sinclair. Bulloch eventually got out of Wilmington on a Fraser & Company's blockade runner, *Annie Childs*, taking with him the engineer McNair. What became of the rest of the Scots crew left behind with the *Fingal* is not known. The British consul at Charleston reported that they had travelled overland to Fort Monroe as a group seeking to enter the North. The garrison commander turned them back on the orders of General Wood.

To Washington, the '*Fingal* incident' was a spectacular breach of British neutrality and a damning indictment of the complacency, or even passive collusion, of Palmerston's government. While Adams clamoured for action on the building of the cruisers in British yards, the British press gloated over the ease with which Bulloch had hoodwinked the British authorities and the Yankees.

While Russell struggled to manage the damage done by the 'Fingal incident', the war at sea took a dramatic turn that threatened to undo Anglo-American relations. The day after the Fingal left Bermuda for Savannah, Wilkes on the USS San Jacinto – three hundred miles away in the Old Bahamas Channel – stopped and boarded the British mail packet Trent. After her release, the Trent resumed her course, carrying the shocking news of this gross insult to a vessel of the 'mistress of the seas'. She approached her home port just as a new outrage was rapidly unfolding in British waters. This was the arrival in the Solent of the armed Confederate privateer Nashville under Pegram.

After his rendezvous with Bulloch and the Fingal at Bermuda, Pegram had crossed over to the west coast of Ireland. There he stopped a large Union clipper Harvey Birch, bound from Le Havre to New York. After taking off her crew and passengers, he burned her (19 November). Immediately afterwards a storm rose that damaged the Nashville and, being low on coal, Pegram headed for Southampton.

The emotions aroused by her arrival in British waters flying the Confederate flag were tremendous. Moran at the US London Legation was incensed at 'that pirate flag of the South at her peak . . . there is something perfectly vile to me about the rebel flag, and I never see it without itching to burn it.' The mood of local onlookers was by then on Moran's side. When Pegram landed his prisoners to hand them over to the local US consul, he was met by a hostile crowd who loudly jeered that his most recent act was nothing less than piracy.

Yet only days later, the mood of the mob swung dramatically around, such was the impact of the news of the abduction of Commissioners Mason and Slidell off the Trent. Punch magazine captured the whimsical nature of the moment in a poem:

> But when in Southampton free, grim,
> The prisoners you've caught, Captain Pegram,
> We are placed in a fix, to pronounce your tricks
> Are a hero's or a pirate's, Oh Pegram.

A midshipman on the Nashville recalled the sudden shift 'from abuse to a more friendly attitude towards us. In fact they wined, dined and toasted us on every hand, as heroes.'

Close on his heels came Captain Tunis A.N. Craven on the sloop of war USS *Tuscarora* flying the Stars and Stripes. He moored his ship in Itchen Creek opposite Southampton Docks where the *Nashville* was undergoing repairs. The Admiralty responded by sending HMS *Phaeton* from Portsmouth to stand watch over the two belligerents, should they decide to attempt to engage in any form of hostilities while in British waters. The *Scotsman* noted that the Federal captain was ready for instant action as he kept his furnaces banked and rode to two springs that allowed him to slip his cable at a moment's notice.

Craven was anxious that the *Sumter* might also be nearby (she was then at Gibraltar). He twice left his moorings to circumnavigate the Isle of Wight in search of her. On his second tour, he dropped anchor in the bay off Osborne House, the Queen's residence. He was promptly told to leave by his Royal Navy shadow.

The press assumed that, if it came to a sea battle, the lightly armed *Nashville* would be hopelessly outgunned. The *Illustrated London News* described the larger *Tuscarora* as 'a smart, handsome-looking craft, heavily armed, with eight Dahlgren guns: two of them, placed amidships, are the famous columbiad 120-pounders; and a rifled 30-pounder of Parrot's design on her forecastle'. She also had two hundred of a crew, twice that of the *Nashville*. The aggrieved owners of the *Trent* joined in and petitioned the Foreign Office not to allow Federal cruisers a supply of coal – other than what was needed to get them out of British waters.

The *Scotsman* took the long view that the real danger was political rather than physical. The prospect of American shells flying off the shores of Britain was, simply, unthinkable. The editorial held the opinion that any such act 'will tend to stimulate the war feeling of the mob and may further embarrass the cabinet'. It also noted that France was certainly anxious for 'something to be done' about the *Trent* affair.

As the weeks passed, the stand-off showed no signs of breaking. With public sentiment on his side, Pegram was in no hurry to hand the Federal captain a propaganda coup by engaging and losing a one-sided fight. With the *Sumter* still on the loose, he would wait Captain Craven out.

Russell, having taken stock of the traumatic diplomatic events of the past few months, ordered a rigorous tightening up of Customs surveillance at the ports in a belated attempt to stop further direct armament shipments such as those carried by the *Fingal*. So prompted, the Board of Customs and Excise sitting in London issued an order (7 December) to their Greenock Collector:

The Board, having strong reason to believe that it is in contemplation of certain persons to ship large quantities of Arms, Ammunition and other articles in violation of her majesty's Proclamation . . . the proper Officers and the Collector at the principal Out ports are to take immediate steps to appoint a sufficient number of Officers to keep watch over all suspicious shipments of packages to be made as will satisfy them that Her Majesty's Proclamations are not being infringed.

The Board in issuing this order reply on the discretion of the superior Officers to employ force sufficient to carry out efficiently their instructions and they will take special care not unnecessarily to disturb the legitimate business of the Port.

The Board have also received information that large quantities of Arms are prepared for shipment under the disguise of Hardware, Saws, Machinery etc. and Saltpetre under that of Sugar and Guano, but the goods are expected to be sent by railway to the ports of shipments. The Board consider that by judicious private enquiries at the Stations or the employment of intelligent Officers, Shipments of prohibited goods may effectively be intercepted.

Confederate agents were desperately seeking saltpetre, the European supply of which had been bought up by Henry Sanford for the Union. On 24 December the Collector at Greenock took measures to stop the export or theft of this prohibited commodity. This involved dispatching a 'Principal Coast Officer' to oversee the stores at the Kames Gunpowder Works on the Isle of Bute.

During the stand-off in the Solent, the Confederates woke up to their dire plight and strove to safeguard their supply line from Europe. Their remaining coastal fortresses defending the approaches to Charleston and Wilmington were hastily equipped with the best available heavy ordnance run in from Europe. Massive defensive earthworks were thrown up and surmounted with cannon to deter seaborne assaults and provide covering fire for incoming runners.

In Washington the Federal strategic planners were under no delusions as to the task ahead. While these two ports remained open to the runners, the Confederate armies in the field could be fed, clothed and armed. On 1 December Admiral Du Pont wrote: 'The rebel defences of Charleston are still progressing. The English officers who have been in and the blockade runners whom we capture, smile at the idea of its being taken, and say it is stronger than Sebastopol – but they said the same of New Orleans.' However, his commanders had not rested on their laurels since Port Royal. In the months following Bulloch's successful run into Savannah with the *Fingal*, the Federal navy had expanded rapidly. The increase in numbers and better access to bases made a close blockade along the entire length of the Confederate-held seaboard a reality. To maintain this massive undertaking, the blockaders were divided into three fleets – the North Atlantic, the South Atlantic and the Gulf squadrons.

Rear Admiral Farragut of the Gulf squadron was optimistic that he was close to achieving his mission of eradicating the blockade runners. Only days after Du Pont's reserved comment, Farragut confidently reported to him: 'We have either taken or destroyed all the steamers that run from Havana & Nassau to this coast, except the *Cuba* and *Alice* . . . I have all the coast except Mobile Bay, and am ready to take that the moment I can get troops.' His squadron had indeed done well. In the eight months since the fall of Fort Sumter they had chased and captured almost all the sailing vessels engaged in blockade running – such was the superiority of steam over sail. Those still running had quit the Atlantic seaboard and heavily patrolled eastern Gulf coast for the relative safety of the remote waters off the Texas–Mexico border.

This success hid the fact that most of his blockaders were commercial steamers adapted for the service: ill-suited and slow. As Du Pont remarked on their conversion to armed naval units, it was like 'altering a vest into a skirt'. When pitted against a thoroughbred Clyde steamer, racing on an open sea, they had little chance of catching one.

Chapter 3
The Boom Years 1862–4

The first blockade-run Confederate cargo arrived in the Clyde in early June 1862. The *Greenock Advertiser* reported her docking under the heading 'The American Blockade':

> On Tuesday afternoon, the fore and aft schooner *Sue*, 77 tons, Captain Smith, hailing from Nassau, New Providence, but supposed to be Southern property, arrived at the 'Tail o' the Bank' from Georgetown, South Carolina, after breaking the blockade, being the first arrival in the Clyde that has accomplished that feat. Her cargo consists of turpentine and a few barrels of rosin. She left Georgetown about the middle of April, and affected her escape during the night without any interruption. She reached Queenstown [Cork] on the 30th ult., short of provisions, and after receiving a supply proceeded to this port, whence she has gone to Glasgow. She ran the blockade on a previous occasion and got safely to Nassau.

US Consul Prettyman immediately informed Seward that her cargo of 498 barrels of turpentine and thirty-six of rosin was consigned to the Glasgow firm of McLeash & McNutt. This firm was known to him as 'violent sympathisers . . . they having done all they could to forward the cause of the secessionists in this country and also to send them relief and assistance'.

He was sure that they were already gun-running under the guise of shipping 'hardware' from Glasgow to Nassau on their sailing bark *Leeburg*. This was in addition to the large profit they had already made on their share of the armaments shipment run into Charleston on the *Bermuda* the previous year. They had since converted their credit for this into 300 bales of cotton and registered this cargo as 'British owned' with the British consul there.

The *Sue* had escaped South Carolina just as the gaps in blockade were being closed, transforming what might have been described by its detractors as a 'paper' blockade into an 'effective' blockade. By the time she docked in the Clyde, the first wave of larger munitions carriers out from Britain had been intercepted. The latest, Fraser, Trenholm & Company's *Gladiator*, was blockaded in Nassau harbour. Carefully watched, she was too slow to try and outrun the Federal steamers patrolling offshore. Transhipment to smaller swift steamers became the only viable alternative for delivering her cargo to the South. By the time the *Sue* arrived in the Clyde, thirty such steamers had already congregated at Nassau.

To organise the shipments, a New Orleans businessman, Louis Heyliger, had been sent to Nassau on the *Theodora* to act as the local Confederate agent. Around the same time the Federal Secretary of the Treasury, Salmon P. Chase, acted swiftly to plug a rather embarrassing hole whereby war contraband was purchased in New York and delivered to Nassau on steamers burning US coal. He ordered all Federal port authorities to implement an immediate embargo on the 'shipments of coal and dry goods and shoes, and quinine and other drugs and Tin Ware and Munitions of War, and sundry other articles to Nassau and the West Indies'.

Lord Lyon, the British ambassador to Washington, lodged a stern protest with Seward over these new restrictions in trade to a British Crown possession – but to no avail. Chase's action had the effect of confining all future Confederate procurement operations to Europe with delivery via Canadian ports and British-owned islands.

Around the same time, Federal cruisers were given the go-ahead to step up their aggressive 'stop and search' policy in the international waters off the Florida Channel. The seizure of three large steamers, *Bermuda*, *Columbia* and *Memphis*, while attempting to run cargoes of arms and munitions flying the British flag – as the *Fingal* had done – effectively ended regular direct shipments from Britain. Only the *Economist*, another new Denny-built large screw steamer owned by Fraser, Trenholm & Company, managed to get out from Charleston on April Fool's day. She carried the cargo that had been unloaded from the entrapped *Fingal*.

Part of the Federal blockade strategy was to send cruisers to patrol in international waters off the Bahamas. One of the first vessels to be captured was the old Clyde steamer *Tubal Cain*, heading for Charleston from Nassau with half a million pounds worth of munitions. She was taken (24 July) after a six-hour chase by the USS *Octorara* and carried into Fort Monroe.

In August 1862, Major Caleb Huse wrote from Liverpool to Colonel Josiah Gorgas (Head of the Confederate Ordnance Bureau based in Richmond) that he now considered Nassau 'so dangerous, even as a port of destination for arms in British ships, that [he] thought it prudent not to order anything more to that port, for the present at least.' The port of St George on British Bermuda offered the perfect alternative. Located almost 700 miles directly out in the Atlantic from the American eastern seaboard, it offered an expanse of ocean in which to disappear when running in and out of Wilmington or Charleston. This increasingly became a deciding factor as to where to base a runner as the war progressed, especially after Federal cruisers took to lying in wait in the Nassau Channel.

Bermuda's more remote location also doubled the distance from a coaling station for the Federal cruisers that periodically cruised off St George's harbour. Very early on in the war they had been refused coaling and repair facilities by the British governor, which greatly reduced the time they could stay on station. The blockade runners, on the other hand, had access to all facilities and to the British naval base on the island, which had a dry dock, secure warehousing and powder magazines.

By December 1862, routing arms through Bermuda was well established under the cover of a number of private local firms. The Bermudan agent John T. Bourne believed he had a special position with the various Confederate agencies, similar to Heyliger's in Nassau. He was soon divested of that notion with the arrival of Major Norman S. Walker CSA and his wife from Europe, where they had delivered $2 million in Confederate bonds to Huse.

Walker was empowered by Gorgas to manage the necessary disbursements for the heavy munitions delivered to Bermuda from Britain in large deep-hulled steamers. The Walkers took up residence in a grand house overlooking St George's harbour. It soon became an open house for endless social functions for the numerous pro-Southern supporters, agents and naval officers. Such was the universal sympathy for the South on the island that the resident US consul claimed that he went in fear of his life and was regularly abused in the streets.

Walker left the overseeing of transhipments to his two aides, both of whom were on detached duty from the Ordnance Bureau. This left Bourne with the more mundane business of squaring the demands and bills of the private running captains and companies. He did so stoically and with much diligence and care. He made sure that the more sensitive and 'combustible' shipments were kept locked up in stone warehouses away from prying eyes. With his organisation, the runners were able to turn round in three or four days and not left lying in the harbour for long periods with armaments visibly stowed on board.

By then the competition for the Clyde shipbuilders' speciality – fast shallow-draught steamers – had been gathering such momentum that most yards on Clydeside were gearing up to meet the demand. Paddle wheelers were in the greatest demand. They could sprint to their maximum speed much faster than a single screw, turn and reverse more quickly, and were better able to free themselves if they grounded on a sandbar. They alternated the drive to each wheel so that the steamer simply 'waddled off' into deeper water.

As new keels were being laid down in the stocks of the Clydeside yards, there was an immediate and profitable business in modifying the existing stock for their new role and the Atlantic crossing. The first paddle steamer dispatched to Bermuda was the *Herald*, built by Wood & Reid of Port Glasgow for the Dublin & Glasgow Sailing and Steam Packet Company. She had been purchased by a local agent, Charles Taylor, around the same time as the acquisition of the *Fingal* (late 1861). He was acting for Charles Prioleau of Fraser, Trenholm & Company.

Although she was ten years old and slow by the standards of the day (eight knots), this 'channel class' ex-mail boat suited his purpose as she had a large cargo capacity similar to the *Fingal* (450 tons burthen) and a draught of only ten and a half feet when fully loaded. Her survival was very much in the hands of her master and pilot and their ability to sneak her in and out without being challenged.

For her new role, she was stripped of most of her passenger-lounge accommodation to make room for berths for her large crew (fifty men) and cargo. Her spars and masts had been adapted with hinges, so that they could be readily dropped onto the deck, and she was fitted with telescopic funnels. These measures were all designed to reduce her visibility while running. She arrived at Liverpool from the Clyde, having been adapted for her new role, in the spring of 1862. There she was loaded with her cargo of heavy munitions and artillery under the watchful eye of Louis M. Coxetter. This mild-mannered and soft-spoken Confederate master of Dutch extraction had left Charleston on the *Theodora* expressly for this run.

On the transatlantic leg, however, she flew the British flag and was under the command of Captain Tate, a British master. On her arrival at St George from Madeira (24 March), the plan for a peaceful handover to Coxetter fell apart. Her crew, led by Fraser, the chief engineer, mutinied when they learned that she was destined for Charleston, not the West Indies as they had signed up for. In this incident there were no rousing speeches, as in Bulloch's tale of the *Fingal*, to sway the reluctant crew. Captain Tate was, apparently, in sympathy with, if not behind, the mutiny and it took some well-directed bribery and the threat of imprisonment to evict Tate, Fraser and the rest of the irascible crew from the *Herald*.

The fracas had the undesired effect of awakening the US consul on the island to this latest subterfuge. This was almost certainly the reason why a small group of specialist engravers, carrying the 'stones' (the blanks from which banknote plates were engraved) and sixty-three cases of printing materials for the Confederacy Treasury, were hurriedly transferred to another large runner then in port.

Three months later, Coxetter finally accomplished his mission when he brought her safely through the blockade into Charleston in early July. There she was sold to the newly set up blockade-running firm, the Chicora Importing & Exporting Company of Charleston, and renamed *Antonica* that September. Thereafter, her exploits as a runner under Coxetter (complete with a Colt revolver in his pocket) became the stuff of legend. On one return trip in December 1862, he found the entrance to Nassau blockaded by a flotilla led by the newly promoted Commander Wilkes (of Slidell and Mason fame) on the *San Jacinto*. Wilkes was lying in wait for the Confederate raider *Florida* that had escaped from Nassau under the command of John N. Maffitt.

Rather than run back out to sea, Coxetter chose to speed past him at first light, gaining the bar before the Federal gunners could react. Wilkes, in his typical high-handed manner, fired a number of shells after him, some of which landed in the fairway of the crowded harbour. He then anchored the *San Jacinto* opposite the main channel entrance in defiance of a direct order from the island's governor to quit British waters. He only left when artillery was hauled across to Hog Island and brought to bear on the *San Jacinto*.

By then Wilkes had received considerable intelligence from the US consul on the island that redirected him to the Gulf of Mexico in his pursuit of the *Florida*. He left behind his two gunboats, *Sonoma* and *Tioga*, hovering off the entrance hoping to catch any runners trying to break out after his departure. Denied coal by the governor, they did not stay on station long.

The charmed life of this one-time Dublin–Glasgow mail boat ended a year later. By then Coxetter, who had been declared a 'pirate' by the Federal government, had left to take over her sister ship *Havelock*, renamed by the Chicora Company the *General Beauregard*.

His replacement on the *Antonica* (ex-*Herald*) was the veteran Captain W.F. Adair. Under Adair's command her luck finally ran out when he ran her aground on the Frying Pan Shoals off the Old Inlet at

Wilmington. He had been trying to squeeze past the blockader USS *Governor Buckingham*. Adair and his crew of twenty-six men were captured as they tried to row ashore. Unable to tow her off, the *Governor Buckingham* destroyed the *Antonica* by gunfire. By then she had already made a fortune for her owners by carrying over a thousand bales of cotton on each one of her twenty-five return journeys.

The *Herald* and the *Havelock* were two of ten 'channel class' steamers that had been covertly acquired in the Clyde during 1862 and sent to the blockade. The others were *Giraffe*, *Leopard*, *Adela*, *Tubal Cain*, *Antona*, *Thistle*, *Britannia* and *Princess Royal*. They were joined by five smaller 'river class' paddle steamers: *Kelpie*, *Eagle*, *Pearl*, *Ruby* and *Dolphin*. Together they represented the cream of the Clyde's Irish Sea mail boats and inshore Highland and Islands steamers.

During the second half of that year, a steady flow of newly launched steamers, many built on speculation, joined the trek to Bermuda and Nassau: *Queen of the Wave*, *Wave Queen*, *Georgiana*, *Memphis*, *Cornubia I*, *Minho*, *Amelia*, *Corinth*, *Granite City*, *Ranger* and *Leeburg II*. The risks involved can be underlined by the fact that all of the 1862 sailings were captured or sunk by the end of the following year.

Only one, the small elderly Denny-built *Eagle*, had a second life as a blockade runner. She was taken by USS *Octorara* in May 1863 and condemned as prize at New York. At her sale, she was bought by private interests and sent back to Havana. Renamed *Jeanette* she ran the Gulf to Galveston towards the end of the war under her Scots Captain, William Watson. Both Captain Watson and the *Jeanette* managed to survive the war.

It would be tedious to relate the exploits of each and every Clyde steamer that crossed the Atlantic that year. It might suffice to select a few whose careers illuminate different facets of this 'peculiar business'.

Of the 'channel class' steamers, the most famous was the iron paddle steamer *Giraffe*. Her tale offers insights into the way things were managed on the Clyde immediately prior to the war and how agents for the government of the Confederate States went about procuring her.

Her pedigree as a pre-war Clyde steamer was impeccable. She was built by James and George Thomson of Finnieston and Govan in 1860 for the Glasgow shipping company G. and J. Burns. As their newest and fastest vessel, she was their flagship on the highly competitive Glasgow to Belfast mail and passenger run.

The owners' instructions to the builders were that she should be able to complete the summertime round trip (seven hours each way) in daylight. This gruelling schedule involved leaving Greenock at eight in the morning and returning in time to meet the seven o'clock evening train for Glasgow. She would then continue upriver to discharge her third-class passengers at the Broomielaw by late evening. The cost was £1 for a first-class return ticket, which included the train and a cabin on board. Third-class fare was six shillings (30p) without the train option. During the great annual summer holiday, the Glasgow Trades Fair, she was diverted to day excursions from the Broomielaw around Ailsa Craig, stopping at piers along the Clyde Coast. On these cruises she regularly carried 700 passengers.

In her day, the *Giraffe* was considered the ultimate compromise between 'sea boat' and 'racer'. She was able to withstand the wild cross-currents and seas of the North Channel between Scotland and Ireland, while retaining the allegiance of the more discerning customers. They expected a speed and comfort superior to that of her older Company consorts, *Leopard*, *Stag* and *Lynx*, which plied the same route.

For stability in rough seas the *Giraffe* had a beam of over twenty-six feet and a depth of hull of thirteen feet. She was schooner rigged and on the Belfast run her sails were often set to stabilise her when running on a course abeam to heavy waves. For speed, she had a hull of great length and knife-edge bow, driven through the seas by twin oscillating engines (each 90 horsepower) served by six boilers.

At the time of her launch – to great pomp – it was hoped that she might be the first to break the magical twenty knots speed barrier. During her sea trials in the Gareloch, however, she logged just over thirteen knots – good for the day but well below the overblown expectations drummed up by the press.

Her first paying passage was to carry a party, led by the lord provost and magistrates of Glasgow, on their annual inspection of the Clyde's lighthouses (7 July 1860). It was more of a grand outing rather than a serious inspection. Her departure from Greenock attracted local crowds and a salute from the cannons of Fort Matilda as she carved her way past Gourock at high speed. After a cruise round the isles of Little Cumbrae and Ailsa Craig she made for Campbeltown on the Mull of Kintyre, where the whole town turned out for her arrival. On the way back to the Clyde her party of 125 gentlemen sat down for dinner in the fore lounge. This culinary experience was enjoyed in 'great comfort' as they glided past the grandeur of the lofty peaks of the Isle of Arran.

Once in regular service, great things were expected of her. On her first run to Belfast, however, she failed to beat the Glasgow–Lamlash ferry *Hero* in an impromptu race. This defeat greatly disappointed the hundreds of onlookers on board. Much was made in the local press as to the reasons why: 'shortness of steam', 'one engine unfortunately overheating' and 'unfavourable circumstances' were given as excuses. A fortnight later she redeemed herself in a repeat encounter when she 'completely' beat the *Hero*. The account of the second race was reported at length in the *Illustrated London News* and *The Times*, which circulated in America.

Some two years later (1862) Christopher Memminger, Secretary of the Confederate Treasury, having secured the services of a few master engravers, was anxiously looking for ways to import engraving machinery and presses. His need was to mass-produce high quality paper money, bonds and securities for the new state. Scotland was identified as a prime source. Its banking system pre-dated the setting up of the Bank of England and so each of the numerous independent Scottish banking companies (most were regionally based, like the Clydesdale Bank) retained the right to print their own banknotes.

Then there was the problem of shipping such a unique and precious cargo. As this was a particularly sensitive mission, it was understood that it could not be entrusted to third parties and private runners. One of his agents, Major Benjamin Ficklin CSA, had done his research. He told Memminger of a Clyde steamer he knew of, one that was 'admirably adapted for blockade running . . . called the *Giraffe*'. Ficklin appears to have been following her progress in the British press. He had it from his contacts in Glasgow that she was losing money for her owners and would soon be put up for sale.

Part of Ficklin's proposal was that, after she had delivered her 'one-off' consignment, he would relieve the Treasury of their outlays by purchasing her for his own private running venture. Much to his chagrin, this was rejected in favour of a partnership with the forward-looking Ordnance Bureau. Once this was settled, a young naval officer, Lieutenant John Wilkinson, was selected to accompany Ficklin to Britain. Their remit was to purchase this vessel and return with the cargo of printing equipment and whatever munitions Huse could deliver to the Clyde.

Wilkinson relates in his memoirs how they sneaked out of Wilmington on Fraser & Company's *Kate* during a dark stormy night. From Nassau they crossed to Havana and on to St Thomas, where they took passage for Britain on the splendid Cunarder *Atrato*.

In the interim, the *Giraffe* had made her last Irish Sea passage for her owners. Arriving in Glasgow from Belfast (10 October) she was moved up to Tod & McGregor's Meadowside Yard to join the others in dock awaiting conversion to blockade runners.

As usual, her arrival did not go unnoticed. On 17 October, US Consul Prettyman reported to Seward that she was the latest addition to 'the fleet fitting out in this port. She is one of the fastest and best steamers sailing from this port.' Five days later her registration was transferred to a Liverpool speculator. Almost immediately, he sold her on to Edward Pembroke of London, a well-known Southern sympathiser who acted as a front for the armaments dealer Alexander Collie & Company of Manchester and London.

By the time Ficklin and Wilkinson arrived in London, Collie had his mind firmly set on using her in his own private running operation and refused to sell her when approached. After much pleading he relented. His price was £32,000, the same as he had paid for her, with the proviso that – should the Confederate government decide to sell her on the open market after her mission – he should have first refusal. It was a shrewd move as it granted him great standing and favour with the new Secretary of War, James A. Seddon, who remarked on his 'spirit of liberality and friendship in the sale of the *Giraffe*'. Thereafter, Collie's runners were given official preference in future government contracts.

With ownership of the *Giraffe* settled, Ficklin and Wilkinson enjoyed a month's sojourn in London while she underwent her refit and conversion (to take 360 tons cargo) in the Clyde. Receiving news of her completion, they journeyed north to a Confederate safe house in the quiet Stirlingshire village of Bridge of Allan. It had good railway links to Edinburgh and Glasgow, enabling Ficklin to set about his task of purchasing engraving and printing machinery and materials. In the process he recruited twenty-six lithographers who agreed to return to Richmond with him to set up an engraving shop and run the presses.

On 15 November 1862, the *Giraffe*, painted an 'off-white' and fully laden with printing machinery, medicines and munitions, left the Clyde for Madeira. Like the *Fingal* before her, she departed flying the Union Jack, under the command of a Scottish master and manned by a locally raised crew. It was a rough passage, during which Wilkinson was greatly impressed by her 'superb qualities as a sea boat'. At Funchal they spent three days taking on coal from lighters before heading out across the Atlantic for San Juan, Puerto Rico. She eventually steamed into Nassau on 19 December 1862, where her Scots crew were paid off, having fulfilled their contract. By not trying to coerce these men into running the blockade, the time-wasting and costly experience of Coxetter on the *Herald* was avoided.

Nine days later, under Wilkinson's command and with a new and willing crew, two pilots and a signals officer, she slipped through the blockading lines into Cape Fear River via the New Inlet. The passage was not without a major scare. A couple of miles outside the bar and in complete darkness, she grounded on the notorious offshore sandbank known as the 'Lump'. Travelling at speed she came to a shuddering halt, bowling the crew off their feet, close by an unsuspecting blockader. Wilkinson immediately ordered his party of terrified Scots lithographers into the long boats and had them rowed ashore. A few hours later, with the aid of kedge anchor and a rising tide, the *Giraffe* was got off and ran over the bar at full speed without being discovered.

Two days later the *Giraffe* docked at Wilmington and was handed over to the Confederate government. Ficklin was waiting there as he had returned independently, via a fast New York packet, and made his way south in time for her arrival. He cajoled Memminger at the Treasury into agreeing to sell her to him but the War Department would not have it so.

For the first steamer acquired by the government as a regular runner, Secretary Seddon thought it fit to put his name as owner in her new register. She was renamed *Robert E. Lee* and embarked upon what was to prove to be a very profitable enterprise. Over the next eleven months she made twenty runs carrying munitions in and 7,000 bales of cotton out under Wilkinson's command. On his final approaches he always flew the Confederate flag, to the great annoyance of his pursuers.

Wilkinson was one of the wiliest of the Confederate blockade-running commanders. He had studied the methods the blockaders used to direct their vessels towards a speeding runner on a dark night. This required the gunboat that first spotted the runner to fire a small cannon, followed by a signal rocket, the colour of which indicated the channel the runner was making for or out of. Wilkinson's solution was to have a set of decoy rockets made up by a New York pyrotechnic company, which he fired from the *Giraffe* if rumbled during a night run. This was usually enough to send his pursuers steaming off in the wrong direction.

Wilkinson also made a number of famous daylight dashes straight through their midst. He trusted that they would be caught napping by his unexpected gambit and then reluctant to fire so close, should their shot miss and hit one of their own.

He claimed in his memoirs that he was the first to resort to burning cotton, soaked in turpentine, in her furnaces when he was pursued by the fast modern cruiser USS *Iroquois*. On that occasion he managed to escape her grasp with a sudden change in direction. He executed this manoeuvre behind the cover of a smokescreen sent up by deliberately piling dirty bituminous North Carolina 'brown' coal into the over-worked furnaces. The heat was so great that the deck plates imme-diately above the furnaces began to buckle. Wilkinson recounted that he had to go below, remove his smouldering shoes and stick his feet out of a porthole in his cabin to cool them down. The sight of them prompted a mischievous young lady passenger, the daughter of Senator Gwin, to tickle them in her appreciation of their narrow escape. Wilkinson's association with the *Robert E. Lee* ended when he was dispatched to Halifax, Nova Scotia on a forlorn secret mission to liberate Confederate prisoners held on Johnson's Island in Lake Erie.

On her return passage the Ulster-born John Knox was her new commander. While still some way from Wilmington, he decided, to the exasperation of his officers, to hove-to close inshore off the North Carolina coast for the night, while he considered his options. At first light (9 November 1863) she was sighted by USS *James Adger* escorting the recently captured *Cornubia* to Beaufort. After a short chase, the *Robert E. Lee* was also taken. Highly incriminating letters between British shipbuilders and Confederate businesses were found on both these runners. Seward later used these to counter claims from Ambassador Lyon that their 'British' crews were harshly treated and kept in custody for overlong periods. Also on board the *Robert E. Lee* were ten passengers, two of whom were British military officers. When questioned, they claimed that they were on two months' leave and enjoying 'an excursion of pleasure'.

Of the 'river class' paddle steamers that left the Clyde in 1862 the *Ruby* serves to complement the details of the *Giraffe*. She was launched by Henderson & Son of Renfrew in May 1861 and was typical of the 'river' paddle steamers' class at the outbreak of the war, a long hull with a narrow beam and shallow draught – less than nine feet when fully loaded. She was of lightweight construction suitable for fast cruising in the relatively sheltered waters of the Firth of Clyde. As such she was only one-third of the registered tonnage of the 'channel class' *Giraffe*. Her two 120-horsepower engines ensured that she gained her place as a high-speed 'racer' on the prestigious Rothesay–Broomielaw route.

In January 1862, the *Ruby* was sold to the engineer and shipowner William Coulborn of Liverpool, who was soon to be a full partner in the Henderson & Son shipbuilding firm which built her. She changed hands again in early November when Robert Heddell of Manchester purchased her for Alexander Collie. Having parted with the *Giraffe*, he had been looking for a replacement in his blockade-running scheme. Once the *Ruby* was secured, Collie expended only four days on a refit before sending her out to Bermuda manned by a 'roguish lot of engineers'. She left one day ahead of the *Giraffe* but seems to have been detained at Nassau for some reason, perhaps for repairs. It was not until mid-February 1863 that the *Ruby* entered Charleston on the first of her eight successful runs. On 11 June, however, she was chased ashore near the Lighthouse Inlet and destroyed by shellfire.

For those following her from the Clyde, there was more than just the adverse weather to face in the Atlantic crossing. By late 1862, following Wilkes' example, many Federal commanders took the widest possible interpretation of their orders to stop and search in international waters – and conducted forays on both sides of the Atlantic.

The experience of the composite (wood on iron frame) screw 'channel class' *Thistle* illustrates this new development. She was built by Laurence Hill & Company of Port Glasgow in 1859 for the Glasgow & Londonderry Steam Packet Company and was acquired by George Wigg of Liverpool in early October 1862. He was acting for the Navigation Company of Liverpool, one of six blockade-running firms in which he held an interest.

Wigg sent her south to Bramley Moor Dock, Liverpool to be converted for her new role. In early December, the *Scotsman* reported her departure with three other steamers, making 'no secret' that they were off to run the blockade. The *Thistle* arrived at Funchal flying British colours, a week after the *Giraffe* had passed through, and dropped anchor near HMS *Leopard* which was in passage from China to London. A short time later Craven on the USS *Tuscarora* came in and anchored uncomfortably close – keeping his steam up so as to leave at a moment's notice. Captain Maxted on the *Thistle* felt it prudent to leave Madeira as soon as he had completed his coaling from the lighters.

On clearing out for St Thomas, West Indies, he was chased by the *Tuscarora* and shadowed by the *Leopard*. All this warlike activity just outside the three-mile limit was, apparently, a source of great annoyance to the local Portuguese authorities, who were wholly ignored. In what promised to be another international incident in the making, the *Leopard* looked on as a boarding party from the *Tuscarora*, led by a German-accented lieutenant, clambered onto the *Thistle* within sight of Funchal.

They checked her papers and rummaged her cargo but found nothing. By then most small runners making the crossing had stopped carrying

contraband and sailed in ballast to Bermuda to minimise seizure in
transit. They then turned to questioning her officers. One of the *Thistle*'s
mates was identified as having previously served on the CSS *Florida* but
no action was taken and the *Thistle* was allowed to proceed.

This incident did not go unchallenged. Ambassador Lyon lodged a
note of protest with Secretary Seward that 'a more un-neutral use of
port could not be well conceived than lying in wait in it for the vessels
of a neutral state, as they entered and left it, and, on passing the limits
of three mile, boarding and visiting them, and then returning to the
port.' Seward's response to Lyon was that he would reprimand the
officer in charge, if the details were as described. No such reprimand
was issued.

While the diplomats wrangled over the legalities of this incident, the
Thistle sailed on – intent on making a profit. On her first run into
Charleston from Nassau on the night of 27/28 January 1863 she had a
very narrow escape. The *Irish Times* published an eyewitness account
of this daredevil exploit some months later entitled 'The Perils of
Running the Blockade'. The author was credited as a local Charleston
resident who was normally a correspondent for the *Scotsman* but he
may well have been her pilot on that night.

He partially blanked her name in his dispatch, by then the standard
format for a front-line report of a run:

> It was night, and all danger seemed to have passed. At length,
> however, a blinding flash and stunning report, followed by the
> peculiar half scream, half roar of a shell as it flew overhead, broke
> the stillness of the night. This shell had been fired from a gunboat
> ahead, and directly in the track of T—e, whose presence had been
> betrayed by the escape of some sparks from her funnel. In a moment
> the surface of the sea was illuminated by the meteor-like flashes of
> innumerable rockets, while as many blue lights threw a sickly glare
> over the scene. It rendered for a moment almost every vessel in the
> blockading fleet clearly visible, as it did too, the helpless little T—e
> in their midst.
>
> While this had been taking place, however, the engineers had
> weighed down the safety valve, shut off the feed pipe, and piled up
> the furnaces with resin, oil and turpentine, and the captain and
> pilot, having, thanks to the Yankee illumination, discerned their
> enemies' whereabouts, had headed the T—e clear of them, and she
> quivered in every plate as she fairly flew on her way under an
> immense pressure of steam.

All this time shot and shell had been plunging over and around her, but, thanks to her rate of speed, they began to fall astern, or where the Yankees reckoned she should have been. A large and very fast steamer, the *Quaker City*, of eleven guns was now in pursuit, firing her bow as fast as it could be loaded. At this point a vessel was seen nearly ahead, and though painted of the blockade running colour [a dirty whitish grey], the T—e's course was altered, though not a moment too soon, for as she passed across the stranger's stern the latter bumped hard and fast against a sand bank.

A little twinkling light ahead of the T—e showed another Yankee and again was the T—e's course altered. The *Quaker City*, though now far behind, still maintained her harmless fire and her pursuit, and so matters continued till the lead [line] announced that the T—e had crossed the bar, and was within range of Fort Sumter's guns. The T—e held on towards Charleston up the narrow and intricate channel, and had got abreast of Fort Beauregard when she grounded. There was now no alternative but to wait patiently for sunrise, which was already heralded by the first faint streaks of morning light.

As the morning grew, the *Quaker City* was seen about a mile from the bar, and she slowly went about, and returned to her station, a movement that was considerably accelerated by a shot from the guns of [Fort] Beauregard.

The steamer that had grounded could now be distinctly seen some five miles off, surrounded by a little fleet of armed Yankee schooners. She was recognised as the *Princess Royal*, laden with arms and steam machinery for the Southern Government, to whom her loss is a very great one, even if they have since been amply revenged in kind. The Yankees got her off later in the afternoon, and took her alongside of the flagship *Powhatten*. Soon after daylight several batteries of artillery were posted along the shore of Sullivan's Island, so as to cover the T—e, in the event of the Yankees attempting a cutting-out expedition; but they seemed too much engrossed in their prize, to molest the prey that had escaped them. At high water the T—e floated safely off, and proceeded on her way up to Charleston. Out of six vessels that attempted to run the blockade on the 27th and 28th of January, three are now in Charleston, one (the *Princess Royal*) has been captured, and two are missing.

While the blockade off Charleston and Wilmington gathered strength, the New Year brought much-needed relief for the runners in the waters off St George, Bermuda. In Bourne's letter to Caleb Huse in London, he reported the safe arrival of his most recent shipment of armaments on the *Justitia*. In passing he mentions that: 'We have had no visits from Yankee cruisers and are not likely to have any, the [British] Admiral and fleet have returned from Nassau and will winter at Dock yard [anchorage].'

He also took the opportunity to reassure Huse that he had spoken to the island's Attorney General and the status quo with regard to arms running had not been changed, despite Lord Russell's recent posturing:

You will read in the *Royal Gazette* of this island a proclamation prohibiting the exportation of Arms and ammunition but as no law of this kind has ever been sanctioned by the Home Authorities it is necessary to make it known by proclamation, but it is only intended for the Governor and Council to act on in case of hostilities with England, and I learnt to my satisfaction that it will not affect the cause at issue, as far as I am concerned.

By the end of January, two more large arms shipments had arrived directly from London on board the *Harriet Pinckney* and the *Merrimac*. These were spirited ashore to Bourne's warehouse and those of his associates, A.J. Musson and A.W. Penno. The gunpowder was dispatched to the 'Whale House' magazine. Once transferred to the small runners, the cargo manifests hid the true nature of the iron-bound cases under the innocuous general headings 'manufactured goods' and 'combustible materials'. Their declared port of destination was invariably given as British Nassau or Halifax, Nova Scotia.

By the start of 1863 the blockade-running business had entered a new phase. The Federal blockading squadrons had doubled in numbers as Welles' building programme churned out gunboats. These were supplemented by captured blockade runners – the ultimate 'poachers turned gamekeepers'. The *Scotsman* reprinted a spurious lampoon on this situation which first appeared in the *New York Herald* the previous November:

The government and people of the US rather hope that the [running] trade will now be continued: for they know the result will be largely in their favour and will continue to be so every day. 'John Bull' builds excellent steamers and furnishes first rate goods which he expects to realise large profits; consequently, all we now take from him is admirably suited for the use of the army and navy, and saves much trouble purchasing elsewhere and paying contractors exorbitant prices for worthless articles.

The captured steamers were greatly needed. It took fifty vessels to maintain the blockade off Wilmington alone. These had to be split into two distinct groups to cover the Old and New Inlets. It took a minimum of four hours' steaming to make the passage between the two stations. This involved a forty-mile detour around the great Frying Pan Shoal which extends some ten miles out from Smith's Island into the Atlantic. In adverse weather, the blockaders had to stand out to sea or risk wrecking on the numerous shoals. During this time runners could slip in and out unchallenged.

Whilst the forts guarding the Cape Fear River inlets remained operational and in Confederate hands, the topography greatly favoured the runner. On an outgoing run, a master would drop down channel to the small town of Smithville. There he had a clear view of both exits and the latest advice on the blockaders' deployment from the commanders of the great coastal fortresses, Caswell and Fisher. After this it was a matter of choosing the right channel and the right moment. Running out under cover of darkness and keeping close to the breakers to mask the sound of the paddles, most masters retained the element of surprise until they were well clear.

The blockaders adapted their tactics accordingly. At first they rode to their anchors or cruised slowly, fully lit, giving away their positions. When this was realised, a complete blackout regime was imposed on the squadron. The exception was a single light on the commander's vessel which was anchored in the midst of the fleet as a point of reference. Even this became a handy marker for the runners and this practice too was soon stopped.

The offshore cruisers were also now closely at blockading the main storage islands involved in running: the Danish West Indian island of St Thomas and the British islands of Bermuda and the Bahamas. Gideon Welles' decision to promote Charles Wilkes of *Trent* notoriety to commander of the Federal West Indies Squadron was a political folly of the first magnitude. Following his example, his officers regularly overstepped their authority and blatantly ignored the sovereignty of the three-mile limit in their pursuit of suspects.

The most potentially explosive incident happened on 30 May 1863 when Captain Stephen D. Trenchard on the uss *Rhode Island* chased the runner *Margaret & Jessie* ashore on Eleuthera Island, part of the

British Bahamas. Trenchard crossed the three-mile line to closely bombard the runner (the 'CB' ex-Isle of Man ferry *Douglas*) while her Scots captain William Wilson was landing his passengers. Shells from Trenchard's great parrot cannons – with a range of five miles – not only ripped through one of the stranded runner's boilers but also struck the island, destroying trees and ploughing up the soil. The British press was furious at this 'ferocious outrage'. The *Army & Navy Gazette*, referring to the threat posed by the uss *Tuscarora* stalking the css *Nashville* in British waters blasted: 'If at Eleuthera, why not at the Isle of Wight, in Southampton Water?'

It was a clear-cut case which demanded the firmest protest from the British Foreign Office. The Washington administration realised the folly of letting such actions by their officers continue unchecked or, indeed, condoning them. Captain Trenchard was brought before a Court of Inquiry the following April. He blamed his pilot for not warning him that he had entered British waters. As the captain of the *Margaret & Jessie* failed to attend the hearing it was assumed that he was indeed a runner. Trenchard was exonerated on the grounds that he had not intended to shell the island.

There were very good reasons why the runner's master had not appeared in court. Captain William Wilson, described as a 'careful quiet Scot', was something of a hero for the Southern cause. He was one of the first to fly the Palmetto flag of the seceded state of South Carolina from the mast of the Fraser, Trenholm & Company vessel *Emily St Pierre* while in Liverpool. He had since voyaged to Calcutta for gunny cloth to make cotton bales and had been captured trying to get into Charleston. A prize crew of fourteen men was placed on board and ordered to proceed to Philadelphia. Thirty miles off Cape Hatteras, Wilson (with the help of his cook and steward), overpowered the prize master by placing a loaded pistol to his head.

One month later, Wilson, almost demented by lack of sleep, sailed into Liverpool. Fêted as a hero by the British press and mercantile interest, he was considered a 'pirate' by the acutely embarrassed Federal navy. He jumped at the chance to command the runner *Margaret & Jessie* for his old company.

While Trenchard got off lightly, an understanding was reached that, given the range of the latest naval weaponry, six miles was now the *de facto* limit of national sovereignty. This was respected for the rest of the war, removing a great bone of contention between the United States and the European powers. That November, the *Margaret &*

Jessie, under a different commander, was captured trying to enter the New Inlet on her twentieth run.

As the blockading squadrons geared up and refined their tactics, control of the running business was also evolving. Bulloch had advocated from the start that the Confederate Navy Department should follow the example of the Ordnance Bureau and acquire its own small fleet of runners to avoid 'the killing prices on private steamers'.

While his boss Mallory, the Secretary for the Navy, reserved his judgement, Seddon, the Secretary of War, acted independently to acquire a new fleet of runners for the Commissary and Quartermaster Bureau that supplied the armies with everything from blankets to medicines. His plan took the form of a semi-private contract that authorised the artillery officer and one-time Richmond merchant, Captain William G. Crenshaw, to go to Britain and form a partnership with a British company. The deal was that the War Department would meet three-quarters of the costs and Crenshaw and his British partner would find the remaining quarter between them. The cargo space was to be allocated along the same formula, with the two partners receiving a commission on the purchase and sale of the cargo carried on the War Department account. As was to be expected, Alexander Collie of Manchester was the chosen partner, with Commissioner James Mason overseeing the proceedings from his office in London.

All of this was done without the knowledge or approval of Slidell, Gorgas or Huse. It seriously undermined their position, especially with Isaac, Campbell & Company of London which had greatly extended itself – to the point of bankruptcy – to provide them with funds and credit.

The fallout was terrible. Huse refused to deal with Crenshaw or sanction his purchases. Crenshaw retaliated by writing directly to Seddon accusing Huse of misappropriating Confederate funds. He urged Seddon to promote him to the same rank as Huse so that he might act independently. While his allegations of bribery and corruption were being investigated, Crenshaw and Collie went about ordering a fleet of four new steamers. They also visited the Clyde, where they bought the *Venus*, yet another large paddle steamer recently launched by J. and G. Thomson of Finnieston and Govan. In the space of a few days she was sent to Bermuda under Captain Charles Murray.

She was one of thirty Clyde steamers to cross the Atlantic in 1863. During this year the war reached its peak. Lee's victory at Chancellorville in May marked the zenith of the South's military achievements.

This incited a flurry of acquisitions in the Clyde for the blockade. The newly appointed US consul at Glasgow, Underwood, reported to Seward in Washington:

> Within the last three weeks . . . not less than thirteen of the fastest and best light draft steamers of the Clyde have been purchased by various parties to run the blockade ports on our coast. Some of these purchases have been made, I have reason to believe, by agents of the Confederate Government and for it. Most of them, however, have been made as bold and gambling ventures, allured by the enormous, but in most cases no doubt falsely reported, profits of the enterprise. One successful venture fires the minds and excites the competition of hundreds.

There can be no doubt that a boom had started. As the best steamers disappeared from their usual routes, the local papers carried angry 'Letters to the Editor' and reports of public protests over the disruption to local passenger services. Their replacements were old, slow and uncomfortable in comparison. What was being built was being sold off the stocks. In April alone eleven steamers were launched on the Clyde and immediately headed out to sea.

The boom was, however, short-lived, with the news of the Confederate disaster at Gettysburg in July. This devastating defeat wiped out any hope that the South could win the war. In the retreat, Lee's shattered army were forced to leave most of their equipment on the field. Driven back into Virginia, Lee now faced the enormous problem of feeding and clothing his army in what was rapidly descending into a brutal war of siege and attrition. The war in the West was going no better for the South. Vicksburg was lost and at Chattanooga the defeat turned into rout when Confederate soldiers fled, discarding their rifles. Morale was ebbing away and the desertion rate soared. When all this grim news reached Europe, the number of new subscribers and the value of Confederate Cotton Loan Bonds slumped.

In August, Seddon was facing both military and financial collapse. The very survival of the Confederacy demanded that the armies in the field were quickly re-equipped, clothed and fed. To revitalise the supply and financial situation he took the unprecedented step of ordering his commanders at the key ports to take control of the runners. They were empowered to enforce his new ruling that half of their outgoing cargo space must be set aside for government-owned cotton. It was a fraught time as the private runners threatened a boycott, while over-zealous local army and naval commanders bickered over who should enforce what.

To stabilise the financial situation in Europe, General Colin J. McRae was appointed 'supremo' over all procurement operations. He had arrived in Britain in May to investigate Crenshaw's allegations against Huse. These he found groundless and under his firm hand all discord ended and European confidence in Confederate bonds was restored.

Back in 'Dixie', the dramatic reversal of military fortunes finally galvanised a number of state governors into taking direct action to secure a supply line for their own troops. The first to act was the dynamic Zebulon B. Vance, the newly elected governor of North Carolina. His state was the epicentre of the textile industry which clothed the Confederate armies. As the supply of raw materials – leather, spun cotton and wool – ran out, he decided to use the government funds allocated to his state to pay for uniforms and to buy materials from Britain. His plan required that a fast steamer be purchased to run in his cargoes.

His two agents, John White and Thomas Crossan, arrived in Manchester around the same time as McRae. They were carrying cotton bonds worth $1,500,000 drawn on the state of North Carolina. Alexander Collie, by now entrenched as the Confederates' preferred British business partner, took charge of these bonds. They were highly preferential to the more adventurous holder as they guaranteed redemption of every £100 borrowed against twelve cotton bales (400 lb each) – delivered to the quay at Wilmington on sixty days' notice.

Underwritten by Collie's credit, White (the merchant) went about acquiring a cargo while Crossan (the naval expert) sought out a suitable runner. His choice was the Glasgow–Dublin ferry *Lord Clyde*. She was a six-month-old 'channel class' built by Caird and Company of Greenock the previous year. He moved quickly. Within the month she was purchased for £35,000, loaded and dispatched to Bermuda. She got into the Cape Fear River safely on 28 June 1863, where she was renamed *Advance* – as more befitting her new and highly successful career as a state-owned runner.

During that summer, more states concluded a similar agreement with a local running company. By now a system was developing whereby the preferred company bought a string of fast steamers for the blockade run and a large freighter to convey the contraband and luxury goods from Britain to the warehouses on Bermuda and Nassau.

Governor Joseph Brown entered into one such agreement with the Importing & Exporting Company of Georgia to carry his state's goods on commission and with priority to load cotton. The agents involved were Gazaway B. Lamar and Henry Lafone of Lancaster. Lafone was a regular visitor to the Clyde where he bought four of the six steamers acquired for the company over the next year. South Carolina soon followed suit but, as the boom took off, had to compete for steamers with the growing number of private joint-stock companies that had formed to exploit what was by now an exceedingly profitable trade.

As the pace of blockade running gathered momentum, so too did the rate of capture. Acting Rear Admiral S.P. Lee, commanding the blockading squadron off Wilmington, reported with some satisfaction that his vessels had captured or destroyed seventeen runners between 1 August 1863 and the end of the year. Eight were Clyde-built steamers. One was Crenshaw and Collie's *Venus* running under their contract to supply foodstuffs for the Commissary and Quartermaster Bureau.

The report of her destruction on her fourth run gives insights into both the tactics of the day and the composition of her crew. The *Cork Examiner* published a report of her loss in November 1863 which first appeared in the *New York Tribune* the previous month, under the title 'From the fleet off Wilmington N.C. Capture and destruction of the *Venus*':

> The US steam gunboat *Nansemond* came into this port this evening from the blockading fleet off Wilmington, bringing news of the capture and destruction of the Anglo-Confederate blockade runner *Venus* . . . early on the morning of the 21st inst. [October] . . . she was running down the coast close to the shore about eight miles north of New Inlet.
>
> An exciting chase then ensued, during which the gunboat fired several well directed shots and gained upon her steadily. Seeing that escape was impossible, the blockade runner played the usual game of running onto the beach. She went on under full speed and at falling tide, and after a full hour of the most vigorous and un-successful efforts to get her afloat, it was decided the only course was to burn her . . . She was carefully fired in three places, and in the morning was completely burned out . . . The *Venus* had an assorted cargo, the principal article being bacon. She is a splendid vessel, nearly new . . . divided into four compartments, each of which was perfectly and independently watertight. Her engines were magnificent.

Only the pilot managed to escape, leaving the crew of five officers and eighteen men to be taken prisoner. Three of the officers – the first mate, chief and second engineer – gave Scotland as their domicile. The Captain, Mr W.O. Pinchon, was an Englishman:

> a small, quiet man, and very uncommunicative. This is his first trip, and he feels the loss of his command very seriously. The rest are a rather brutish looking set. They admitted that the *Nansemond* put three shots into their vessel, killing one man.

The *Venus* had been flying British colours when she was shelled and her novice captain, assuming some sort of immunity, had failed to destroy his signal book or his personal notes. The latter listed the sixty-three runners that were operating that year. Against half their number he had marked 'captured' or 'destroyed'. Twenty-two on that list were Clyde-built steamers. Five were recent arrivals, the rest were the survivors of the 1862 sailings.

During the remaining two months of 1863, four more were added to this tally. The last was the *General Beauregard* (the old Belfast–Glasgow ferry *Havelock*) driven ashore and destroyed by USS *Howquah* just north of Fort Fisher, Wilmington on 15 December. Up until then she had been highly successful (seventeen runs in) for the Chicora Company of Charleston. Her capture reduced the number of Clyde-built steamers still running to twenty-three.

As the war entered its last full year, President Davis approved the radical 'New Plan' devised by secretaries Seddon, Benjamin and Memminger to give the government control of its finances abroad. In one sweep, all private contracts in Europe were withdrawn; General McRae was given a free hand to control all credit and funds held abroad; and future purchasing was settled on two officers – Huse for the army and Bulloch for the navy – overseen by McRae.

As cotton had effectively replaced Confederate money as the medium for exchange in the running trade, its purchase and export were now to be tightly controlled at a price fixed by Congress. These measures received the President's signature on 6 February 1864, the same day as a second law was passed prohibiting 'the import of luxuries or articles not necessaries or of common good'. This consolidated the early decree that set aside half of the cargo space on a private runner for government cargo.

This ruling included those vessels owned by state governors, sparking a revolt in Congress. Governors Vance and Brown led the challenge, demanding exemption for their runners. Despite their violent protestations and threats, President Davis pressed on. He raised the small 'Bureau of Foreign Supplies' to a paramount position over all other departments engaged in running cotton. Henceforth, all cotton for export belonged to the Treasury. At each of the main ports a disbursing agent from the Bureau of Foreign Supplies was empowered to regulate the exchange of run goods and foodstuffs for cotton at a fixed price. All excess cotton stock landed at Bermuda and Nassau on the government account was shipped directly to Fraser, Trenholm & Company in Liverpool. The proceeds of these sales were immediately put at McRae's disposal.

The result was that the Confederate procurement effort in Europe enjoyed a sixfold increase in revenue from every bale sold. The backlash from the private running companies was immediate and most laid up their steamers at Nassau and Bermuda in protest. The boycott did not last long as the running trade, even with the new controls, was still extremely profitable. There were also ways around the restrictions, as Begbie and his business associates found to their profit. Most were back in business by the end of March 1864.

By the spring of that year, the fortunes of blockade-running companies seemed secure – for the foreseeable future at least. The advance of the Federal 'hordes', as Begbie liked to refer to them, had been checked and reduced to trench warfare in front of Richmond and Atlanta. The coastal defences at Charleston, Wilmington, Mobile and Galveston were holding firm. The South was becoming increasingly dependent on the runners for virtually every basic commodity, including food, and profiteering took hold. Despite the new regulations, incoming cargoes of luxuries did occur and readily passed into the hands of unscrupulous local companies. There was also a fortune to be made in redeeming the Cotton Loan Bonds at the quayside inside the Confederacy by those bold enough to run the blockade on their own account.

The surge in demand, coupled with the revival of Confederate credit and the cotton bond market, encouraged a wave of speculative shipbuilding the length of Clydeside. As the *Dumbarton Herald* reported in late April 1864:

> At present there are no fewer than forty-two deep-sea steamers building for blockade running alone. Of these, fifteen are building at Glasgow, four at Whiteinch, six at Renfrew, six at Dumbarton, two at Port Glasgow, and nine at Greenock.

The report estimated that when the value of these new vessels was added to those already sold to the blockade (sixty-four) over the two previous years, the total price tag was a staggering £1,388,000. This is a massive amount by the money values of the day. Approximately a third of this was war-inflated profit.

By 1864 the shipbuilders along the banks of the Clyde were well aware of the clandestine activities of the Federal intelligence agents. Security was very tight at the yards, inspections were discouraged and the launching ceremony cut to a minimum. As Consul Underwood moaned:

> There is not a shipyard on the Clyde that is not . . . impenetrable to outside observation . . . and should an unlucky workman dare speak of anything progressing in the yard, he is instantly black-balled and expelled. Vessels are frequently launched with steam up and scarcely stop before proceeding to sea. Hence it is impossible to keep up with the operations [going on at the shipyards] extending over a distance of more than twenty miles.

He reckoned that twenty-seven yards were then involved in churning out runners, employing as many as 25,000 men and boys. Seventeen were start-up companies, set up specifically to exploit the seemingly insatiable market for runners that summer.

He later concluded that they had launched fifty runners in that year. Almost all were of the new design of large paddle steamers with a broad beam and clear deck capable of carrying 1,000 bales of cotton. Most had an exceptionally shallow draught, suitable for running the Gulf ports if need be.

The most technically advanced custom-built runners were launched between June and August. These were Collie's five 'Flamingo class' paddles for his new contract with McRae. They were highly distinctive, with three raked funnels. Their large bunkers and high speed (over twenty knots) meant they could make the long run between Halifax, Nova Scotia and Charleston. Collie's new steamers were on a mission of such importance that exceptional security surrounded their outward passage. The British government was now impounding new large freighters which were plainly earmarked for conversion to gunboats or cruisers.

The first to go was the *Flamingo*, followed in quick succession by the *Falcon* and the *Condor*. The report of the departure of the *Condor* reveals how easy it was to slip away. A few days after being handed over by her builders, Randolph, Elder & Company, she left from the East Dock, Greenock (16 August) supposedly on a 'pleasure cruise' around the Firth of Clyde. She sailed under the command of the adventurer 'Captain A. Roberts' (in reality Augustus C. Hobart-Hampden RN). She reappeared at Limerick on the west coast of Ireland the following day, causing a great stir. As the *Irish Times* noted:

> On Friday evening the Confederate steamer, the *Condor*, a new vessel just arrived from the Clyde, where she has been recently built, slackened her speed at Foynes, although she had been running at the rate of twenty-five miles an hour, for the purpose of taking on board a pilot who would conduct her to the port of Limerick.

Her departure was equally dramatic:

> On Saturday, about 2 o'clock, the *Condor* quitted the Limerick docks, not waiting to take in a full supply of coal ordered. Although wagons were wheeled along as fast as horseflesh could accomplish the task, yet several wagons were left behind; and the *Condor* after being visited by thousands, was almost in an instant out of sight.

Two months later, the last of Collie's new steamers, the sister ship *Evelyn*, steamed into the same Irish port. Her register had been transferred to new Irish owners there in early August, so it would appear that the Limerick link in the conspiracy was well laid. It was a flying visit as 'she went out again this morning, her name unknown, as she would not wait for coast guard men to board her . . . and went at the rate of eighteen knots an hour against a flood tide'.

The reason for this subterfuge only became apparent six months later when the *Greenock Telegraph* ran two stories on her exploits in February 1865:

> A story is current of the success of one of the most spirited speculations in the annals of blockade running, and by which it is said its originators have realised profits to the amount of £100,000. It is stated that Mr. Tait, the well known army clothier of Limerick, Sir John Arnot, a native of Auchtermuchty [Fife], and the firm of Cannock & White of Dublin, going shares in the enterprise, had 60,000 suits of military outfits manufactured. A steamer possessing all the qualities necessary for blockade running

was purchased for £40,000, and the clothing put on board. Captain Burgoyne, a dashing sailor, son of the late Sir John Burgoyne, was appointed commander of the craft, with £1,000 a month, and with instructions that if he succeeded in landing his cargo in Wilmington he should have 5 per cent as his share of the profits, and on arriving at Liverpool with a cargo of cotton he should be rewarded with 2½ per cent additional on the latter transaction. Everything was got ready with as much dispatch and as little noise as possible . . . she steamed out of Limerick port on her hazardous expedition.

As she neared her destination the Federals were bombarding Wilmington [late December], and in the thick of the fray Captain Burgoyne slipped in unnoticed, unshipped his military stores, put on board a cargo of cotton [for Nassau], and [weeks later] a telegram from Liverpool has announced her arrival at that port without so much as receiving a shot from the Federals.

By the time the *Evelyn* recrossed the Atlantic, Fort Fisher had finally succumbed to a ferocious bombardment and frontal assault. With its loss Wilmington was closed to runners. Consequently, the *Evelyn*'s last run was into Galveston. On her return to Havana she was put up for sale alongside her sister vessels *Falcon*, *Ptarmigan* and *Flamingo* and another fourteen runners.

The *Condor* was missing. On 1 October 1864 she safely ran under the guns of Fort Fisher from Halifax. Unfortunately the pilot ran her aground while avoiding the recently stranded runner *Night Hawk*. One of Hobart-Hampden's passengers was the Southern belle and infamous spy, Rose O'Neal Greenhow. She pleaded to be put ashore rather than risk capture and a certain trial and execution for treason. He agreed to her request but her dinghy overset in the surf and she was drowned. It was reputed that she was weighed down with vital dispatches for President Davis and $2,000 in gold on her person. The latter was said to be her royalties from her book, *My Imprisonment, or The First Year of Abolitionist Rule in Washington*, which had caused a sensation in Europe. Her body was later recovered from the beach and received full military honours.

In the same month as the *Falcon* was lost, her sister ship *Flamingo* was back in Greenock under the command of the veteran Captain T. Atkinson. He had been forced to return for urgent repairs to her engines after only one trip into Wilmington. The recurring problem was the great difficulty her engineers had in trying to stop her complex engines. The problem had first appeared on the *Flamingo*'s maiden voyage when she was attempting to get alongside the quay at Green-ock after her launch. Her engines ran on after the steam was shut off and she rammed the bulwarks.

With the fault finally fixed, Atkinson was keen to return to the blockade but faced a further delay when his chief engineer, Dickson, was arrested for violently obstructing Customs officers who tried to board her. The police were summoned and he was arrested and charged. For a man used to dodging shells this was a simple matter to resolve. Just as the *Flamingo* was about to sail for Madeira, Dickson jumped bail and sneaked back on board.

Collie's super racers were just five of a flotilla of over fifty steamers that left the Clyde for the blockade that year. Most were new launchings as only two had been serving Clyde ferry boats. These two, the *Fairy* (put on the remote Havana to Matamoros run) and the ancient *Blenheim* which had been launched back in 1848, had both previously been passed over as being too slow. The *Blenheim* had the distinction of being the last runner to be captured trying to get into Wilmington after the fall of Fort Fisher. Her master was duped into making the attempt by the invading Federals who kept the signal lights burning as an enticement for unsuspecting runners. Begbie referred to this piece of deception as 'a regular rat trap' when he heard of it weeks later.

The *Greenock Advertiser* (26 January 1865) informed its Clydeside readership of the capture of the last of the few:

> Unaware that Fort Fisher had been taken the *Blenheim* the last of the Belfast Steamship Company vessels sold to Richard Eustace in 1864 was captured attempting the New Inlet passage by the ex-blockader USS *Tristram Shandy*. The other – the *Charlotte* – was taken by the *Malvern* inside the Old Inlet bar after the fall of Fort Fisher, January 1865.

The previous year's departures from the Clyde were new purchases jointly owned by the individual Confederate states and private run-ning companies. The majority had left for the blockade while the prospects for the South were still looking reasonably good. The *Greenock Advertiser* reported in mid-October 1864 that 'in the last nine months no less than thirty-six new vessels have left the Clyde, as was understood, to run the American blockade'.

It was during that autumn that the first signs of a collapse in confidence by the private runners appeared. The trouble had started that summer when yellow fever had again swept the storehouse islands, decimating the crews and leaving a legacy of quarantine restrictions which reduced trade to a snail's pace. In the Gulf, Farragut had finally taken Mobile early in August. On the Atlantic seaboard, the assaults on the forts guarding Charleston were increasing in ferocity and determination. Forts Wagner and Sumter were in ruins, and only the Confederates' much-feared new weapons – the spar 'torpedo' and the submarine – kept the Federal 'monitor class' vessels from running into the harbour to bombard Charleston itself.

At sea the capture rate was rapidly reaching breaking point for the runners. To stop the haemorrhaging of fast steamers to the Federal blockaders via the prize courts, Mallory issued orders that government runners were not to be allowed to fall into enemy hands intact. Captain Maffitt, now commander of the runner *Owl*, was informed by telegram on 19 September:

> It is of the first importance that our steamers should not fall into the enemy's hands. Apart from the specific loss sustained by the country in the capture of blockade runners, these vessels, lightly armed, now constitute the fleetest and most efficient part of his blockading force off Wilmington.

Henceforth it was expected that a blockade-running captain facing capture should not surrender his vessel but charge her full pelt onto the beach. He should set fire to her rather than let the Federals acquire another fast steamer to add to their blockade squadrons. By then, there were twenty ex-runner Clyde steamers patrolling the blockade under the US Stars and Stripes.

Amongst the last of new steamers to leave the Clyde for the blockade late that year were those ordered by Captain James Carlin. He had been a crack commander who had run the blockade on numerous occasions. He had arrived in the Clyde to buy replacements for the ageing fleet of the Importing & Exporting Company of South Carolina. This firm is often referred to in the accounts by the name of its principal shareholder and manager, William C. Bee of Charleston.

Carlin was no stranger to Clyde-built excellence. He was raised in Carrickfergus, Antrim, the old Irish ferry port in the North Channel, and had emigrated to America. Earlier in the war he had served as master on two Clyde-built blockade runners. Late in 1863 he was dispatched to Britain on his procurement mission. He crossed the Atlantic from Havana on the Spanish steam packet, *Infanta Isabella*, built by Peter Denny. He was greatly impressed by her and sent a photograph of her back to William Bee with a note that she was 'one of the finest ships afloat'. He also held the opinion that Robert Napier had 'the best name and stood the highest' in marine engineering. He was, therefore, pre-disposed to pay an inflated price for their hulls and engines when he arrived in the Clyde.

Carlin toured the shipyards of Britain in January 1864, most of which had full order books, before settling on Denny. His order was for three super racers substantially bigger than Collie's '*Flamingo* class'. He gave Denny exact specifications: they had to be 225 foot long, with a 28-foot beam and a 13-foot hold; and driven by two great Napier oscillating engines (200 horsepower) working on 40 pounds per square inch pressure. Peter Denny gave Carlin his personal assurance that they would be 'adapted in every way for blockade running'. His price was £22,000 each. They were called *Ella*, *Caroline* and *Imogene*.

Carlin also ordered a large screw steamer (225 foot long with a 35-foot beam and a deep 16-foot hold powered by 65-inch diameter oscillators) at an agreed price of £35,500. Her specific mission was to carry two complete marine engines for the Confederate ironclads. Named *Emily II*, she left the Clyde on 23 November 1864 and reached Bermuda with her cargo but failed to run the blockade.

That March he tentatively placed a further order for two more of the same design, called *Charlotte* and *Maude Campbell*, with Peter's brother Archibald. It would appear, however, that he was over-committed and the contracts were soon acquired by other closely connected blockading firms.

The *Ella*, the first of his paddle steamers to be completed, had already arrived in Bermuda that June. She managed six runs before she was chased ashore and destroyed in the Old Inlet of Cape Fear River in December. Carlin had the courtesy to write to the 'Keeper of the Shipping Register' at Glasgow to inform him of her fate so that he might close her entry. Her sister ship *Caroline* arrived too late to attempt Wilmington or Charleston and was sent to Havana where she was laid up.

Carlin's third paddle steamer, *Imogene*, was the last to leave the Clyde for the blockade, clearing out of Greenock on 10 February 1865. She managed two runs into Galveston during April 1865. On her return to Havana she was put up for sale and her crew was paid off – bringing to an end the Clyde's contribution to blockade running into the Confederacy.

Chapter 4

The Clyde's Private Runners

In Jules Verne's blockade-running tale, the owners of the *Dolphin* were Playfair & Company of Glasgow. This company is an invention, no doubt prompted by the need to avoid a libel suit. Verne reports Playfair & Company as 'having a principal of business in Glasgow'. The closest fit is the Albion Trading Company, whose managing director was Thomas Stirling Begbie.

Although Begbie had been born in Chelsea and lived most of his life in London, he was intimately connected with Scotland and the Clyde. His mother was a Scot and he appears to have spent his formative years in the Clydeside area, where he probably served an apprenticeship. This was then the normal route for a well-connected young man seeking to enter into the higher echelons of mercantile management. He certainly acquired his working knowledge of all aspects of marine engineering and ship management there. He married his Canadian-born wife, Gertrude Duvernet, in the village of Barony, Lanark (now a suburb of Glasgow). They spent the earlier part of their married life there, where their eldest son and daughter were born. For a while his neighbour was his future rival in the running trade, David McNutt.

As a 'London Scot' he frequently indulged in the vernacular Scots dialect in his letters to his Clydeside partners. All were leading businessmen whom he regularly hosted on their visits to London. He invariably took his family north for their annual holiday. The Begbie family usually stayed with their close friends, the Wisemans, who resided in Ardencaple Castle, Helensburgh, on the northern shore of the Clyde estuary, opposite Greenock.

At the outbreak of the war he was residing in Wantage House, a mansion in fashionable Ladbroke Road, Kensington, with his young family of two sons and three daughters, attended by four live-in servants. Aged thirty-nine, he was already a highly successful ship-owner and broker with business premises at 4 Mansion House Place, London and 19 West Nile Street, Glasgow.

Since 1855, and perhaps earlier, he had been deeply involved with
two of the foremost shipbuilders on Clydeside, John Scott of Greenock
and Peter Denny of Dumbarton. They were typical Victorian family
businesses. John Scott had taken over his father's yard and was
introducing his young son to management when the war broke
out. Peter Denny was the most energetic of the brothers who ran
their father's world-famous yards of William Denny & Sons. Both
Scott and Denny maintained a close relationship with Begbie. He
regularly visited their yards, placed numerous orders with them and
acted as their broker in chartering or selling the vessels they built on
speculation during the war. Their wives attended the launch of his
vessels – often named after a family member – and took tea when the
Begbies were in town.

With his extensive 'London Scottish' connections, he was the perfect
go-between for Confederate agents looking to acquire steamers to run
the blockade or cruisers and armoured rams to smash it. In his
correspondence he rarely named the 'Southerners' he was involved
with, referring to them only in a non-specific manner, such as 'a rich
gentleman from Mobile'. He only broke this rule when he mentioned a
meeting with 'Captain Bulloch'. He presumably took these measures
as a precaution against his mail being intercepted by Federal agents.
Indeed, there were occasions when he complained to Scott that the
letters he received from him were found open on arrival.

He had just cause to be suspicious. The Federal spy network in
Britain had marked him as a major blockade-running player from the
very start of the war. He first attracted their attention when he sold his
large transatlantic steamer, *Melita*, to Isaac, Campbell & Company of
London for £24,000. This company was then extending a vast amount
of credit to Major Cabel Huse, who was setting up his procurement
mission in Europe and was chronically short of funds.

They immediately chartered the *Melita* to Charles Prioleau, the
chairman of Fraser, Trenholm & Company. He was charged with
the delivery of Huse's first cache of arms bought in Europe. On
1 February 1862 the *Melita* sailed from Antwerp, under Captain
Corbett, bound for New York, which was then still being used as a
conduit to the South. She carried 16,000 old flintlock muskets that
had been converted for percussion cap firing at Liége (at a cost of
£3,000). These she successfully delivered before the Federal authorities acted to close the use of New York. Thereafter, she ran arms
from Europe, to the West Indies isles of St Thomas or Cuba, until she
was retired from the business in May 1863.

In direct contrast to the precautions Begbie took to keep his Southern clients' identities secret, he took scant care to conceal the names and features of the steamers he sent across the Atlantic to run the blockade. He seems never to have doubted the legitimacy of his actions as he had the ear of influential people in both Parliament and the Admiralty. Besides, he was no stranger to controversy. A few years earlier he had chartered one of his vessels under the command of his Dundee captain, David Leslie, to land Garibaldi's thousand 'red shirts' on Sicily.

Begbie, like the fictional James Playfair and Rhett Butler, initially held an ambivalent view of the Civil War. He was troubled by the loss of life and sensed the ultimate futility of it all, but this did not stop him seeing it in stark business terms, the success of which required a pro-South stance.

At the height of the *Trent* affair (November–December 1861), he rushed – as a good British patriot – to offer his crack transatlantic *Mauritius* to the government as a troopship to carry reinforcements to Halifax, Nova Scotia. He gleefully told Scott that there was 'great excitement' in his London shipping circle, 'like the good old Crimean times again, and I am caught napping!' He pulled enough strings and his bid was successful.

Begbie immediately saw the profits which were to be had in running the blockade and made his first enquiries for acquiring rifles around the same time. He also bought his first small fast blockade runner in the winter of 1861. She was the three-year-old ex-Cornish packet paddle steamer *Cornubia*. Following an inspection of her at Bristol by his technical manager, E.S. Paddon, he clinched the deal that November. This greatly pleased him: '*Cornubia* is mine: the best buy of the lot or I'm very much cheated!'

Thereafter, Begbie's interest in blockade running cooled considerably. He held the opinion that, since the '*Trent* incident' had failed to trigger a war between the USA and the European powers, the South would now concede that they stood alone in a war they could not win in the long run. This would force them to settle for a negotiated peace while their armies were still winning battles. The opportunity to make a handsome profit was, he believed, about to evaporate. Early in January 1862 he wrote to Scott warning him that the enormous personal investment he was pouring into building a new yard at Greenock in anticipation of war orders – 'the cream of the affair' – might prove premature. As he put it: 'If it is to be peace, the builders should not be over busy with you on the Clyde.'

Within a matter of weeks he had wholly reversed his opinion. The catalyst for change was the news that the Confederates had abandoned their restrictive policy and had thrown open their trade and ports to all-comers. They were determined to go it alone, with or without Europe. The moment for compromise had gone. This he referred to as 'another shuffle of the cards'. As part of his renewed enthusiasm for the blockade-running business he offered to show Scott around his latest running acquisition, the paddle steamer *Ouachita*, on his trip to London. She was then lying in the Victoria Docks and was about to leave for Nassau.

As part of his 'about face' he now urged Scott to extend himself. With the prospect of orders galore for iron-hulled steamers, he pleaded with Scott to stockpile pig iron from the Consett or Blackburn ironworks in England. Both companies, he assured Scott, were 'howling for orders'.

In his self-appointed role of mentor to the younger Scott (who was then thirty-one years old) he counselled him in his usual clipped manner: 'Americans going at it – apparently North sending large expedition to the South and not all improbable that France and England won't stand by and see ports closed. Arms are now permitted to be shipped hence, restrictions removed.'

By the end of March 1862, Begbie made his first move into the 'direct' blockade-running business. He was spurred by the enormous profit the *Bermuda* had made on her round trip to Savannah from the Mersey with munitions out and 2,000 bales of cotton back. She was then loading at Liverpool preparing to repeat this feat in a second round trip.

Begbie's first deal was to charter his large 1,000-ton steamer *Memphis* to Zollinger, Andreas & Company of Manchester. They were armaments dealers who were, almost certainly, fronting yet another delivery for Fraser, Trenholm & Company of Liverpool. The *Memphis* was brand new, having just been delivered by Peter Denny (who retained a share in her) and was still in the Clyde awaiting her sea trials when the deal was struck. The hire terms required that the charterers heavily insured the *Memphis* against 'all risks', including seizure on her voyage from Liverpool to Charleston and back. The insurance premium was set at 40 per cent of her value (£26,000) – part-redeemable if the blockade was raised at any time during her passage. The charter fee was £2,500 per month in cash, which he considered a 'rattling rate', with all operating costs to the hirers. The *Memphis* underwent her sea trials in the Gareloch on 24 April, achieving just over eleven knots, which 'pleased' Denny. A few days later she left for Liverpool to pick up her outward-bound cargo of war contraband.

At around the same time, the *Bermuda*, some four thousand miles away and flying the British flag, was being stopped and boarded off Nassau by the USS *Mercedita*. Found on board the *Bermuda* was a complete set of shore light signals used to guide runners at night to the safest channel when entering Charleston. The Federal Secretary of the Navy, Gideon Welles, had these copied and distributed to the block-ading squadrons.

Having such intelligence did not, however, stop the *Memphis* safely running into Charleston from Nassau on 23 June. Almost a month later she was successfully got out with a cargo of cotton. Five days later, in a replay of the *Bermuda* incident, she was intercepted in international waters by USS *Magnolia*, and taken prize.

Not that Begbie was put out in the slightest. Being fully insured, he sardonically reported her loss to Scott that August: '*Memphis* taken – bless the Yankees! It is pleasant, very, to see them get such a steamer and so loaded!'

At the time he was then quite optimistic that his latest venture, the newly launched iron screw steamer *Columbia*, would get through with a cargo of iron plate, arms and munitions. The field artillery pieces – the largest item was a large calibre Austrian brass field howitzer – had been shipped at Hamburg on Caleb Huse's account.

Archibald Denny (brother of Peter) had built her with a view to selling her, once 'inside', as a gunboat. To this end her deck was reinforced and her bulwarks cut with wide ports ready for conversion. The iron plates she was carrying were intended to be used as armour for the two ironclads then being constructed in Charleston. Denny was again a part-owner and she sailed under the command of the re-doubtable David Leslie, Begbie's veteran master.

On 2 August Leslie sailed for Charleston from Nassau, carrying wood to supplement his coal reserves. Three weeks passed without Begbie receiving a word as to Leslie's safe arrival 'inside'. He began to fear the worst. Even so he wrote to Scott that he reckoned that 'if nabbed, not a cruel thing for me – if she gets in, a splendid thing – if she gets back to Nassau I [will] lay down *instantly* another pair of 'wee ones' ['river class' steamers] which should suit you nicely.'

The *Columbia* got nowhere near Charleston. Only one day into her passage, she was stopped and boarded off the coast of Florida, after a six-hour chase, by the paddle steamer USS *Santiago de Cuba*. Learning from the *Bermuda* incident, Leslie was not carrying any incriminating papers. When boarded he stuck to his claim that he was making a lawful passage to St John's, New Brunswick, under the British flag.

His captor, Commander Ridgely, having rummaged her holds, thought otherwise and escorted her to Key West. She was soon transferred to New York. While moored at the Brooklyn Naval Dock, Secretary Gideon Welles had her cargo of munitions laid out on the quay for the benefit of the American press. Like the *Bermuda* and the *Memphis* before her the *Columbia* was condemned as legal prize and immediately acquired by the US navy, converted to a gunboat and sent out as a blockader.

After the loss of the *Columbia*, Begbie abandoned sending large steamers directly into the Confederacy. He left such high-risk ventures to others driven more by sentiment than business sense. By the end of July, he had taken delivery of her replacement, the brig-rigged auxiliary screw steamer *Harriet Pinckney* (714 gross tonnage), at a price a little above £10,000.

She was central to his new plan to deliver large cargoes of contraband to British-owned Bermuda, which was much further away from the Federal base at Key West. Once there, the contraband would be transhipped to small fast shallow-draught steamers, his 'wee ones', for the seven hundred mile or so final dash 'inside'. To cover the possibility that she too should be captured, he also ordered a new steamer from Denny, with engines from Scott, to be delivered that August.

By mid-September, Begbie was resigned to the condemnation of the *Columbia*. He lodged an appeal with the Prize Court sitting in New York. He did not expect a reversal but hoped it 'will delay her immediate conversion into a dispatch or gunboat'.

His fears of his own 'poachers' being turned into 'gamekeepers' was soon realised. On 14 October the (now USS) *Memphis* chased and captured his paddle steamer *Ouachita* off Cape Romain on her first run into Charleston from Nassau. It would appear that during the boarding, the crew were roughly handled, much to Begbie's indignation: 'I am informed by my New York lawyer that the Yankees used her men shamefully.'

The previous month Begbie's second runner *Cornubia* had left Greenock, having received new boilers at Scott's Foundry yard. Her preparations prior to departure were closely followed by Prettyman, the US consul in Glasgow. Prettyman lodged a formal request that the *Cornubia* should be stopped from sailing and searched for war contraband by the local Customs officers. This request was rejected by the Board of Commissioners of Customs sitting in London, with the final comment, 'we see no ground to interfere in this matter'. The *Cornubia* under Captain John Burroughs arrived at Bermuda in December 1862, just as the first of Begbie's new 'wee ones' was undergoing her sea trials in the Clyde.

Some time around late August or early September 1862, Begbie convinced Peter Denny and John Scott to co-ordinate their blockade-running ventures and related shipbuilding interests. His timing was triggered by events both at home and abroad. He told Scott that 'next month *all* the American cotton [in Britain] will be used up – an extraordinary event truly'. He thought this would finally push France and Britain into recognising the Confederacy. This momentous event would, almost certainly, be followed by a joint naval mission to break the blockade:

> how the blockaders are to fare – time only can show? But the war I look upon as not nearly ended, provided the North can succeed in obtaining men. If the French join in, again there will be no difficulty on this score, if indeed, it be possible to form any judgement in such complicated and extra-ordinary affairs.

At the beginning of September, General Lee's army crossed the Potomac into Maryland. Begbie was on tenterhooks:

> American news next to nil per the *Scotia*, next Cunarder . . . should bring important news – one way or the other; ammunition not failing, it looks a tight fit – very – for the Federals during the next fourteen days. But the future of war is proverbially fickle.

And so it proved to be. The news of McClellan's great success in checking Lee's advance at the battle of Antietam (17 September) put paid to the hope of a quick Confederate victory and a negotiated settlement to end the war.

Begbie's correspondence reflects this change in outlook. He heard of the Confederate defeat and bloodbath less than two weeks after the event. This was very fast for the methods of communication of the day – telegraph and transatlantic packet steamer. He immediately wrote, in sombre mood, to Scott: 'if true is sorely bad for the Southerners, a terrible fight . . . it appears almost incredible. Pennsylvanians going to give the Southerners a warm reception apparently – it is terrible work.'

He chose to see this reversal for the Confederates as a costly invasion attempt from which a lesson had to be learned. Once Lee's army was back defending their own soil in Virginia, he was sure that they would once again be victorious in stopping any advance south by McClellan. If anything, he thought this would create a military stalemate as 'a smash up would necessitate a close-up'. In such circumstances direct European intervention to secure cotton supplies was, he thought, almost inevitable.

With the war certain to continue, his interest in the runners was once again revived. In typical style, he shook off the Southern defeat in a paragraph and returned to the business in hand. He offered Scott his opinion on recent purchases of runners in the Clyde. The *Giraffe* was the best of those already sold – but for 'too much money'. On consideration, he 'vastly' preferred his own stout vessel *Cornubia* to the more elegant *Iona*, then undergoing modifications in the Clyde for the crossing (and sold for double the price), as 'speed is not everything'.

He noted that three runners from the first wave to go out from the Clyde – *Minho*, *Kate* and *Adela* – had recently been 'nobbled' by the Federal cruisers. Their loss was his potential gain, as it was bound to fuel the demand for Clyde steamers at Bermuda and Nassau. This prime business opportunity was also a great source of irritation to him as he saw his chances slipping away for lack of suitable vessels being available.

So annoyed was he that he railed at Scott for being behind in constructing the oscillating engines for the 'wee ones'. At that time Barclay, Curle & Company of Glasgow was ahead of schedule building the hulls, which were close to launching. All now rested with Scott:

> don't pitch into me for nagging at you about the small boat engines . . . under the peculiar circumstances in which affairs are placed you can hardly conceive the importance it may be to me of having the boats early – if I had them at present I could do splendidly with them.

Between tirades, Begbie took time in one of his letters to Scott (15 October 1862) to report that his steamer *Ouachita* – his first runner – had arrived at Bermuda. As he penned his letter, he was not to know that, only that day, she had been captured heading for Charleston on her 'death or glory job', as he put it.

The hull of his first 'wee one' was launched in late November, followed a few days later by her sister ship. They were named *Emma* and *Gertrude* after members of his family, before being towed down river to Scott's Greenock yard to receive their engines.

The news from Bermuda and Nassau remained very encouraging. Both Clyde steamers, *Leopard* and *Herald*, were safely back at Nassau with cotton after 'clean trips'. Begbie was particularly impressed by a report on the performance of John Fraser & Company's old steamer *Kate*, which had left 'Dixie' on 14 December on her twentieth run: 'pretty fair for an eight knotter!'

That month, the first meeting of the informal partnership was convened at Edinburgh, attended by all three – Begbie, Scott and Denny. It is not recorded what was discussed but they seem to have reached a consensus that the blockade-busting business had long-term prospects. It was agreed that they should expand their share of the business by a mixture of solo and joint ventures. This meant acquiring more steamers. Begbie, acutely aware of the four to six month lead time in having a new runner built, wanted to repeat the *Cornubia* formula by buying a fast older hull in need of new boilers. He had already identified a paddle steamer launched by Scott back in 1858, *Flora*, as a likely candidate.

By their actions, it can be deduced that their plan was to extend operations to include both Bermuda and Nassau. The new steamer *Gertrude* was assigned to Nassau while her sister *Emma* was earmarked for Bermuda. Following the success of his 'Bermuda model' of business, Begbie chartered the bark *Springbok* to undertake the role *Harriet Pinckney* had performed at Bermuda – carrying contraband out from London to Nassau and running cotton back.

At the time the *Springbok* was dispatched, Scott was still struggling to complete his side of the 'wee ones' contract. In stoic mood, Begbie mused to Scott on the prospect of the Federal armies being beaten again in their own backyard, and the breaking of the blockade followed by a formal split of America. Writing on the last day of December 1862, he was fully resigned to an abrupt end to the running trade before his new vessels could make his fortune. This turn of events he thought would be most likely to occur some time in the coming spring. As a prudent business move, he contemplated reducing his exposure by selling his 'wee ones' as they neared completion, 'as it really looks as if these small things might possibly be too late for their errand'.

Yet he held back. His plan for Nassau promised much and, in any case, the demand for fast Clyde steamers was undiminished and outstripping supply. In such a market he believed that he held a winning hand either way:

> I believe I shall, against my better judgement, be drawn into selling one of them to a man bothering me today and offers cash and at such a price! If he does buy I think I shall repeat [an order] for a pair at once of these craft.

Captain Leslie was back in the Clyde by late November 1862, having been released by the Federal authorities after the capture of the *Columbia*. As an unarmed British subject caught conveying contraband he was declared *persona non grata* and freed. He managed to return to Bermuda on a small hired schooner and took the first mail steamer back to Britain.

Begbie gave him command of the *Emma* on New Year's Eve. His orders were to take her out on sea trials as soon as possible, with the view to making the crossing to Bermuda within days. This was done with all expediency. Her coaling for her outward passage to Cork commenced as soon as Scott's workmen were off her – 'in red-hot haste with paint all wet and not decent to start on a voyage'. The plan almost came unstuck at the last minute. While Leslie was up in the Gareloch adjusting her compasses prior to departure, he came down with a terrible cold and rasping cough. Begbie immediately instructed his site manager Paddon to telegraph Liverpool for a replacement master. He insisted that the man chosen had to be as tough as Leslie in mastering the 'difficult' chief engineer and his unruly mate. As it transpired, Leslie recovered sufficiently to retain his command and sailed off in the midst of a winter gale.

Begbie wanted the *Gertrude* under Captain Raison to follow immediately. This was not to be. The weather deteriorated so badly that she had to ride out the storm to both her anchors in Lamlash Bay on the Isle of Arran. During her enforced stay it was found that the soft soldering around a heat exchanger had melted under the high temperatures reached when working under high-pressure 'dry' steam. This fault had to be remedied at Scott's yard before she could finally clear for the Atlantic.

By mid-February 1863 things were looking up. The news from Bermuda was that the *Cornubia*, under Burroughs, had returned with 300 bales of cotton from her second run to Wilmington. This was a small payload for her size, as much of her deck cargo had been jettisoned in a chase. The cotton was immediately transferred to the *Harriet Pinckney* which was then in St George's harbour.

Begbie related Burroughs' tale to Scott with some pride. Having shaken off his inshore pursuers, he was sighted and chased in a heavy gale by the giant USS *Vanderbilt*, the largest full-rigged steamer in the blockade service. In a classic manoeuvre Burroughs turned the speeding *Cornubia* directly into the teeth of the wind and heavy seas, forcing the *Vanderbilt* to bear away to take in her sails. In this way he 'dropped the big one in five hours' and made his escape. Begbie took some satisfaction that her passengers reported that 'there was not a craft out there can look at her for speed, especially in a heavy sea' even though 'they put very little in her to keep her at this'. Burroughs reached Bermuda at the same time as the *Giraffe* came in with 900 bales in her hold and on deck. These successes, Begbie thought, would 'give the [Confederate] Cause an excellent lift!'

Around this time the Charleston blockading fleet was blown off station by the severe weather. Unlike many commentators, Begbie did not see this as a lifting of the blockade and held back to wait to see what the next twenty-four hours of clear weather would bring. Meanwhile, the new Confederate cotton bonds, in which Begbie was a heavy investor, were selling well in Paris and London.

Just as Begbie turned his attention to other matters, disaster struck his blockade-running scheme for Nassau. On 3 February 1863, the *Springbok* was stopped by USS *Sonoma*. It was almost certainly a planned interception instigated by the American Legation in London. The incident took place while on her first voyage out from London while about 150 miles east of Nassau. Being on a legal voyage between two neutral British ports, her officers did not try to run or put up any resistance. Nor did they attempt to destroy the ship's papers.

The search of her cargo found that her 'bills of lading' did not match what was stowed below and so she was taken into Key West. There it was discovered that concealed among her cargo were three cases of brass buttons, many stamped with 'CSA' or 'CSN'; a case of swords and cavalry sabres; rifle bayonets; forty-seven pairs of cavalry boots; and close to a hundred pairs of army boots. The manifest did not, however, give the names of the owners. They were, in fact, Thomas S. Begbie and Isaac, Campbell & Company of London.

At New York's prize court, Judge Samuel R. Betts condemned both the vessel and its cargo. He ruled that the concealed contraband was on a 'continuous voyage', one that would ultimately end at a quay in a blockaded rebel port. The fact that this cargo was to be transhipped to a runner at Nassau for final delivery was considered immaterial.

Her seizure was followed three weeks later by yet another orchestrated interception. The *Peterhoff* was heading for Matamoros, on the Mexican side of the Rio Grande, from the Danish-owned St Thomas in the West Indies. Her cargo was an array of artillery and cavalry trappings, blankets, shoes and medicines. She too was condemned at New York under the same ruling.

These two incidents were a dramatic and unilateral shift in the American interpretation of the Rules of Neutrality and created a storm of controversy in Europe. Begbie was cynical about demands for direct action in response to these latest outrages against international law. In late March he scribbled in the margin of a letter to Scott, 'a rumour obtained this afternoon that the [British] Government have ordered off [i.e. dispatched] other vessels to America to stop such seizures as the *Springbok* and *Peterhoff* – I don't believe it!' As it turned out, the *Springbok* was released on appeal, though the condemnation of her cargo was upheld. No doubt Begbie had his share of her cargo heavily insured.

His optimism was buoyed by the good news that both *Emma* and *Gertrude* had reached Nassau safely with 820 bales of cotton. Indeed, they were already on their way back to Wilmington and Charleston respectively, when he wrote, 'if true, sharp work, say five days at Nassau to discharge and load'. The *Cornubia* was also reported safe at Bermuda. Burroughs' last inward run cargo was such as to credit Begbie and Scott with 1,100 bales at Charleston, 'so that the cotton is going to relieve us and in a very agreeable manner'. Purring over this performance, he wrote to his partner: 'I feel disposed to revert to my old opinion that they are the safest craft to lay down', and was considering a repeat order, though for vessels slightly greater in length.

There was, however, a problem. The war-fuelled shipbuilding boom sweeping the British and French yards had created an acute shortage of iron, driving up prices and causing delays in the completion of ships already on the stocks. Scott was particularly vulnerable as he was building three large vessels for a French company on a fixed-price contract which carried stiff penalties for late delivery.

Begbie viewed Scott's dealings with the French (Scott had a small yard at St Nazare) as a great mistake. Instead of getting caught with large long-term projects he struggled to finish, he could be making a fortune churning out small steamers on speculation for the 'running trade'. Begbie was on the very brink of ordering two more 'wee ones' and called a meeting at Greenock to check out whether Scott's yard was in a fit state to deliver their engines. He had already decided that someone else would construct the hulls as he wanted them ready in four months.

Begbie's visit to Scott's Greenock Foundry yard at the end of April left him gravely concerned. Scott's only senior manager had been headhunted by an English rival and was working his notice period, 'leaving no one apparently in charge when you are away – which is fair ruin!' This was at a time when Scott was on the verge of securing yet another contract for a large Royal Mail steamship.

In such circumstances, Begbie had no qualms in placing the order for his latest 'wee ones' (two paddle steamers) with the Thames firm Ash & Stewart, for delivery in four months. The price was fixed at £15 per ton which Begbie thought was 'a bit of a steal'. To expand the running business he also placed an order for two screw steamers, in which he had great faith, with the tried and trusted Glasgow firm Barclay, Curle & Company.

While he awaited delivery, Begbie was planning ahead. He wanted to break into the lucrative trade in running in heavy ordnance by small steamer. This required designing holds that were both accessible and strong enough to take these large items of great weight. At the beginning of March 1863 he wrote to Scott:

Do you think you could design something exquisite – qua – dispatch boat, iron . . . flush, fastest possible and light draft – say twelve feet to carry heavy armaments. Boilers and machinery not cramped under the waterline – do the dimensions to please you.

It can be taken as certain that he intended to sell this vessel to Gorgas' Ordnance Bureau at some stage.

Begbie was not in the least sentimental about parting with his vessels, if the price was right. As soon as his favourite, the *Cornubia*, was established at Bermuda he had her run the local measured mile. She achieved over eleven knots against a strong head wind. This he considered 'not too bad'. The whole exercise was to impress Major Walker, the resident Confederate procurement agent, who had been instructed by Gorgas to acquire suitable steamers for the War Department.

In June, Begbie's plan succeeded, as Walker bought her for £10,000 for the Confederacy. Secretary Seddon renamed her *Lady Davis* in honour of the President's wife and sent her back to Bermuda under

Lieutenant Richard H. Gayle. On 8 November 1863 he ran her aground while trying to get into Wilmington and was captured with his crew by the USS *James Adger* and USS *Niphon*.

In the interim Begbie's first pair of 'wee ones', *Emma* and *Gertrude*, had been taken. The first captured was *Gertrude*, commanded by Captain Raison. Unlike Burroughs, he was unable to shake off the USS *Vanderbilt* when chased off the Bahamas on 16 April. He was on his third outward run. Leslie, on the *Emma*, fared much better: he was on his eighth run when he was finally taken coming out of Cape Fear River by USS *Arago* on 26 July.

Begbie did not hear of the loss of *Emma* until early August. His response was typical of the man: 'Very annoying but well done, wish I had a dozen like her.' He related the incident to Scott at length. Leslie, his 'best captain', had got clean out of the Cape Fear River and was some thirty miles out in the Gulf Stream when he was spotted by the *Arago*. This large steamer was then conveying troops for an assault on Charleston's coastal defences. Leslie turned the *Emma* out to sea and made a run for it, throwing overboard a hundred bales from the deck cargo. His flight was checked by the approach of two other gunboats that cut him off from the open sea. Cornered, he was forced to surrender.

Even before he received the news of these latest captures, Begbie had been reconsidering his personal level of exposure in the 'trade'. By then the land war was approaching its climax at the small Pennsylvanian town of Gettysburg. He wrote to Scott on 17 June 1863 – unaware of the outcome of this desperately fought battle – that he believed the military deadlock was holding fast and the Confederacy would, at the very least, extract a negotiated peace from the North. Were this to happen, he planned to extract himself on the best possible terms: 'I hold Confederate bonds [£60,000] which hamper me and which I do not like selling at all at the present, or at a loss.' He thought mid-September would be the right time to sell them: 'I should get out [of] the Confederates the considerable amount I have lying in English gold, in cotton, in property and in dollars at my credit with two firms.'

Fate was to decide otherwise. Begbie took most of July off to go fishing and shooting at Banavie, Fort William. In doing so he missed his best opportunity to extract himself with minimum loss. When he returned to London and his desk in early August, the markets were reeling from the news from America. Even he could not pass off the Confederate defeats at Gettysburg and Vicksburg as minor setbacks: 'The South has caught it and no mistake.'

Begbie still clung to the hope that there might yet be a businesslike peace settlement, one in which Confederate debts would be honoured. He reasoned that Lee would not be caught again so far away from his supply lines. And if Charleston's defences held firm against all assaults, his battered army and that in the West could be readily re-equipped and fed by sea. Furthermore, Lincoln's administration was racked with internal problems and faced riots in New York over the planned conscription.

The most pressing problem for the Confederacy, he thought, was its finances abroad: 'the Confederate Loan here [is] used up – several people and the Northerners banging away at it to destroy the Confederate credit.' By late August his holdings in the Erlanger Loan Bonds had crashed in value by 36 per cent.

The blockade-running business was also reeling from a new Confederate government edict issued that month. Secretary Seddon, faced with a dire shortage of munitions and basic equipment of all kinds (as well as the money to pay for them) ordered his military governors at Charleston, Wilmington and Mobile to take control of the running trade. They were empowered to enforce his order that all departing steamers set aside half their cargo space for government cotton. The uproar from the private operators did not last long as they soon found ways to reduce the rail space demanded by the quota.

Begbie concluded that blockade running was 'the oddest game altogether that I have ever seen played, the most difficult to estimate and [to] calculate to play with safety'. Nevertheless, he urged Scott to continue to build small steamers for the blockade on speculation.

By then things were not going well on Clydeside either. The price of materials and wages at the shipyards was rising fast. The latter was caused by bad weather locally, which resulted in a poor harvest for the second year running and rising food prices. While Denny skilfully managed his labour unrest, Scott, on the rack with fixed-price contracts, resisted all claims and stamped on any moves to unionise with characteristic bull-headedness. To relieve his shortage of skilled tradesmen he imported carpenters from Aberdeen, which greatly annoyed his already disgruntled indigenous workforce.

Just as Begbie was recovering his business nerve, a personal disaster struck. His youngest daughter Mary – known to all as 'Minnie' – ruptured a tumour that had been developing in one of her lungs. She was on holiday with the Wisemans at Ardencaple Castle when it happened. For a while it seemed that she would not live more than a few days (though she did in fact recover). Stuck in Helensburgh with his wife attending their desperately ill daughter, Begbie fretted as his business affairs were pushed onto the back burner.

Even so he found time to scribble a note to Scott, hoping to entice him into a scheme to buy back his old screw steamer, *Melita*, from Isaac, Campbell & Company. She had been lying at Liverpool since May, having been retired from the running business. He thought that if her boilers and engines were refurbished, as Scott had done with the *Cornubia*, he could sell her at a handsome profit to the Confederate government as a transatlantic carrier. Scott was simply not interested as he was grossly over-committed and late with the French contract.

With that idea dropped, Begbie turned his mind back to smaller runners. He knew that the recent and dramatic reorganisation of Confederate finances and procurement operations would bring out even larger funds to pay for the besieged South's escalating needs. Everything from basic foodstuffs to clothing, from blankets to lead ingots to make bullets, would have to be run through the blockade. This, he confidently predicted, would create a 'tremendous rush for boats out there during the next six months'.

Throughout November 1863 he was tempted by offers to sell his next two screw steamers when launched by Ash & Stewart in the Thames. But he resisted all such approaches as they were to be key assets in a new joint-stock venture he was on the verge of floating – the Albion Trading Company.

Begbie's scheme was both elegant and simple. With the funds he received from his subscribers to his new company (£160,000) he would travel to Paris and purchase a £50,000 Confederate Cotton Bond at 40 per cent discount. This guaranteed access to 11,250 bales of government cotton at Wilmington or Charleston at a pre-set and highly preferential price of two and a half pence per pound. The going rate was then sixpence a pound.

After factoring in the cost of freighting the cotton from Bermuda or Nassau to Britain and the selling commission, the final cost would be four and a half pence per pound. At Liverpool this cotton could easily realise twenty-five and a half pence per pound. This gave the company a profit of £40 per bale from which the expense of running the blockade had to be deducted (he reckoned £2,250 per round trip per vessel). The potential net profit, if all the 'loan' cotton was run out without loss, was a tantalising £420,000 – over three times the original capital outlay and to be realised in a matter of a few months. This was without considering the earnings from running in goods on private account and government supplies (at £8 per ton freighted). The latter was only redeemable against cotton at the undiscounted price of sixpence per pound and was paid as credit that would only be used in subsequent runs.

The plan called for five company steamers (two screws and three paddles), two of which were about to be launched on Begbie's account. The Cotton Loan Bond was issued in quadruplicate at Paris so that four of his captains each carried a copy, thereby minimising the chance of its loss to capture.

In mid-December 1863, Begbie, as nominated managing director, put a fixed price on each of his steamers which was commuted into shares in thousand-pound blocks. As soon as the company was registered (14 January 1864), Begbie sold much of his personal stock for cash. This move greatly concerned Scott who was also a major shareholder.

Begbie already had one steamer out at Nassau, *City of St Petersburg*, a large paddle built earlier that year by Scott's neighbour and rival, Caird & Sons of Greenock. Under Captain F.W. Fuller she had done two 'absurdly good' runs into Wilmington before her ownership passed from Begbie to the new company. The second steamer to join the company was the newly launched screw, *Emily*, built by Barclay, Curle & Company at their Stobcross yard. Begbie had her propeller up-rated for more speed before she was sent out to Bermuda. She was joined by her sister ship, *Minnie*, within a few weeks.

The launch of his 'twa wee beauties' which were to complete the Company fleet was delayed by bad weather until January 1864. Built by Ash & Stewart at their Thames yard, these large paddle wheelers were identical in design, with a wide beam and shallow draught. At £30,000 each, they were twice the price of the smaller 'river class' he had ordered in the Clyde. Begbie gave command of these two new racers (they managed over sixteen knots on their trials) to his most experienced masters, David Leslie and John Burroughs. Leslie took out the *Helen* while Burroughs sailed on her sister ship *North Heath*. They both departed in January and in very heavy weather which never let up during the entire crossing.

Just before they sailed (12 January) Begbie was fretting to Scott about, of all things, a lull in what had been a soaring capture rate up until late November as well as the resilience of the Confederacy infrastructure:

I am absolutely getting alarmed at the absence of captures – hoping they won't commence upon us [Albion Company]. I cannot imagine how, with their railways in such bad order, they can manage to get down cotton sufficient to keep them all going at the rate they are. Then [there is] the question of pressing must be a large question and to have no bales well pressed is a matter of 20–25% of our carrying capacity.

To increase his carrying capacity and protect his profit margins he shipped 20 tons of baling hoops in each of his new Ash steamers – enough to bind 800 compressed bales.

The news that the first 1,000 bales under the Cotton Bond scheme had been delivered to Nassau was a great fillip for the Confederate bonds market. Begbie was swept along with the rising tide and immediately placed an order for four new paddle steamers with Scott on speculation. He wanted their delivery staggered so that, as two were delivered (having, hopefully, been sold in advance), he could fund the next two rising in the stocks. To finance these new purchases he needed to liquidate more of his stock. He bluntly asked Scott if 'any of your men' wanted stock in the Albion Trading Company: he was ready to sell 'so as to ease myself in funds'.

His target for selling the first two 'April beauties' was Alexander Collie. Collie had London offices at 17 Leadenhall Street, just around the corner from Begbie's premises, which he shared with the Nassau agent Theodore Andrae. Collie had enjoyed much 'grace and favour' ever since he parted with the *Giraffe* to agents Ficklin and Wilkinson on favourable terms over a year ago. Since then Collie had gained the confidence of Commissioner James Mason in London. Mason introduced him to Captain William G. Crenshaw of the Commissary and Quartermaster Bureau, who had been sent to Europe to set up a running fleet along the lines of Gorgas' Ordnance Bureau operation.

Crenshaw and Collie went into partnership, acquiring five steamers. It was an ill-fated venture, as three were captured before the end of 1863, one was destroyed and the last remaining was missing – presumed lost at sea. It had never been an amicable partnership, as Collie acquired a personal dislike for Crenshaw. With the loss of the last steamer he deemed himself a free agent and quickly secured a contract with General McRae, who had recently arrived in Europe to oversee all Confederate procurement operations. This placed Collie back in the market for new vessels.

Begbie was very wary of him: 'I do not approach Collie myself – it is cutting our own throats . . . I better steer clear of him meanwhile.' In such a climate it took little to frighten Begbie off and drop the Collie connection. This did not pose a problem for Collie as he had already signed a contract with Randoph, Elder & Company to build five '*Flamingo* class' super racers for his new fleet.

Begbie was right to be suspicious of Collie. During his time touring the Clyde he headhunted one of Begbie's crack masters, Captain Raison, in order to deliver a new boat, *Let Her Be*, which was lying at Liverpool. Raison had only just returned from delivering the legendary *Syren* for Andrew Lamb of the Charleston Importing & Exporting Company.

Begbie also tried Collie's ex-partner Crenshaw, whom 'I do not know but can get at him perfectly well'. He met him in early March in London, 'brought by the first southerner man here', General McRae.

At this time, Begbie's imagination was fired (as with all Clydeside) by the exploits of *Denbigh* and *Donegal*, two Gulf of Mexico runners. They were doing great business running cotton from Mobile to Havana. Mobile had the added attraction that it was free from the trading constraints imposed by the Confederate government's recent 'New Plan'. He wrote to the owner, H.O. Brewer of Mobile, proposing a partnership. This approach was shunned as Brewer had already formed a company, the European Trading Company, with much bigger fish: Shroeder of Manchester and Erlanger of Paris. Their intention was to monopolise the Mobile market.

Forced to look elsewhere, he ran across the shady 'Mr Beach', who was then in London looking for vessels for a 'rich Mobile man . . . [who] will surely buy when he arrives from Havana on the next steamer'. Within days Begbie had drawn up a 'Mobile Scheme' involving six new steamers, each costing £14,000 and built by Scott on their joint account. This paper plan, he assured Scott, would strengthen their bargaining position.

While Begbie 'wheeled and dealed' in steamers that had not yet been built, those of his Albion Trading Company were making their runs from Bermuda. The first to make it 'inside', carrying a copy of the £50,000 Cotton Bond, was Fuller on the *City of St Petersburg*. He got into Wilmington safely on 18 January 1864. Three weeks later, Halpin on the *Emily* was not so lucky. She had been severely strained in the crossing and sank off Wrightsville Beach on her final approach to Wilmington. There she was blown up by a boat party from USS *Florida*.

In his old age, the veteran runner James Sprunt recalled that he could see *Emily*'s wreck from his cottage half a century later. He remembered, as a seventeen-year-old, seeing her in Wilmington:

'a beautiful vessel . . . superior to any other blockade runner of the Fleet'. Begbie was not affected by such sentimentality when he heard the news of her loss. His only comment to Scott was that, as she was only carrying general cargo inwards, it was 'cheaper for us by £3000–£4000 than losing her cargo [of cotton] coming out'.

The upsurge in running out of Bermuda brought other problems. Begbie found it 'most galling' that Gilpin on the *Minnie*, having arrived at Bermuda from Madeira, missed a 'moon' for lack of a pilot. Marshall, Beach & Company of Wilmington were the agents responsible for providing pilots. Begbie denounced them: 'these men being very saucy and most exorbitant. £1,000 has been paid in advance by the *Thistle* and they pick and choose their boats.' The arrival of the old hands Leslie (*Helen*) and Burroughs (*North Heath*) at St George's harbour did much to expedite matters for the inexperienced Gilpin.

In addition, there were problems getting Confederate officials to exchange cotton for the bond certificates held by his captains. Begbie directly intervened, using his contacts in the Confederate Navy Department to clear the way.

Despite these issues, the spring of that year (1864) was prime time for the Albion Trading Company. Most independent running companies had withdrawn their vessels in protest at the devaluation of the Confederate dollar and the government's 'New Plan' to control the running trade. As the resident Bermudan agent John T. Bourne noted that April: 'The restriction put on the Blockade trade by the Confederate Congress is likely to cramp all connected with the Trade. The present holders of Cotton Bonds are the only persons likely to do any business with the Confederacy.' Being the bearers of Cotton Loan Bonds, Begbie's captains were preferred under the new regulations. Indeed, they could afford almost to ignore what was carried in the hold on the inward run as Begbie declared 'bonds in – cotton out!'

Just as things were looking well set for the Company, the *City of St Petersburg* developed serious mechanical problems and had to retire to Halifax for urgent repairs. The first trip of the *Minnie*, however, more than compensated. She brought back over 731 bales of cotton and 330 boxes of tobacco from Wilmington. The local agent, Bourne, calculated that this one trip paid for her and the loss of the *Emily*.

For a while thereafter the business went from strength to strength. On her second trip 'inside', the *Minnie* was joined by the much larger *Helen* and *North Heath*. By early May, the *City of St Petersburg* was back from Halifax and again in harness. As they clocked up run after run, Begbie wrote to Scott in jubilant mood: 'so it's a case now of "Look Out"!' He urged him to push on with his new steamers – 'so hammer, hammer away – you can't be ready for sea too soon – a regular blaze after blockaders seemingly!'

At St George, his three masters had formed a group to be reckoned with. In a dispute over which local agent would meet their bills, they stormed Bourne's office with his rival agent in tow, and extracted satisfaction in a 'very offensive and dictatorial manner'.

Even with the capture of the *Minnie* (9 May) leaving Wilmington, on her fourth round trip, the Company's fortunes were assured. Begbie thought that she had not only paid for herself but 'all existing debts'. Her last cargo of cotton (663 bales), and that of the *Helen* (871 bales) had arrived at Plymouth on the *Harriet Pinckney* that June. The bales were a mixture of non-compressed and badly compressed cotton as supplied by the Bureau of Foreign Supplies agent. This sad state of affairs at Wilmington convinced Begbie that the unrestricted ports in the Gulf of Mexico – Mobile and Galveston – were now a much more attractive business proposition. All that was needed were runners of very shallow draught – ideally drawing only seven foot when fully loaded.

By the beginning of April, the first of his new batch of paddle steamers of this design was launched from Scott's yard. Another four were also rising in the stocks. All five were named after Sir Walter Scott's novels – *Ivanhoe*, *Redgauntlet*, *Talisman*, *Kenilworth* and *Marmion*. In his correspondence to his partner Scott, he referred to them by their initials *I*, *R*, *T*, *K* and *M*. They were identical in design, with the required exceptionally shallow draught and broad beam to accommodate a 1,000-bale payload.

His original intention was to play the rampant sellers' market with a pair of them to recoup his outlay and retain the others for his own Mobile scheme. But, having wasted months showing Confederate buyers and their agents round Scott's yard, he came to the inescapable conclusion that none had any real money – only more Confederate bonds to exchange. Besides, such associations threatened to compromise his position as the managing director of an independent running company.

The deciding factor seems to have been his brushes with the well-connected but slippery 'Mr Beach': 'clever and cute, complimentary in his admiration for you [Scott] but rather unprofitable to us . . . I will keep him at arm's length now.' It only took a couple of meetings before Begbie realised Beach's plan was to keep his Southerner partners all to himself, while trying to separate Scott from him and the Albion Company.

Begbie finally decided that the easiest and least risky option was to sell the first two steamers to his own Albion Trading Company. At a board meeting, held in early May, he convinced his fellow directors to buy the newly launched *Ivanhoe* immediately for £16,000 with the view to open up the Mobile route from Havana. At the next meeting, two weeks later, he was thwarted in his attempt to include the *Redgauntlet* in the deal by 'one haggling man I allowed foolishly to stop the sale of *R*'. Not to be deflected from his plan, he called a special meeting the following week and had that decision reversed.

Having ordered them at £14,000, he made an instant and handsome profit of around £2,000 on each. Flush with funds, he decided to re-invest in the company: '[I] fancy myself five hundred of Albion Company stock at par today, which is not rash.' Learning a lesson from his encounter with Beach, he became anxious to tie Scott closer into the running of the company. He urged him to nominate directors to dilute the domination by 'London Scottish' worthies on the present board: 'but this being a Scotch affair we require your men as an indication of the genuineness of the concern'. He reassured him that the company's capital was insured against failure, so he should have no apprehensions in commending seats on the board to his Clydeside associates.

With *I* and *R* accounted for, Begbie played the market for a while as *T*, *M* and *K* were launched in quick succession. By June, he had Collie back in Greenock looking over *T*. A month later Captain Bulloch paid a visit to Scott's yard to look over the paddles and joined Andrew Lamb on board for the sea trials of *T*. To push the sale, Begbie recommended that Scott employ a veteran blockade-running master to put her through her paces, 'whose acquaintance you will make at once, introducing yourself in my name'. His choice was the dashing 'Captain A. Roberts' (real name Augustus Charles Hobart-Hampden RN), then in Glasgow looking for a new command.

As the new steamer raced between the Cumbrae and the Cloch lighthouses for the benefit of his guest buyers, Begbie made a snap decision to keep all of them. The solution to all his problems was to set up another blockade-running firm: 'rather a neat thing in the way of concocting companies – is it not?'

Collie was not at all put out when he was told the *T* was no longer for sale. Once again he used the opportunity to recruit a crack captain. He appointed 'Roberts' as the master of his latest racer, the *Condor*, when she was handed over to him by Thomsons of Finnieston and Govan a few days later.

To implement his new scheme Begbie closed the subscription book on the Albion Company on 1 August 1864. It would henceforth continue to operate while there was still cotton waiting to be collected on the old Bond and credit. But there would be no further capital injections or purchases of new Cotton Bonds. The prime assets – the steamers – would be run until they were captured or destroyed or the war was concluded.

Just over a month before, the *Ivanhoe* had been driven ashore close by Fort Morgan by the ex-runner uss *Glasgow*. The *I* was on her first run into Mobile. Under the guard of a Confederate shore battery, she was stripped of her cargo and engines before the blockaders arrived and smashed up her hull with shellfire. This left the three surviving runners, *North Heath*, *Helen* and *Redgauntlet*, as the Albion Company's last assets. The first two continued to bring out cotton from Wilmington on what was left to redeem on the old Cotton Bond. The *Redgauntlet* was sent to Havana to replace the *I* on the Mobile run.

Unfortunately, she was involved in a collision in the harbour and was laid up for repairs there until the beginning of August. She had the distinction of being the last runner to enter Mobile before Farragut's invasion fleet closed the trap. With no escape possible, she was commandeered by the local military commander as an army transport with the promise of settling in near-worthless Confederate dollars.

In his summing up to his shareholders the following month, Begbie reckoned that the company's vessels had brought out 3,200 bales of cotton in the nine months that the company had been in existence. Their sale at Liverpool had netted £110,000 in gross profit. Against this, £70,000 had to be deducted for the cost of the two steamers and one cargo lost in running and the purchase of their replacements. This left £40,000 clear profit, which allowed him to declare an immediate cash dividend of 25 per cent, irrespective of the future fate of three surviving steamers. This was a remarkable achievement, given that the Bank of England's interest rate hovered around 7 per cent throughout the war. He reassured Scott that 'your Albion speculation is now perfectly safe . . . so that Albion Trading Company shareholders adventuring in the Universal Company are trading on very sure ground.'

This new firm, the Universal Trading Company of Glasgow, was almost an exact duplicate of the Albion Company, with the same

registered office, office-holders and capital stock, but with a new
Cotton Loan Bond and four new vessels. Following the old pattern, he
sold the remaining three of his newest paddle steamers *T*, *M* and *K*,
to the new company as they were launched for a reduced price of
£14,000 each. He also bought a new Blackwall-built paddle steamer,
named *Lady Sterling* in honour of a close relative. She cost £66,000,
was very fast (16 knots) and large (twice the size of Scott's paddles),
and could carry 1,400 bales. Her large coal bunk capacity gave Begbie
the option of running her from Halifax to Wilmington – a 'killer
distance'. When launched she was, arguably, the greatest runner then
afloat.

In his new company prospectus he listed the outlays and anticipated
returns. He intended to use £94,000 of the company's capital on
acquiring the new steamers. He set aside £6,000 as working capital to
cover coal, provisions, oil, wages and insurance. This time, however,
he only purchased £35,000 worth of Confederate Cotton Bonds from
former Commissioner Slidell in Paris. This guaranteed the company
vessels access to 7,875 bales of cotton at the preferred price. The
remaining £25,000 was set aside as reserve stock.

He calculated that, if all four steamers made one successful round
trip fully loaded, they would bring out 3,700 bales. This, at current
prices at Liverpool, would amount to a net operating profit of
£138,000 after expenses – exceeding the original capital outlay by
£3,000. He concluded his business plan with a glittering forecast of
£276,000 net profit – if the remaining 4,175 bales on this bond were
brought out on their second run. There was also the potential to earn a
further £38,400 from government freight run in under the 'New Plan'
on the two trips. Begbie chose not to include this in his revenue
forecast as it was not a hard cash transaction.

This proposition was irresistible to many of Clydeside's most noted
businessmen, led by James Lumsden, the future lord provost of
Glasgow. Even the canny shipbuilder Peter Denny of Dumbarton
took £5,000 of the one pound shares. John Scott of Greenock signed
up for a more modest £2,000 stake.

Within nine days of being floated, Begbie had the subscription book
filled. He was supremely confident and invested heavily in his new
company: 'I shall have a fistful with Universal.' But he was already
over-extending himself. Only the previous month, he had bought as a
private venture the old P &O transatlantic steamer, the *Columbian*,
lying at Southampton. He sent her up to Scott at Greenock to have
new boilers, engines and a full refurbishment. It was a large gamble as

he paid £30,000 for the vessel and spent half again on the refit. He was banking on selling her for £55,000 on the open market and in a very short space of time.

The month of August 1864, despite the loss of the *Ivanhoe* and the entrapment of the *Redgauntlet* in Mobile, proved to be the high water mark for Begbie and his blockade-running schemes: 'I hope to have a good winter campaign of it, if Wilmington is left alone, as at present, and fever gets out of Bermuda.'

In a matter of weeks all his assumptions and assurances floundered in the deep slump that set in that autumn. Just as business was returning to normal, yellow fever swept through the islands, decimating the crews. This severely curtailed operations even for those captains who could muster enough fit men for a run. They faced an enforced twenty-one-day quarantine at their home port and a further forty-day-quarantine at Wilmington or Charleston.

This was not the only harbinger of bad times ahead. His engineer reported that the company's newest paddle steamer was plagued with faults and problems. The bearings overheated on *Talisman*'s maiden run to Falmouth. She sprang a leak and her coal consumption was reported as 'enormous'. Begbie blamed Scott's shoddy workmanship, which put him in 'a bad position with the shareholders'.

His neglected Albion Company was faring no better. The *North Heath* had retired from Bermuda to Halifax for major repairs after being almost overwhelmed at sea in a violent storm. On her return she was badly damaged by shellfire while entering Wilmington. Without any prospect of a replacement, her captain, John Burroughs, switched employers and took up command of the *Stag*, owned by a Liverpool consortium. This left only Leslie on the *Helen* still running into Wilmington.

Much more serious for Begbie was the slump in cotton prices at Liverpool. As the depression-hit mill owners of Manchester began to close their gates and lock out their workforce, demand for raw cotton collapsed. Begbie declared that their orchestrated action 'plays "Old Harry" with sales of cotton or sales of anything . . . I believe the long dreaded panic would come at last, though I hear of no difficulties except in the most speculative and weak traders.'

By mid-October Begbie could report the sale of only ten bales out of the Albion Company's swelling stockpile at Liverpool. His attempts at a cash call on his shareholders flopped: 'with my cotton unsold at Liverpool, a good number of my subscribers down, leaves me short at present with a heavy month before me in November'. Defiantly, he stuck to the line that 'the mills cannot all stand still' and that the market for cotton must revive soon.

In such a depressed market, the refitted *Columbian* was unsellable and rapidly turning into a serious liability as her maintenance bills were unrelenting. He tried to put a brave face on his looming liquidity crisis with Scott: 'The Albion Company owes me £50,000 in cash outlay on their behalf and I have £60,000 to £70,000 of cotton at Liverpool and on the way home to cover me. But this is vastly different from having proceeds in the till!'

By now the Federal use of captured runners as blockaders was having a devastating impact on the trade. The capture rate soared to one in every two runs attempted. Such losses were simply unsustainable. Begbie thought it all a bitter irony when he quoted to Scott the latest Federal success: 'Peter Denny's *Ella* captured I see, [by] my old screw *Emma* – a tremendous fleet they have of old blockade runners now converted into blockaders.'

Unfortunately, all correspondence with Scott ceases from mid-October until early December. Whether this was because the relevant letters have not survived or because Begbie was ill or gone to earth to escape his creditors, is not known. When the correspondence resumes, the running game was all but up.

The first clear sign of the beginning of the end for Begbie was the return of the barque-rigged auxiliary screw *Hawk* to Liverpool. Begbie had her built earlier in the year by Henderson & Coulborn of Renfrew for the Virginia Volunteer Navy. They intended to modify her to serve as a privateer once she was got into Wilmington. While on the slipway her strengthened deck attracted the attention of the US consul in Glasgow and Adams in London, who tried to have her detained. They failed and she reached Bermuda safely, but her patriotic would-be buyers had since run out of funds and defaulted. A more ominous fact was that there were no other takers for her where she lay at Bermuda. This situation was only retrieved when Bulloch was ordered by Mason and Slidell to square things with Begbie with compensation to the tune of £15,000. Back in British waters, the *Hawk* was in collision with another vessel and had to be sent up to Greenock for costly repairs.

Blockade runners in the United Kingdom and at Nassau were by now aware that the long awaited Federal assault on Fort Fisher was imminent. If this key fortress was taken, then the Federal monitors would have the free run of the Cape Fear River, cutting off Wilmington and Lee's main railway supply line. For all but the most committed to the struggle, the time had come to get out of the running trade.

To Begbie's great annoyance, it was now taking three or four weeks for news to reach him. At the time of the first assault on Fort Fisher (end of December), the most recent account he had was that brought out by the runner *Hansa* the week before. He received intelligence that the invasion preparations were in hand: 'dreadfully bad for the Confederates – if true'. Still in denial, he dismissed as 'bosh!' claims that Savannah was already taken by Sherman and that the forts guarding Charleston had been reduced to rubble.

Unpleasant as it was, he had to face the grim realisation that he had left his exit from the running trade too late: 'How I wish I could realise on the entire fleet at twenty-five per cent loss and close up – and I sent there [to Bermuda] instructions to do so six weeks ago.'

The appearance on 19 December 1864 of Rear Admiral Porter's grand invasion fleet off Cape Fear River prompted a mass exodus of runners. Begbie tried to make the best of it: 'News very bad for the Confederates if Wilmington is taken it will be entirely up with blockading – I see several vessels [still] get in and out of Charleston.'

The end of his Bermuda-based operation was also in sight. Just days before the assault, the *Talisman* of his Universal Company raced out of the New Inlet, only to run into the wreck of the Confederate ironclad *Raleigh*. She had to limp back upriver to Wilmington for repairs. On her second attempt, two weeks later, she managed to get out but her weakened hull broke up in heavy seas. The crew were lucky to be rescued by a passing schooner and taken back to Bermuda.

With the fall of Fort Fisher, on the second assault that January, the military commander of Wilmington tried to stop the Federal monitors reaching the town by sinking blockade runners in the river. This was the fate of the badly damaged *North Heath* of his Albion Company. She was commandeered, filled with stones and scuttled off Fort Strong on 15 January. Adding to Begbie's miseries was the collapse of Confederate Cotton Loan Bonds in Europe. His response to this was 'I feel very blue.'

Soon afterwards Begbie had what he thought was some good news – his instructions to his captains to stop running had finally arrived at Bermuda and Nassau. The *Marion* and *Kenilworth* were now both safe in Nassau, having been chased back after narrow escapes off the Charleston bar. They were soon joined by the *Helen* and put up for sale 'which relieves me immensely'. He firmly believed he could yet salvage some of his capital by offering them at £16,000 each to Lafitte & Company, the local agents for Fraser, Trenholm & Company in Nassau.

But as the weeks slipped by without news of any buyers, he became more and more despondent: 'To be sold there under the present crisis is most irritating, aggravating and ruinous.' All he wished now was to extract himself and the 'business brought to an end [so] I am left free to work at some decent calling'. His worst fears were soon confirmed. Without Wilmington, running out of Bermuda was abandoned. Those still willing to risk a run into Charleston in the last weeks before it too was evacuated, debunked to Nassau. Its anchorage was, by now, packed with laid-up steamers for sale. There was the little isolated Texas port of Galveston still open but it was barely feasible as a business proposition.

By early February Begbie was feeling 'terribly squeezed for want of something out of the West'. There were still no buyers: 'If not saleable [I must] send the steamers home, which I fear I must make up my mind to: a terrible sacrifice and such a wait!' The cotton market at Liverpool had not improved: 'dead forever I think . . . some men have absconded there, with enormous losses'.

On 24 March 1865, with his fleet gone or laid-up, Begbie faced the wrath of his Universal Company shareholders at a meeting attended by Peter Denny. Begbie let his (unnamed) 'worthy banker' take the chair and act as 'inspector' into his handling of the firm's affairs. He told Scott that it was 'a most nervous affair for me' as he rose to present the company's financial position. All he had to offer his shareholders was ten shillings in the pound on their investment. In an attempt to soften the blow, he held out the wholly illusory hope that the Confederate government would make up the loss when they paid their debts some time in the future. He confessed to Scott 'my account declared it is a perfect turtle feast – it's excruciating work for me'.

His key partners abandoned him, badly damaging his reputation and standing in this tight-knit shipping community. During the Easter holidays he joined the crowds strolling round the Victoria Docks where his recently returned steamers, *Helen*, *Hawk* and *Kenilworth*, were moored alongside the others back from blockade running and awaiting a buyer. His indefatigable spirit for once seemed to fail him: 'Dreadful heavy work to get on here – business awfully bad, and distrustful. But we are surely, bar some failures, about the bottom and should have some upward movement – *something* doing!' He hoped that with the end of the war in sight, there would be immediate resumption of trade with America and some sort of cash settlement by the victorious North for the destruction and capture of his steamers.

By June, he confessed to Scott that he was still in a malaise: 'I can't get on at all with the sale of the steamers and I don't appear to be getting nearer it at all!' He also had the large *Columbian* still on his hands – without a buyer in sight. All hope of any monies from the cotton bonds he was left holding had vanished: 'Confederates clean wiped out!'

Over the next three months he attended to the paperwork surrounding the acrimonious winding up of the Universal Company and the resulting litigation. He had managed to sell the *Helen* at a loss but realised little else of the outstanding £80,000 he claimed that the company owed him. At the same time he wrote endless proposals for new large steamers, visited P & O offices with the returned Captain Leslie, and generally went 'cap in hand' to Scott and Denny. Gone were his weekly tirades to Scott as to how to run a successful shipping business.

He saw opportunities for his fast steamers everywhere: the revolt against Napoleon's scheme in Mexico; the movement of 100,000 men to the Texan border; and outbreak of war between Chile and Spain. But without sufficient capital of his own or backers, he did not have the means or the nerve. One year to the day after the founding of the Universal Company he confided in Scott: 'I wish I had the backbone I had twelve months ago.' Plainly, blockade running had claimed its price in the short term. Indeed, it is not until late 1866 that he makes a reappearance in the speculative market for steamers.

Begbie was not the only private speculator to be caught out. Many of the shallow-draught runners that had switched to running into the Gulf ports of Mobile and Galveston were withdrawn too late to find buyers. By February 1865 – four months before the closure of Galveston – seventeen steamers were already laid up at Havana. Most of those were recently built for the various state trading companies. They were all put up for sale, and the few that found a buyer went for half their original price.

In the following months, a sense of panic had set in amongst the Confederate owners of runners still lying at Nassau, Bermuda and Havana. Their fear was that the triumphant Federal consuls and naval officers would seize their vessels where they lay in neutral ports as the property of the defunct Confederate States of America. To avoid this scenario they were all transferred back to private ownership. Alexander Collie, the well-connected and highly adventurous investor, took possession of the fleet of four 'racers' – *Flamingo*, *Falcon*, *Ptarmigan* and *Evelyn* – which Thomsons of Finnieston and Govan had built for the McRae contract. He tried to sell them to the

Admiralty as fast patrol boats capable of catching the illegal slave traders off the West African and Brazilian coasts. This offer was not taken up.

Rejected, they joined other 'CB' company runners – *Little Hattie*, *Wild Rover* and *Susan O'Beirne* – on the trek to Rio de Janeiro that spring. After the ramming of the css *Florida* incident in Bahia harbour the previous year, Brazil was guaranteed safe from Federal interference. There was, however, no ready market awaiting them. Indeed, it took the outbreak of the rebellions against Spanish rule in Chile and Cuba six months later to resuscitate interest in small cargo-carrying 'racers'. By then prices had slipped further, to around a third of their wartime value. Collie reckoned the sale of each lost him £18,000 and, unable to wait out the slump, he was forced to close his company.

To play the wider European market, others followed Begbie's example and sent their runners back across the Atlantic to the safety of a British port. The Anglo-Confederate Trading Company's *Banshee II* (sister to the *Susan O'Beirne*) was sent to Liverpool after her last run (March) into Galveston.

James Carlin, the British agent for the Importing & Exporting Company of South Carolina, also chose Liverpool to liquidate his fleet – *Imogene*, *Ella* and *Caroline*. Power of attorney was signed over to his lawyer to dispose of them as best he could. Ironically, it was the rising prospects for steamers in Brazil that finally found buyers for all three the following year. They were sold to small partnerships made up from the old blockade-running circle of Peter Denny, James Galbraith, J.N. Beach and Thomas S. Begbie. The selling price was £15,000 each – approximately a third of what Carlin paid Denny at the time of their launch – but an improvement on the immediate post-war slump prices.

The last to leave Nassau were diverted to Halifax, Nova Scotia, in the hope of finding a market that was not already glutted. This was the fate of the *Rothesay Castle*, which left in June 1865, days after the uss *Cornubia* (Begbie's old runner) had steamed into Galveston to take the last Confederate port for the Union.

Chapter 5

The Search for Speed

In May 1863, at the height of the replacement boom for runners, the London-based Thomas Begbie engaged in a lengthy debate with his shipbuilding partner John Scott of Greenock. The issue was the size of a massive multi-tubular boiler Begbie wanted Scott to squeeze into a new hull the former was having built for the blockade. She was one of a pair of small iron screw steamers (253 registered tons) he had ordered from William Simons & Company's yard at Renfrew.

Begbie's technical manager Paddon had inspected the original drawings and counted no fewer than 5,670 tubes in this monster boiler. These, somehow, had to fit into hull space twenty-one feet across and just over eleven feet high. Scott argued that the firemen (stokers) working the boiler in what was left of the interior space would be cramped and find it very hard to do their job for long periods. He wanted to cut the number of tubes by 20 per cent to reduce the boiler's overall size to allow more workspace. Begbie's response was that for the money these men would be paid on a blockade run, they would put up with the cramped conditions. The only thing that mattered was speed!

At one stage he had to spell it out to Scott in the most brutal business terms:

For the trade she is intended for, it is a short life she has before her. A careful engineer – whom I have – can by extra care prevent salting. The 'cutting' you make, [will lose] I estimate at upwards of a knot when pressed. Although, as you rightly put it, nothing on ordinary service – but it is for a spurt that this great power is put in her. When at trial, a knot will make a great difference in her value as a saleable article . . . but do you not think, on reconsideration, that for a trade where two voyages yield a large return of capital and profit, or where a sale depends on speed, that it might be better to leave the tubes in – as I suggest. Or do you consider them fatal even for three months running and with a careful man?

Begbie sought to reassure Scott that 'she will be a fast craft when finished, faster far than anything . . . you ever had a chance to build'. As usual, Begbie had his way and the number of tubes remained untouched. He did, however, compromise on their diameter and allowed a reduction of a quarter of an inch to save a little space.

His 'winning design' was finalised in June and was in the stocks at Renfrew that September. Named *Emily* in honour of his youngest daughter, she was launched in December.

This relentless search for speed by the blockade runners was driven by the universal adoption of steam propulsion by their naval pursuers. There had been a few small steam-driven warships during the previous Mexican and Crimean wars. But the first year of the American Civil War saw a wholesale changeover to steam. Steam propulsion liberated the warship from the constraints of wind and tide. Within months of the outbreak of war, only fast steamers had a chance of survival in the blockade-running trade to the main ports.

Being chased by a blockader was highly dangerous. Developments in the armament industry during the intervening five years since the Crimean War had also enormously extended the range, accuracy and destructive power of naval armaments. By 1861, this new generation of cannon shot and shell, together with the steam-driven ironclad ram had rendered the 'wooden walls' of Nelson's navy obsolete.

The French started the naval race the year before the outbreak of the American Civil War, when they launched *La Gloire*, the world's first ironclad. She was a crude affair – essentially a traditional wooden warship with iron plates bolted onto her sides. The British response was launched within that year, and was of quite a different class. The revolutionary HMS *Warrior* built at Blackwall on the Thames was the first 'raven amongst the daws [crows]' – a true iron-framed, steam-driven ironclad with a retractable propeller and watertight compartments. Her sister ship HMS *Black Prince* was built in the Clyde by Robert Napier. This was a great step forward for the region as a naval shipbuilding area.

The American Civil War was the first arena in which the new technology was put to the test: smooth-bore versus rifled cannon; armour-piercing projectile versus armour plate; broadside against turret. Clashes between warships of differing designs, as with the classic struggle between CSS *Merrimac* (broadside) and USS *Monitor* (turret), were studiously analysed by the European newspapers. Virtually all the major maritime powers turned a blind eye to their officers 'visiting' America as observers. Those found in Confederate-held territory or on board a blockade runner invariably claimed to be on leave and 'pleasuring'.

Breech-loading cannons were much faster to load. Fortunately for the blockade runners, they were then in their infancy, few in number and mostly in Confederate hands. The Federal blockader squadrons were armed with muzzle-loading smooth-bore and rifled cannons. In a sea chase most blockading captains preferred to fire solid round shot from their smaller smooth bores at the speeding low-profile runner. They took less time to reload and the ball bounced in a straight line if it hit a wave, increasing the chances of a hit as it skipped. Loading a rifled pointed projectile or studded canister with time fuses on a heaving deck took more care and more time. The spinning shot also ricocheted in an unpredictable way if it clipped a wave top. Even, so many captains had small-calibre rifled cannon on the fore deck with which to harass a runner at long range, hoping for a lucky hit. Most pursuers continued the chase as long as possible in the hope that a boiler would burst or one of the engines break down on the speeding runner. The lure of prize money provided the main inducement to persevere. The crew of the gunboat uss *Eolus* each received $2,000 in prize money for assisting in the capture of Begbie's *Lady Sterling* off Wilmington. Their pay was then $16 a month. The prize money also served to keep the casualty rate on the runners very low as their pursuers' aim was to capture rather than destroy the valuable steamer and its cargo.

The strategy of a runner was dictated by the deployment of the opposing blockaders. The picket lines blockading the major Confederate ports extended as much as thirty miles offshore and often formed three distinct cordons. The outer line was made up mainly of the larger full-rigged steam-driven 'bona fide' warships that cruised offshore in open water. Shallower draught armed ex-commercial steamers patrolled within a few miles of the entrances to the main channels. Smaller gunboats kept station as close inshore as the Confederate coastal batteries would permit. In the case of Wilmington they formed a crescent, with the smallest vessels stationed on innermost horns riding to a kedge anchor almost in the surf.

By the end of the war, around twenty Clyde-built ex-runners were performing excellent service with the blockading squadrons. They had been bought by the US navy after being condemned as lawful prize. Those of the 'river class' carried a single light cannon on their fore deck, as their primary function was to send up rockets to illuminate the runner and signal the particular channel she was attempting. Only the larger 'channel class' steamers were strong enough – after their decks were strengthened – to withstand the shock of recoil from heavy ordnance.

Survival for the hunted blockade runner, once discovered, depended solely on speed. If rumbled in daylight while still in open sea, the runner's captain used his advantage in speed and manoeuvrability to turn and run back out to sea. This was usually successful, so long as her boilers and engines were in good condition.

Detection closer inshore posed greater risks. On the Atlantic seaboard runs most captains crossed the turbulent influence of the Gulf Stream towards dusk and ran in close to the shoreline. There the silhouette of the coast blended with their grey hulls to mask them from view from the sea. Hugging the shore in darkness, they worked their way up one of the inlets. The ultimate test usually came in the final approaches while sneaking through the inner picket lines. If all went well they would attempt to slip past, throttled back to minimise noise and with dampers down on the flues to reduce the risk of a shower of telltale sparks escaping from the funnels.

The Federal commanders learned early on that the shallow draught of the Clyde-built paddle steamers allowed them to run over shoal banks or creep up very close inshore, amongst the breakers and places where their pursuers could not follow. As often as not, they were spotted. Exposed under a glare of signal rockets and flares, the only viable option was to sprint the last few miles under shellfire to gain the protection of the Confederate coastal defences. The principal Confederate forts had great rifled muzzle-loaders which easily out-gunned anything a chasing blockader had to offer in retaliation. Indeed, the largest fortress cannon could fire a shaped shell over two miles.

The commander of the famous coastal bastion Fort Fisher, Colonel Lamb, had a detachment of smaller rifled cannon on carriages. These were rushed by mule train to the beaches at New Inlet, to cover any runner forced onto the shore. It would be fair to say that without their combined covering fire, the risks of running the blockade would have been unacceptable much earlier in the war.

Many fortress cannon were English-made and supplied by Fraser, Trenholm & Company of Liverpool or the personal gift of Charles K. Prioleau. These massive muzzle-loaders were mostly constructed to the Whitworth design whereby a red-hot wrought-iron coil was shrunk onto an inner cast-steel barrel. This was then encased by a succession of wrought-iron hoops also shrunk on with heat. The other British cannons much sought after were those built by the Blakely and Armstrong companies. Armstrong produced a few smaller calibre breech-loaders which had a higher rate of fire but they were prone to malfunctioning. All fired shaped or studded projectiles with time fuses that required a slow-burning propellant (mammoth gunpowder) which had to be run past the blockade.

Both sides soon had home-produced versions. The North mass-produced cannons for the navy to the designs of Parrott and Dahlgren. The Confederates produced small numbers of the indigenous Rodman design. Their ordnance department also sought to increase its output and ability to manufacture specialist rifled solid, canister and armour-piercing projectiles by importing the machinery and technicians from Britain.

One such cargo was on board the screw steamer *Princess Royal* (the most probable match for Verne's fictitious *Dolphin*). She was built by Tod & McGregor in 1862 and was considered one of the finest sea-going steamers of her day. She was acquired in early 1863 by Fraser, Trenholm & Company from her original owners Langland & Son of Glasgow. Her captain was a company veteran who had just returned from the China Seas. His mission was to run a cargo of rifled cannon and machinery (accompanied by a specialist technician) into Charleston. It was a desperate gamble as she was highly visible (large and high-rigged) and the blockade was then at its height. Needless to say, she was captured as she tried to enter the main channel and before she could reach the cover of the cannons on Fort Sumter.

The Confederate coastal fortresses and batteries were largely a pre-war legacy. The capture of the great naval base of Norfolk at the start of the war provided the Confederates with a great store of heavy smooth-bore ordnance and munitions. Indeed, throughout the war, it was field cannon for the army, rather than naval fortress cannon, that was in dire shortage.

For the blockade runners making for the Cape Fear River and Wilmington, the all-important sanctuary was the guns of Forts Caswell and Fisher. The latter was a massive earthwork guarding the entrance to the New Inlet. Colonel Lamb had worked tirelessly to remodel his fort along the lines of the famous Russian Malakoff citadel which had defended Sebastapol against all British and French assaults during the Crimean War. His long-range rifled Whitworths offered the ultimate protection for a runner being pursued by Federal blockaders.

In comparison, the contest between 'blockade runner' and 'block-ader' at sea was one-sided. The thin plated iron hull of the unarmed blockade runner offered no defence against Federal shell and shot. Nor could they retaliate without losing their non-belligerent status. As the number of blockaders increased and their techniques improved, speed became the most sought-after attribute when purchasing a new runner.

The seventeen-year-old Glasgow-born purser James Sprunt would certainly have agreed with Begbie's maxim that 'a knot made all the difference' after serving on the *Lilian* under the legendary Captain Maffitt on her last run into Wilmington. Built by J. and G. Thomson of Finnieston and Govan in late 1864, her twin oscillators drove her at fifteen knots loaded 'to the marks'. It was her speed that saved her in an open sea chase off Cape Lookout by USS *Shenandoah*. The pursuit lasted over three hours, during which she was continually shelled.

The Federal commander's clinical entry in his log relates just how much weaponry was brought to bear on the fleeing *Lilian*:

> Saturday, July 30, 1864: At 3.45 p.m. sighted a steamer burning black smoke to the eastward; made all sail in chase. At 4.30 p.m. made stranger out to be a double smokestack, side-wheel steamer, apparently a blockade runner, standing to the northward and westward. At 5.45 he showed rebel colours. Called the first division and powder division to quarters and began to fire at her with the 30 and 150 pounder rifle Parrott. At 6 p.m. boat to quarters and fired all the divisions. At 7 p.m. took in fore-topgallant sail and foresail. At 7.30 took in fore-topsail. During the chase fired 70 rounds from 30-pounder Parrott, 18 rounds from 11-inch guns, and one round from 24-pounder howitzer. At 8 p.m. stopped firing, gave up the chase, stopped engines.

In the decade preceding the war, an entire shipbuilding industry had risen in the Clyde to meet the demand for 'racing' passenger steamers. Robert Napier's Vulcan and Lancefield yards in Govan were regarded as the cradle of advanced high-pressure steam propulsion. Many of the engineers who opened their own yards further downriver during the war were trained there. The builder of the *Lilian*, George Thomson, had served his time with Napier and rose to 'assistant manager' before leaving to set up his own company with his brother.

The largest class of 'racing' passenger steamers regularly launched before the war were those ordered for the deep cross-channel routes from Glasgow to Belfast, the Isle of Man, Dublin, Liverpool, Cork and the Outer Hebrides. In winter, the treacherous tides and currents of the North Channel, Irish Sea and Minches created maelstroms in severe weather which claimed many a fine ship. Subsequently, the ferries working these wild sea areas were designed to match speed with excellent sea-going qualities. The best were screw-driven and deep-hulled with a good cargo capacity. The first blockade runners acquired from the Clyde were mostly of this 'channel class'.

As the blockade tightened and Federal cruisers stepped up their 'stop and search' missions during the spring of 1862, the runners out of

Bermuda and the Bahamas sought to buy smaller and faster craft. The Clyde's 'river class' paddle steamers with their higher speed and shallow draught were ideal for their needs. The 'river class' hulls had the distinctive knife-edge bow and a narrow beam relative to their length. This type of hull was designed to be 'driven' through the short seas of the Firth of Clyde. They were, of course, not suited for the Atlantic swell and suffered badly in the crossing and winter runs into the Confederacy. Their hulls had to be strengthened in the bow with diagonal struts and the fore deck fitted with a 'turtle' cover to shed the broaching waves. Those custom-built for the running trade after 1862 had these fitted as standard, along with watertight compartments and a powder magazine.

To exploit fully the hull's potential for great speed required high-pressure boilers and finely-tuned performance engines. The engineers that served them were in a class of their own and most sought after by the blockade-running companies.

In his memoirs, 'Mack' relates that he once had to draw his pistol to stop the Confederate agents kidnapping his engineer and firemen. The incident happened off Fleetwood, Lancashire when delivering a newly built runner to its new owners. The Southern agents were waiting on a tug that had towed out a barge with a cargo of heavy ordnance under cover. At the critical moment of transfer of documents and crews, they tried to manhandle the engineer and his firemen back on board the runner. After an ugly stand-off the pistol-wielding Mack got his men back, forcing the Confederate agents to resort to bribery. For a substantial sum they secured the services of Angus Macdonald, one of his mechanics. Mack met him ten years later when he was back plying his trade in the Clyde. Macdonald explained that, while racing out of Charleston, a Federal shell had hit the bulwark of his steamer. One of the splinters from the wooden handrail sliced off the top part of his finger, 'as clean as the big shearing machine would cut a bit of boiler plate'.

Both 'channel' and 'river' classes of Clyde steamers have a long technical pedigree. They had evolved to serve the growing trade in 'doon the watter' day excursions and conveying wealthy commuters between their Glasgow offices and their fashionable villas along the Clyde coast. It was a cut-throat business in which the shipbuilder usually was a major shareholder in the ferry company. Their customers were discerning and patronised their favourite steamers. Such loyalty expected to be rewarded by the thrill of their captains racing one another when the opportunity arose.

Such reckless showmanship, particularly in the narrow confines of the River Clyde, was greatly frowned upon by the governing Clyde

Navigation Authority. They imposed fines on any master reported 'racing' but this did little to deter a 'day's sport'. Indeed, the press of the day actively encouraged such behaviour. In June 1861, the *Greenock Telegraph* reported on the three best racers on the local 'blue ribbon' run to Rothesay on the Isle of Bute, under the heading 'The Fastest Steamer on the Clyde':

> The new steamer *Neptune*, built by Messrs Robert Napier & Sons, Glasgow, for the Glasgow and Rothesay station, was out on trial yesterday, and proved herself to be the fastest steamer that has ever been on the Clyde. She ran the distance between Cumbrae and Cloch Lights in 46 minutes, being 1 minute 45 seconds less than the run of the *Windsor Castle* two years ago. She afterwards competed with the new steamer *Ruby*, between Innellan and Rothesay, and beat her by more than two lengths.

These performances did not go unnoticed by the Confederate agents. A short time later the same newspaper carried a report titled 'Another Clyde Steamer for America':

> Messrs Napiers' splendid Rothesay steamer *Neptune* proceeded to Gareloch, on Friday, with a few gentlemen on board, the reputed object being to test her rate of speed, over a measured mile, before closing a purchase of her by gentlemen said to be acting for the Southern States of America. It is said that the bargain has been pending for some weeks back; that Messrs Napier have been shy about parting with the *Neptune*, as being a steamer of thoroughly tested speed and capacity.

The gentlemen in question were agents for Fraser, Trenholm & Company.

Over a year later, one of her rivals for the Rothesay run was also acquired, as the *Morning Journal* reported in November 1862, under the heading 'The Clyde Steamer *Ruby*':

> This favourite steamer, the sale of which was announced some time ago, sailed from the Broomielaw yesterday. She will take her departure from the Tail o' the Bank on an early day for a foreign port, and will steam out with a full complement of Welsh patent fuel being stowed on board for that purpose. Going down the river yesterday her consumption of that fuel averaged half a ton per hour. Had ordinary coal been used, the consumption for the same period would have been one ton at least. The firing was under the supervision of

Mr. Clough the agent here for the Fuel Company. The *Giraffe* we are informed will also use the fuel on her outward voyage.

For a decade before the war, the market for 'doon the watter' racers designed for maximised speed was booming. Hull design was already an established science. Twenty years before the war, John Scott Russell, the author of 'Wave Theory', had first applied his principles commercially to the river steamer *Flambeau* while employed by Cairds of Greenock. In simple terms, his theory was that the maximum speed that a vessel could possibly be driven through water is pre-set by the amount of 'wetted surface area' it presents to the sea. No amount of additional propulsion can change this, unless the hull was designed to ride on top of the wave (as with modern powerboats).

To approach their maximum speed, the Clyde shipbuilders produced the distinctive sleek hulls with knife-shaped bows. Both paddle- and screw-driven hulls were designed to perform at their best when loaded, thereby avoiding 'slippage'. This happened when the paddle or the screw rode too high in the water and the engines over-revved. It followed that during speed trials the steamer had to be at least half-loaded. Calculating the speed of a potential runner over a measured mile became so critical during the war years that two onshore marker poles were placed next to the two Clyde lighthouses, the Cloch and the Wee Cumbrae. The start and finish of the run were timed when the two poles aligned when viewed from the wheelhouse.

The *Juno*, built by Tod & McGregor, was a prime example of the larger shallow-draught 'river class' paddle steamers available at the outbreak of the war. Unlike Verne's *Dolphin*, her launching from the Meadowside yard on 3 March 1860 was a quiet and dignified affair. As the *Glasgow Herald* noted: 'Shortly before 4 o'clock, the ways having been cleared and the dog shores knocked off, the *Juno* took to the water in fine style after being gracefully named by Miss Auld of Partick.'

She had been ordered by McKellar & Sons, the owners of the largest fleet of paddle steamers on the Clyde coast at the time. The head of the family, Alexander McKellar, was the first master of their new flagship. She sported the company's distinctive salmon-pink livery on her two funnels and boasted first-class passenger lounges under deck. Based at Lamlash on the Isle of Arran, her outward daily run was from Brodick to Millport, thence on to Largs, Greenock and finally to the Broomielaw (Glasgow). She managed this run in just over three hours 'including stoppages', the longest of which was at Greenock where first-class passengers could transfer to the railway.

Her acquisition and dispatch as a blockade runner was a rapid process. On 12 April 1863 her captain, Alexander's eldest son Duncan, died suddenly while on board her in Glasgow harbour. It is not known whether this bereavement was the principal reason for his father's snap decision to sell his three fastest steamers (*Juno*, *Jupiter* and *Star*) to the blockade runners. What is certain is that on 8 May, within a fortnight of the burial, the ownership of the *Juno* officially passed to a Glasgow-based middleman Neil Mathieson, acting for George Wigg of Liverpool, then in Nassau.

It took only four days to refit her at Greenock for her transatlantic crossing. The *Glasgow Herald* noted her hasty departure:

> The favourite steamer *Juno* sailed from here yesterday for her unknown destination. She has received a temporary awning from her bow to her paddle box for the purpose of breaking [the] heavy seas she may have to contend with. Her hull has been painted white, which gives her a yacht-like appearance.

Within a month of her leaving the Clyde she ran the blockade into Charleston (8 July). There she was 'forcibly taken possession of' by the Confederate government for Mallory's Navy Department, her owners receiving £21,000 in compensation. For a short time she served as a local defence gunboat, armed with a torpedo spar and a light howitzer, before she was restored to blockade-running duty in March 1864. She was lost in a gale that month after running out of Charleston.

Reaching Bermuda from Scotland on a Clyde steamer was a feat of endurance that put low coal consumption at a premium. Most if not all of the passage across the Atlantic via Madeira was sail-assisted. A fast crossing took around three weeks, with a stopover for coaling at Funchal. The report of the Govan-built *Emma Henry* gives a good idea of the timescales involved. She made the run from the Clyde to Madeira in five days and twenty hours. From there to Bermuda took just over nine days. Her career as a runner was a short one as she was captured on her second run out of Wilmington by the USS *Cherokee* (ex-runner *Thistle*).

To make these Atlantic crossings, the smaller 'river class' steamers had to be stepped with sails (schooner rig) as part of their modifications. They left crammed with Welsh coal, which was also heaped on the deck to the top of the hand railings. After the escape of the *Fingal* from Holyhead, the United States opened a consulate in Cardiff to plug the gap in their surveillance of runners coaling before making out into the Atlantic. To escape such close vigilance many were sent

COME, JONATHAN, WHY SHOULD WE FIGHT—"AM I NOT A MAN, AND A BROTHER?"

1. John Bull inviting Cousin Jonathan to sign the Declaration of Paris, *Punch* 1856 (ESME Library)

2. American view of the European response to the blockade, *Harper's Weekly* 1861 (ESME Library)

3. Chasing a blockade runner, *Harper's Weekly* 1861 (ESME Library)

THE DANGEROUS PLAYMATE—A SINGULAR INSTANCE OF FASCINATION.
That Innocent Infant JOHNNY BULL giving Aid and Comfort to the Reptile.

THE "SENSATION" STRUGGLE IN AMERICA.

LOOK OUT FOR SQUALLS
JACK BULL: "You do what's right, my son, or I'll blow you
out of the water."

4. Johnny Bull feeding the serpent, *Harper's Weekly* 1861 (ESME Library)

5. The British view of the Civil War, *Punch* 1862 (ESME Library)

6. British view of the *Trent* Incident, *Punch* 1862 (ESME Library)

JOHN BULL AS PAINTED BY HIMSELF.

ONE HEAD BETTER THAN TWO.

Louis Napoleon. "I SAY, HADN'T WE BETTER TELL OUR FRIEND THERE TO LEAVE OFF MAKING A FOOL OF HIMSELF?"

Lord Pam. "H'M, WELL, SUPPOSE YOU TALK TO HIM YOURSELF. HE'S A GREAT ADMIRER OF YOURS, YOU KNOW."

ABE LINCOLN'S LAST CARD; OR, ROUGE-ET-NOIR.

7. John Bull's store of contraband, *Harper's Weekly* 1862 (ESME Library)

8. Palmerston and Napoleon confer on intervention, *Punch* 1862 (ESME Library)

9. British view of Lincoln's Emancipation of Slavery Proclamation, *Punch* 1862 (ESME Library)

10. American view of British duplicity, *Harper's Weekly* 1863 (ESME Library)

11. Lord Palmerston passing President Davis, *Punch* 1864 (ESME Library)

NEUTRALITY.

MRS. NORTH.—"*How about the* ALABAMA, *you wicked old man ?*"
MRS. SOUTH.—"*Where's my rams ?   Take back your precious Consuls—there ! ! !*"

12. The question of neutrality, *Punch* 1864 (ESME Library)

13. Capture of Fort Fisher, January 1865. Engraving published by Kurt and Allison 1890.
(Library of Congress)

14. Britannia and Columbia – first move towards a settlement, *Punch* 1871 (ESME Library)

15. The inflated 'Alabama' claims, *Punch* 1871 (ESME Library

16. The launch of Jules Verne's *Dolphin*, 1876 edition (ESME Library)

17. The *Giraffe* undergoing conversion in the Meadowside Dock, Glasgow 1862 (ESME Library)

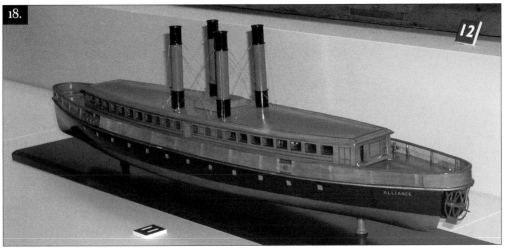

18. Model of the pre-war-*Alliance* (1856) (Maritime Museum of Liverpool)

19. The *Alliance* as the *New Zealand*, *Australian Illustrated News*, 1865
(ESME Library)

20. The blockade runner *Princess Royal* as a Federal armed blockader (ESME Library)

21. A model of the *Evelyn* retained by Captain Burgoyne
(National Museum of Science & Industry)

22. Blockade runner entering Nassau, *Harper's Weekly* 1863 (ESME Library)

23. Run cotton bales at Nassau (ESME Library)

24. John N. Maffitt onboard the blockade runner *Lilian, London Illustrated News* 1864 (ESME Library)

25. The crippled blockade runner *Lilian* preparing to surrender on 24 August 1864

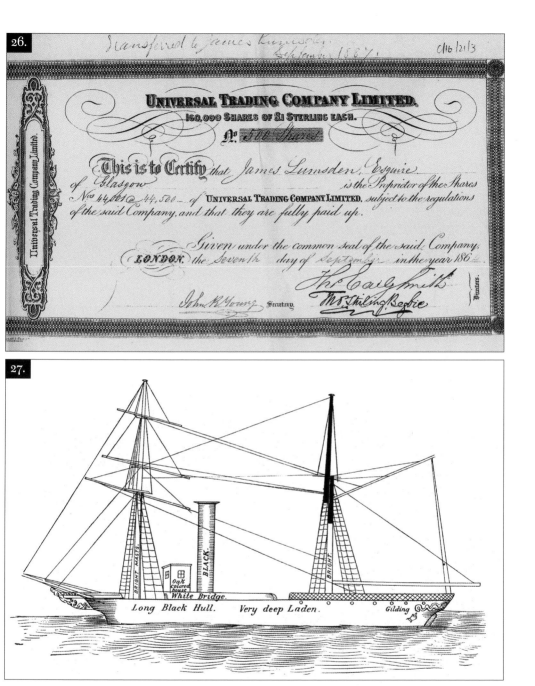

26. Share certificate of the Universal Trading Company (Glasgow University Archives)

27. Drawing of the *Fingal* at Greenock by Detective Brennan (ESME Library)

28. The *Fingal* undergoing conversion to the CSS *Atlanta*, 1862 (ESME Library)

29. The capture of the CCS *Atlanta* by the USS *Weehawken*, 1863.
Phototype drawing by F. Gutekunst c.1890. (ESME Library)

30. The USS *Atlanta* (ESME Library)

31. Pre-war paddle steamers at the Woodyard, Dumbarton by William Clark of Greenock (West Dunbartonshire Libraries)

32. The CSS *Shenandoah* (ESME Library)

Visitors aboard the Shenandoah *in Melbourne.*

33. The CSS *Shenandoah* receiving guests at Melbourne (ESME Library)

34. The *Pampero* laying in the Clyde, *London Illustrated News* 1865 (ESME Library)

35. Scottish Law Officers ponder the *Pampero* Affair (ESME Library)

36. Plan of the North's *Ram* (Hutington Library)

37. The North's *Ram* as the HDMS *Danmark*

38. US Secretary of the Navy Gideon Welles (ESME Library)

39. CS Secretary of the Navy Stephen Mallory (ESME Library)

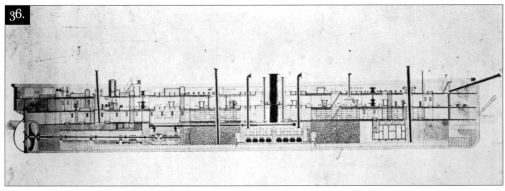

36.

37.

38.

39.

40. US Secretary of State William Seward (ESME Library)

41. US Minister Charles Adams (ESME Library)

42. Prime Minister Lord Palmerston (ESME Library)

43. Foreign Secretary Lord Russell (ESME Library)

44. James D. Bulloch CSN (ESME Library)

45. John Wilkinson CSN, blockade runner (ESME Library)

46. John N. Maffitt CSN, captain of the Confederate *Florida*

47. Captain David Leslie and his family on the steps of his 'Bermuda' villa, Dunoon (Leslie Family Collection)

48. John Scott of Greenock
(West Dunbartonshire
Libraries)

49. Peter Denny of Dumbarton
(West Dunbartonshire
Libraries)

50. Jules Verne (ESME Library)

JULES VERNE

directly out from the Clyde to Cork in Southern Ireland from where communications with London took longer.

Writing to Scott (9 September 1862) Thomas Begbie despaired at the logic in sending out this smaller class of steamer:

> *Iona* may go. *Pearl* appears quite impossible to utilise at seven foot six inches depth [hold], five foot deep [draught] light [loaded] – first strengthening then five days coals [for the run], what remains for cargo – What?

As fate would have it, the diminutive *Pearl* made it to Nassau while the larger *Iona* did not even manage to clear the Clyde. A week after Begbie posted his letter to Scott, the departure of the *Iona* was reported in the *Greenock Advertiser*:

> We understand that the fine steamer *Iona*, one of Messrs D. Hutchison & Co.'s fleet of West Highland steamers, which has been generally acknowledged 'Queen of the Clyde', made her last trip on her route from Glasgow to Ardrishaig on Saturday last, having been purchased. It is said that Mr. Mason, the Southern Commissioner who visited Glasgow recently, had something to do with the purchase. As it is she will likely leave the Clyde, after receiving some strengthening outfit, in a short time hence. It is also said two or three other of our crack steamers, if not already sold, are likely soon to be purchased for the same purpose. Should they go to the South they will likely form a line of steamers between some near neutral ports and one of the smaller Southern ports least likely to be affected by the blockade. The *Iona*'s place on the Highland route has been filled by the saloon steamer *Fairy*.

Hours after finishing her speed trials for her new owners, she set out on her outward passage. Off Fort Matilda, near Gourock, she was in a collision with the *Chanticleer*, another new steamer on her speed test. The captain of the *Iona* refused the services of a salvage tug while he haggled over who was to blame with the other captain, who was drunk. While he squabbled, she slowly settled and sank under him. Today she lies in some twenty metres of water with the great load of coal that had been piled on her decks for the outward passage still in situ.

At the Board of Trade inquiry into the accident, heard in Glasgow, the strengthening of the *Iona* for her transatlantic voyage became a major issue with her Lloyd's insurers. Over £5,500 had been paid to her original builders James and George Thomson of Finnieston and

Govan to reinforce her hull by her new owner David McNutt of Glasgow, a regular speculator in the blockade. At the hearing, an independent surveyor claimed that she would never have made the ocean crossing had she encountered rough seas. He stated that the work done on her was insufficient to stop her rivets and plates parting under the relentless shock of 'hogging, pitching and rolling' in the tremendous ocean waves of an Atlantic storm. It would seem a blessing that she sank while close inshore in the Firth of Clyde as all the crew, including a boy stowaway from Stornoway, got off safely.

The ocean-going resilience of even the custom-built runners was questionable. The veteran Confederate master Taylor reckoned that his last charge, the Will o' the Wisp (built by the recently opened William Simons & Company, Renfrew, in 1863), of which much was expected, was 'shamefully put together'. He also described as an 'Irish cattle boat', the Despatch, in which he left for the Atlantic only the year before with coal up to the railings and only a foot freeboard. He reckoned he only made it across that February because the weather was mild for the time of year.

Hull failure was probably the cause of the disappearance of the paddle steamer Hattie while attempting an Atlantic crossing in mid-December 1864. She had been launched by Caird & Company of Greenock only the month before and was designed for the Gulf running trade – long, beamy and with a very shallow draught. Her owner was given as John Laing, shipmaster, of 34 Houston Street, Glasgow. It would seem likely that he had already sold her on when she departed from the Clyde in ballast on 10 November for Nassau and on to Havana.

Her disappearance was recounted by the Greenock Telegraph six months later:

> She encountered stormy weather, and put into Waterford with damage, and after repair sailed for her destination (15 December) and as she has not since been heard of, there is little doubt that she has foundered with all hands – twenty-eight in number.

It was a locally felt tragedy. The newspaper responded by printing the names of the missing. Poignant as this list is, it offers a unique opportunity to examine the make-up of the transatlantic crew, most of whom were young Scots and Irish men. It also serves as a chilling counterbalance to the swashbuckling heroic tales that were published after the war. The published list of the crew that departed Greenock reads:

Mr. Eugene Lambert, a native of the Southern States, master
Mr. Fred H. Wharton, 24, Manchester, mate
David Cunningham, 25, Renfrew, carpenter
Matthew Montgomery, 34, Dublin 1st steward
Thomas Johnston, 20, Dumfries, 2nd steward
William McIver, 25, 68 Shaw Street, Greenock (unmarried) 1st cook
James Watson, Largs, 17, assistant cook
Thomas Richards, 34, Glasgow, 1st engineer
James Stevenson, 24, Glasgow, 2nd engineer
Alexander Melville, 26, Fife, 3rd engineer
Robert Gilles, 27, Belfast, A.B.
Henry Henderson, 21, Belfast, A.B.
William Robson, 22, Kilmarnock, A.B.
Alexander McKinnon, 22, Edinburgh, A.B.
George Perkins, 21, St. John, N.B., A.B.
James Rooney, 36, Dublin, A.B.
Donald Currie, 22, Argyll, fireman
George Reed, 28, Lanark, fireman
James Arthur, 33, Tyrone, fireman
Laurence Hamilton, 37, Glasgow, fireman
Malcolm Morrison, 34, 30 Bearhope Street, Greenock (unmarried), fireman
Hector Livingstone, 39, Argyll, fireman
John McNair, 32, Argyll, fireman
Daniel Fleming, 23, 7 Stanners, Greenock, fireman
John Boyle, 37, Antrim, fireman
John Riach, 26, Argyll, fireman
H. McLauchlin, 25, Londonderry, fireman
Daniel McDougall, 22, 6 Manse Lane, Greenock (unmarried), fireman.
The others lodged in town, or were boarded in the Seaman's Home.

Her entry in the Shipping Register was finally closed on 8 May 1865 with the entry 'lost at sea'.

The *Hattie* was not the only Clyde steamer to break up or be overwhelmed in winter seas. The *Iona II*, launched in 1863 by James and George Thomson of Finnieston and Govan and acquired by David McNutt for a Richmond client, suffered a similar fate off Lundy Island en route to Nassau in February 1864. Fortunately her crew were saved.

Many had narrow escapes and barely made it to Bermuda or Nassau. Having delivered them, their traumatised crews often refused to continue to serve on them. Others were so badly damaged that they had to limp back to the Clyde for repairs. As the *Greenock Telegraph* reported on 19 January 1864, under the heading 'Bound For Nassau':

A Queenstown [Cork] correspondent of the *Dublin Express*, writing on Friday, says: The good fortune which has attended recent attempts to run the blockade at Wilmington, North Carolina, has caused a small crowd of shipping lately to leave Liverpool and Glasgow, ostensibly bound for a neutral port, but really bent on carrying supplies to those who are willing to pay cent per cent for 'soft goods', and a high premium for certain kinds of 'hardware'. The steamers are so constructed, being shallow and without much breadth of beam, that they are unable to keep out in stormy weather. The recent gale has had the effect of driving in two of these craft, and from their fancy yacht-like build one would say that their former plying on the Clyde was more suitable than the Atlantic in January weather. A few weeks since a slight craft came in so battered and shaken that men worked day and night to complete the extensive repairs, and in the end some of the crew deserted rather than proceed. The *Fairy*, which is up the river in dock for repairs, has come down, and has now steam up, and will probably sail tonight. It was amusing last week to see a 20-knotter from the Clyde tacking about the entrance of the harbour, waiting for darkness and the disappearance of a suspicious hull to the westward. The *Julia* sailed before daylight this morning, so low in the water that her red and green lights could scarcely be seen in the dip of the sea. These boats are deeply-laden, and the captains were most zealous in keeping strangers from going on board. The principal officers come from the 'Land of [Oat] Cakes [Scotland]' but most of the crews are natives of the 'Gem of the Sea [Ireland]' whose sons compose the greater part of the hands of almost every vessel touching here, no matter where from or on what errand, indeed it is extremely probable that if the muster roll of the *Flying Dutchman* were called over, the majority of the hands would hail from the Emerald Isle.

Surviving the Atlantic crossing was just the start of the war of attrition with the elements. In 1864, Sprunt, while serving as purser on the *North Heath*, owned by Begbie's Albion Company, experienced a close shave with death during a storm at sea. His vivid account is worth telling in full:

I believe that under God, Captain Burroughs, by his fine qualities as a cool and capable seaman, saved this ship from foundering at sea when we ran into a hurricane shortly after our departure from St. George, Bermuda, bound for Wilmington. For two days and nights we were in imminent danger of our lives tossed upon a raging sea, every man of our crew of 48 except those at the wheel was lashed to the vessel, while we bailed, with buckets and the use of hand pumps, the flooded fireroom of our sinking vessel. For an entire night she wallowed like a log in a trough of mountainous waves, which broke over us in ever-increasing fury. I can never forget this frightful scene. It seems photographed upon my memory in all its fearsome details. The water had risen in our hold until every one of our fourteen furnaces was extinguished. There was no steam to run our donkey boilers and steam-power pumps. Lashed to one another, in the blackness of darkness, relieved only by the intermittent flashes of lightning which illuminated the giant waves towering around us and threatening to overwhelm and sink the labouring, quivering fabric, we held on in despair until morning, when we began to gain on the leaks until our steam pumps could be used in relieving the boiler room, and our brave captain got the ship under control. Then we succeeded in putting her about and headed back to Bermuda.

After this terrible ordeal the young Sprunt was bedridden by an attack of fever for weeks and missed the *North Heath*'s last run to Wilmington, where she was badly damaged.

As losses mounted in 1863, the Clyde's remaining stock of older 'river class' steamers was trawled for any with a turn of speed. Many were never intended for open-sea work as they were very small and without cover for the helmsman. Two that were acquired in June 1863 were the sister paddle steamers *Kelpie* and *Spunkie*. Both were built by Tod & McGregor for the Rothesay run in 1857 with a 'registered tonnage' of just under 81 tons.

The *Greenock Telegraph* followed the preparations for the first one to go, titled 'The *Spunkie*':

This favourite steamer, which was lately sold to the mysterious foreign potentate for something like £7,500, went out upon her trial trip on Thursday, and gave entire satisfaction. She has been completely transformed since she was bought up; a covering, extending from the bow to the steerage companion way, for the purpose of breaking the heavy seas she may have to contend against, having been built. She has also got two strong masts, in place of the light holiday 'stick' she used to carry, the forward one being square rigged. A large deck-house has likewise been erected aft the funnel, and as she is all painted white inside, she presents quite a different appearance. She has also been fitted up with a patent salt water distilling apparatus, which works very well, thus leaving her a larger space between decks for cargo.

The 'mysterious foreign potentate' was Edward J. Lomnitz of Manchester, who the following year added the larger *Beatrice*, built by McNab & Company of Greenock, to his fleet.

The *Spunkie* caused quite a stir when she made her first run for the Bahamas. Sprunt was one of onlookers at the quayside on her return:

> Many blockade runners were given corresponding names, *Owl*, *Bat*, *Badger*, *Phantom*, *Lynx*, but none seemed to be more appropriate than that given to a little toy steamer from the Clyde named *Spunkie* . . . When I saw her in Nassau I could scarcely believe that this little cockleshell of a boat had crossed the North Atlantic and had run through the blockading fleet.

The pluck of the men who sailed can only be wondered at. The *Spunkie* made two runs from Nassau before running hard ashore in the Old Inlet off Fort Caswell, Wilmington, in early February 1864. She was carrying blankets and shoes for the army.

With the last of the Clyde's existing stock of 'racers' snapped up, the demand for new and faster steamers became insatiable. This forced the pace of marine technology from late 1862 onwards.

If speed was the first consideration, then draught was a close second. This was particularly the case after the summer of 1863 when it looked increasing likely that Wilmington and Charleston might soon be closed to the runners. This left the shallower Gulf ports of Galveston and Mobile as the last viable options. Begbie gave one of his designers the go-ahead to drop the traditional solid iron keel in favour of 'angle iron' (in a box construction for rigidity) along most of the mid-length of the vessel. This saved weight and reduced her draught by two inches when loaded compared to a hull of a similar size being built at the time by a rival Greenock yard.

Begbie's simple 'rule of thumb' was that a steamer sank one inch in the water for every twenty tons of cargo she carried. By saving two inches by reducing her deadweight, his vessel could carry an extra forty tons' payload. Or it could make the difference between scraping over or grounding on the sandbars off Mobile 'which makes an enormous difference in utility for the buyer's purposes'.

Shallow draught and length for speed came at a price. William Watson, the only Scottish captain believed to have written under his own name, found out just how fragile a 'river class' Clyde steamer was during a chase off Galveston, late in 1864. Driving his old steamer *Jeanette* (ex-Rothesay ferry *Eagle* built by Denny in 1852) through a heavy sea with a deckload of cotton, she was hit by a small rifled shell. It punched a three-inch hole just above one of its haystack boilers. Had it hit three feet lower, there would have been a disastrous explosion and instant loss of speed.

In his efforts to protect the vulnerable spot from another incoming shell, Watson ordered bales of cotton moved from the fore and aft decks to shield the damaged area over the exposed boiler. As he relates, 'suddenly, the engineer [from Greenock] came running up to say that the vessel was buckling amidships. I looked and saw her bending up at the bow and stern.' To save the ship from springing her plates and breaking up he had to rescind immediately his order and move the bales back to their original position to redistribute the weight.

The ultimate custom-designed blockade runners were the five paddle steamers *Flamingo*, *Falcon*, *Ptarmigan*, *Condor* and *Evelyn*. These were launched between June and August 1864 – just as the game of 'hare and hounds' with the blockading squadrons was entering its final and most lethal phase. The Federals' capture rate was by then up from one in every seven runs to one in three, and rapidly escalating towards one in two.

They were built for Alexander Collie (for his new Gorgas-McRae contract) by Randolph, Elder & Company, at their new Fairfield yard in Govan. They were numbers 26–30 in Randolph's list of hulls and numbers 48–52 in Elder's list of engines. The contract stipulated that they must be very fast, able to run into the Gulf ports and return with a minimum payload of 1,000 bales of cotton.

The '*Flamingo* class' seemed to meet all these requirements. The hull design was that of a racing thoroughbred with beautiful sleek lines topped with iron 'turtle back' deck covers fore and aft, and curved decks. These were designed to shed water rapidly when ploughing at speed through the rough seas of the Gulf of Mexico. The great length of the deck and wide beam (280 feet long by 28 feet) accommodated the desired number of bales. The draught was extremely shallow for her length (only seven foot when fully loaded), enough to clear the shoals and sandbars off Mobile and Galveston. The paddle boxes were set back aft of the three raked funnels. They had a very distinctive look and an extremely low silhouette.

They were driven by two compound engines (180 horsepower) designed by John Elder, an engineering genius. Each was served by three giant haystack boilers raising a working steam pressure to forty pounds per square inch. Thomas Begbie had Scott regularly report on Elder's progress. He was very impressed: 'The forty pounds pressure is an excellent thing to have if to be relied on without priming at sea as such pressure is mighty useful just for a spurt of four or five hours when under chase.' When launched they had a sustainable speed of seventeen knots and over twenty in a sprint.

Begbie was not the only one watching. Underwood, the US consul in Glasgow, reported to Seward in June that the newly launched *Falcon* had made over twenty-one knots in her trials. He concluded with the comment that this was 'not quite as much as was expected of her'. Even so, such a turn of speed would enable them easily to outrun any pursuer.

A reporter for the *Irish Times*, who witnessed the *Falcon* picking up a pilot at Limerick on her way out, noted:

> she at once shot off like an arrow . . . she is described by a marine officer as being as a huge shark that can bound and plunge in the water and dart through an ocean billow instead of mounting it largely. She appears to have been entirely intended for speed, and must become the fastest of the blockade runners.

Raising pressures to this level severely tested the materials and workmanship of the day and posed new problems for the shipbuilders. Above twenty-five pounds per square inch pressure, sea water could not be used in the boilers as the salt quickly clogged the tubes. No amount of 'blowing out' with steam could clear these deposits. Large and bulky desalination apparatus needed to serve the boilers with fresh water was then only fitted to the ocean raiders and the very latest runners.

With the smaller runners, conserving the reservoir of fresh water within the boilers became a major goal. Randolph, Elder & Company of Govan and Scotts of Greenock, were the first to introduce surface condensers that cooled the spent steam from the cylinders for re-cycling. At first it proved difficult to keep the surface condenser 'tight'. A leak would contaminate the boiler's reservoir with the coolant (pumped sea water) and would increase the salinity and hence erosion in the boilers. It was soon found that, by allowing a thin scale of salt to develop inside the boiler and condenser, an effective seal was formed. Begbie was a great advocate of surface condensers but held the view that they only suited haystack boilers: 'otherwise not for such work as out there [running] – they are immense bother: impossible to be kept clean'.

It was a breakthrough that paid dividends. In his memoirs, 'Mack' boasted that, as assistant manager of a Glasgow firm (which he would not name), he was dispatched to Hartlepool to try and snatch an order for a new runner from their arch rivals, Laird of Birkenhead. His yard manager joked on his departure that he was sent out 'to take a fat bane [bone] from that big dog's mou[th]'. He arrived to find the deal all but closed. He was, however, permitted to present his working drawings to the purchasers, who included a Southern 'naval expert':

> I wrestled with every argument, pro and con, for a whole hour; but the surface condensers did it; their compactness and efficiency, savings in fuel, and increase in power . . . no English builder had yet used them, and only one other Scotch firm; it was a great departure.

He won the contract without having to drop his asking price (£18,000). Her test run down the Firth of Clyde from Greenock to Lamlash Bay was some time around December 1863. She carried a large party of distinguished people including 'a true Yankee' who apparently knew all about the vessel and took a great interest in the engines. Also on board was the African explorer and missionary Dr David Livingstone, who had recently taken ownership of the small twin-hulled screw *Lady Nyassa* from Tod & McGregor for his next exploration up the Zambezi.

Self-feathering paddle floats (under Morgan's patent) maximised the surface area presented by each float at the moment of drive in the water. A number of clients, including Alexander Collie, insisted on them and specified that the floats were to be made of iron, not wood. Iron ones sustained less damage from debris on the water and flying shrapnel. In order to transmit the greater horsepower generated – over four times the nominal horsepower rating of the engines – gearing (rather than direct acting) linkage was introduced between the piston crank and the wheel or screw shaft. This allowed larger propeller blades to be fitted on screw steamers.

It was not always a simple matter to transfer more power effectively into forward motion. At the sea trials of Begbie's 'wee one', *Gertrude*, in December 1862, her screw propeller (upgraded from seven-inch to nine-inch blades) did not produce the expected significant increase in speed. He urgently enquired of Scott what could be done as 'the slip is tremendous – what is the gearing ratio?' It was found that the trim of the hull was the critical factor. Begbie immediately told Captain Leslie to trim his other 'wee one', *Emma*, so that she drew seven and a half feet of water aft and only five at the bow 'so as not to make any great splutter'.

Apart from higher speeds, all of these developments in high-pressure steam technology greatly improved fuel efficiency, so much that these vessels could make the round trip to 'Dixie' on one load of the superior and relatively smokeless Welsh 'steamer' coal (anthracite). By the beginning of 1863 there was a vast stockpile of this high-quality fuel available at Bermuda. Begbie insisted on bunkering for a minimum of seven days when placing new orders for steamers. This avoided having to use the low-grade 'brown' coal available from the Confederate ports. Brown coal had a very high bitumen content which sent up a great pall of dense smoke from the furnaces. In doing so, it left behind a heavy tar residue and slate deposits which quickly fouled the furnace flues.

Burning this inferior coal was the cause of many runners being spotted and easily run down on their return passage. When discussing the 'very important' development of a smokeless engine with Scott, Begbie bewailed that it was 'too late for the *Cornubia*'. She had remained his favourite steamer, even after he had sold her to the Confederate government. She was captured when her fouled boilers had cut her speed by half.

To increase the stealth factor of the '*Flamingo* class', the funnels and masts were collapsible and the entire hull painted white. What little steam had to be exhausted was vented via a pipe under the waterline. This dispensed with the telltale white 'puff' with every engine stroke which was emitted from a pipe normally run along the outside of each funnel. It also served as a safety vent if a steamer had to be brought to an abrupt halt in an emergency – such as the approach of blockaders who had yet to stumble on her. When this drastic manoeuvre was taken, the steam pressure in the boilers surged and had to be instantly reduced to avoid a catastrophic explosion.

Within the hull was a 'lamp room' – a windowless cabin – in which charts could be consulted without so much as a chink of light showing to the outside. Another feature, and one noted by the Customs officers assigned to measure this class for registration, was the 'excessive' crew accommodation. Large crews of thirty men and above were required for an Atlantic crossing and the regular three-day runs to and from Bermuda (over two for Nassau).

The last custom-built runner to leave Scotland for the blockade was the paddle steamer *Imogene*. She was launched by Peter Denny for the veteran Captain James Carlin, agent for the Importing & Exporting Company of South Carolina. She was slightly larger than the '*Flamingo* class' and driven by two great 200-horsepower Napier engines. Like all runners, she was schooner-rigged to save coal on a long passage and to stabilise the shallow-draught hull when speeding through heavy cross-seas.

There was, however, one Clyde-built steamer purchased to run the blockade that did not comply with the 'speed first' criterion. This was the oddity paddle steamer the *Alliance*. Designed by her first owner, George Mills of Glasgow, for passengers' comfort and stability rather than speed, she was launched by Tod & McGregor in 1856. She was a unique steamer for her size, having a large two-deck superstructure of great beam (35 foot) built on top of a catamaran-style double hull. Each of her hulls was just over nine feet in width with a curved outer and square inner side, ending in identical canoe ends. As a 'double-ender', she could be driven in either direction without loss of performance.

Embedded in each hull was a small direct-acting engine (85 horsepower) which drove the single internal large paddle wheel. This was fitted tightly in the gap between the hulls. She also had a small variable direction bow paddle at each end (served by a donkey engine). These enabled her to move sidewards when docking at a crowded quay or turn in her own length in a canal or river. When first launched, she appears to have had four funnels in a square layout.

Her high decks and hull shape restricted her speed to just eight knots. Most of her passengers on her runs along the Caledonian Canal from Fort William to Banavie or day excursions around the Firth of Clyde, however, appreciated her smooth passage in bad weather and the high vantage view from the fully glazed first-class lounges.

On 10 December 1863 she was sold for £3,500 to William J. Grazebrook of Liverpool, who regularly secured purchases for the Confederacy. One can only guess what made him acquire such a misfit to serve as a blockade runner so late in the war. The most probable attraction was her exceptionally shallow draught; only five foot when fully loaded. This would allow her to run the network of inland waterways along the coasts of South Carolina and Georgia.

That spring, Grazebrook had her radically altered by her original builders. Her great internal paddle was removed and replaced by a pair of conventional external side wheels. The small variable direction paddles were also discarded and her hull was lengthened to give her a traditional bow and square stern. The high-sided top deck lounges were cut away and iron whaleback covers mounted on her deck fore and aft. Her engines were upgraded and her funnels reduced to three and aligned abreast. Two masts (schooner rigged) were stepped for her transatlantic crossing.

After this radical refit her appearance still remained highly distinctive. On her outward passage from Liverpool for Nassau she called in to Queenstown, Cork (8 August) where the vigilant US consul, Edward G. Eastman, made a sketch of her. This he dispatched to Washington, together with the comment: 'She is a very curious looking craft and could easily be taken for an Iron Clad or some such marine monster and her officers intend rather to frighten our cruisers than to fight. She is slow and will not steam over eight knots.'

The *Alliance* made it to Nassau badly damaged and could not attempt a run for some months. She finally sailed for Savannah early in April 1864. On the night of the 11th she successfully crossed the bar of the Savannah River only to run hard aground on Bloody Point, near Tybee Island. Stuck fast, she was boarded by a boat party from USS *South Carolina* and eventually taken as prize – along with her cargo of wine, meat, beer and Epsom salts.

The final innovation, introduced late in the war, was steel hulls. Steel construction was pioneered by John and William Dudgeon of Liverpool, but was slow to be taken up by the Clyde shipbuilders. While the saving in weight was undeniable, the cost was prohibitive and there were also difficulties in the supply of steel. With such a short life expectancy, most Clyde shipbuilders stuck with the cheaper plate iron. The young James Sprunt served on the first large steel 'CB' racer, *Susan O'Beirne*. She was one of a pair launched in 1864 by new-start company Aitken & Mansell of Kelvinhaugh, Glasgow, at a cost of over £12,300. She was named after a member of the family of the owner of the Galway Steam Company. Henry Lafone of Manchester bought her for the Importing & Exporting Company of Georgia in November 1864.

Under the command of Captain D.S. Martin the *Susan O'Beirne* came close to getting into Wilmington the following month but was forced back by a terrible storm. Badly leaking and close to foundering, she just made it back to Nassau. She was followed in by Captain Maffitt on the *Owl* who informed Martin that Wilmington and Charleston were now closed and the war was as good as lost.

Chapter 6

The Search for Cruisers and Rams

In Verne's opening scene in *The Blockade Runners* set in December 1862, the more vocal in the crowd roared their approval when the whisper went around that the *Dolphin* was a blockade runner. It would seem that among the urban working classes of the cities of Lowland Scotland, sympathies were then decidedly for the South. It had not always been that way and was certainly not the case in the cotton mills of Paisley, Glasgow and west-coast Scotland – even though thousands were unemployed and faced starvation that winter.

Only the year before, the unleashing of Confederate privateers was perceived as a piratical act by the general British public. Symptomatic of this stance was the hostile reception given to the crew of the css *Nashville* on their arrival in Southampton Water after the burning of the US clipper *Harvey Birch* off Ireland. Yet, within days of the news of the *Trent* affair breaking, public sentiment swung decidedly the other way.

When the *Nashville* finally sailed from Southampton (2 February 1862), she left to the cheers of onlookers. Captain Pegram was now portrayed as 'David' and given a twenty-four-hour head start from the pursuing 'Goliath' Captain Craven on uss *Tuscarora*, with hms *Shannon* present to ensure that the decision of the Admiralty was respected.

This was part of Britain's policy of supposed 'even-handedness' between the belligerents. Begbie spoke for his peer group when he took great delight in reporting to Scott that the most recent Royal Proclamation refused access to British ports to the privateers and naval craft of both belligerents – except under stress of weather. In such circumstances, the steamer in question was allowed to re-coal, but only once, and banned from returning. As Begbie gleefully put it to Scott (4 February): 'Don't they both howl! *Nashville* left for some more friendly region: probably to seek *Sumter* at Gib, possibly Cherbourg?'

Up until then the European stockpile of cotton had cushioned the impact of the war on the workforce. The *Trent* incident happened just as the 'cotton famine' took grip, unleashing a flood of anti-Federal propaganda from the press. Most of the Scottish newspapers, following the lead of the *Scotsman*, took up a decidedly anti-blockade stance and an implicitly pro-South view of the unfolding events at sea. Yet, remarkably, at no time did any of the real economic 'victims' of this war – the cotton mill workers and dockers – openly advocate breaking the blockade.

At the time, the *Trent* outrage struck up a great chord of public indignation with the middle classes. It swept the issue of slave owning and the slave trade onto the sidelines for many liberal-minded and literate Scots. It was well noted that President Lincoln had not gone to war over slavery but solely to preserve the Union. To have stressed the slavery issue would have been to push the slave-owning 'border states' – Missouri, Kentucky, Maryland and Delaware – into seceding. It was a political expedient on which President Davis did not fail to capitalise. The *Scotsman* informed its readership (11 January 1862) that Davis had offered to ban the slave trade in the Confederacy and to declare all newborn black children free forthwith – in return for recognition.

Captain Wilkes' actions on the *Trent* were less tortuous or morally challenging. Here was a clear-cut display of US arrogance and open contempt of international law. As various 'Letters to the Editor' in the *Scotsman* sought to remind its readership – was this not the very high-handed act that provoked the USA to declare war on Britain fifty years before? The editorial put the question: was Wilkes acting on his own initiative or was the whole piratical act ordered and planned by the Navy Department in Washington? Put in this light, the struggle was presented as one against an overbearing, aggressive and expansionist USA.

As the war hysteria mounted in the press, the Chancellor of the Exchequer, William Gladstone, was the first cabinet minister to speak on the '*Trent* difficulty'. He did so when visiting the new episcopalian church in his hometown of Leith (15 January). He called for moderation and cautioned his audience against 'the unmeasured abuse of everything American, and the unmeasured praise of everything British, by which bigoted and vulgar minds insult their country'. In practical terms, he reckoned that the 'Wilkes Escapade' had already cost the Treasury £3 million in additional expenditure on defence.

On the same day, the *Scotsman* published a 'Letter to the Editor' from a local Burntisland shipowner giving his initials 'J.S.C.'. He proposed using the leverage created by the *Trent* affair to take the Confederacy at their word and push them to accept phasing out slavery in exchange for full recognition. He also claimed the North was just as implicated in slavery. Only the year before he had bought at a British prize court a Philadelphia-built slaver, the *Black Joke*, which had 500 enslaved Africans on board when caught. He considered this damning proof of the North's hypocrisy towards the slavery issue. It was her shipyards which built and equipped the schooners that perpetuated this heinous traffic in humans almost fifty years after it had been banned by most civilised nations.

During the winter and spring of 1862, those in the House of Commons pushing for recognition of the Confederate States of America were in full cry. Over the ensuing months, they denounced the use of the 'stone fleets' at Charleston as acts of vandalism and declared the blockade – with over 300 runs already made in – wholly 'ineffective' and hence an illegal barrier to free trade. It was a well-orchestrated propaganda campaign.

Attempts to return to the slavery issue were robustly met in the Scottish press. A 'southern gentleman' who resided in Edinburgh and signed himself 'G.B.T.' put pen to paper in another letter to the *Scotsman* that June. He rebuked a circular letter read in local churches from the Presbyterian Reverend Culyer of New York. Culyer had declared that the war was the 'culmination of irrepressible conflict between freedom and slavery', while the correspondent was quite clear in his mind that it was between 'Free Trade and Protectionism'.

Palmerston's cabinet had already come round to the view that a separate Confederate States of America would be in Britain's best interest. Recognition required just one more decisive Confederate victory to prove the South's cohesion and ability to withstand the military might of the industrialised North. That event seemed imminent on 7 October when Gladstone rashly declared in Newcastle that President Jefferson Davis 'had made an army, and was making a navy, and created something greater still – a nation'.

This was the prevailing climate in which the local Emancipation Societies fought an uphill battle to get over their message to the general public – that the Clyde shipyards were deeply involved in supplying the Confederate war machine. Such societies had existed across industrial Scotland since the 1830s and should have been the perfect vehicle for promoting the Northern cause in Scotland. They were, however, bitterly divided on a number of key issues as to how emancipation was to be achieved and how the transition to a free labour market should be managed. They were all, however, united in their opposition to the building of warships for the Confederacy on the Clyde.

Acquiring large steamers for conversion to commercial raiders had been Commander Bulloch's primary mission when he first arrived in Britain, back in 1861. Before he left for Savannah on the *Fingal*, he had placed orders for two fully rigged auxiliary screw steamers with two Merseyside companies experienced in building gunboats for the Royal Navy. Having left the *Fingal* blockaded up the Savannah River, he was anxious to return to Britain and complete the commissioning of his new cruisers.

In his memoirs, he relates how he almost did not make it back. On arrival at Fayal in the Azores, the resident US consul effectively blocked the purchase of coal for his vessel, the runner *Annie Childs*. She finally arrived at Cork on the night of 8 March 1862, burning her spare spars and dross from the bunkers mixed with rosin.

He arrived at Liverpool two days later with four other naval officers, just as the first of his cruisers was ready to take to the sea. Built by William C. Miller & Sons as 'No. 345' in their order book, she was launched under the cover name *Oreto* and was supposedly intended for purchase by an Italian firm. Bulloch had empowered, in his absence, the resident manager and co-partner of Fraser, Trenholm & Company, Charles K. Prioleau, to ensure her dispatch as a raider. He had, in fact, already offered the command to Lieutenant North, but he had declined.

Bulloch had since been ordered by Mallory to stay in Britain and facilitate the cruiser and ironclad programme, which called for 'six steam propellers'. In this role, he personally supervised the final preparations for the departure of the *Oreto*. He made sure that all pretences were maintained to keep up her cover story that her maiden voyage was to Palermo. To pre-empt any accusations levelled by the ever-vigilant US consul in Liverpool, Thomas H. Dudley, no offensive weaponry was taken on board. To complete her British identity, her captain, James A. Duguid (who was married into the Miller family), along with his engineers and crew, were recruited locally and she was registered as of the 'port of Liverpool'.

Bulloch's first intention was to sail her out to rendezvous with the lightly built and armed *Nashville*. There, Pegram and his crew would transfer to this more powerful raider. This was not to be. After escaping from Southampton, Pegram had set out across the Atlantic heading back to a Confederate port. He had been chased by the USS *Tuscarora* until Craven was summoned back to aid in the blockade of the CSS *Sumter* at Gibraltar.

Dudley was not so easily fooled. His agents had found out that Bulloch was *Oreto*'s owner and that he actively supervised her completion. An informant in the dockyard verbally reported that her deck had been reinforced to receive heavy-calibre ordnance and her bulwarks cut at intervals along her length to permit a wide arc of fire. Dudley travelled to the US Legation in London with this information, which Adams immediately used to remonstrate loudly with Russell, the British Foreign Secretary, that she was clearly intended to be a Confederate armed cruiser.

Lord Russell's response was that the so-called evidence was based on hearsay and informers. Nevertheless, he instructed the Commissioner for Customs to order an inspection of her where she lay. Their surveyor at Liverpool, Edward Morgan, duly reported back that he found the nature of her construction ambiguous but he found no 'warlike stores of any kind' on board. The opinion of the Customs, sent back to Russell, was that, in her present unarmed state, there was no reason why she should not be allowed to proceed to sea unhindered.

Bulloch did not hesitate. On 22 March 1862, he ordered Captain Duguid to sail from her berth at Egremount Ferry in the Mersey for Nassau. Already on board was his secretary, Lieutenant John Low CSN, who had received his written orders only the day before. These indicated that he was to deliver *Oreto* to the local island branch of Adderley & Company, then fronting for Louis Heyliger, the Confederate agent on the island. Low was also instructed to make contact with Captain John N. Maffitt CSN who was the commander designate for her raiding mission.

The Atlantic crossing was done mainly under sail, and she eventually arrived at Nassau thirty-eight days later (28 April). Having completed his part in the mission, Low handed her over to Heyliger. As Maffitt had yet to arrive, Heyliger had Low move her to the more remote 'Cochrane's anchorage', some six miles from the main town and away from prying eyes. This ploy did not succeed in its aim, as she continued to arouse much interest. At the instance of the local US consul, Samuel Whiting, she was twice boarded by Royal Naval officers from HMS *Greyhound*, then in port. As the *Oreto* was still unarmed, they took no further action.

The moment of truth arrived when the *Bahama*, sister ship to the *Bermuda*, arrived with armaments and attempted a rendezvous. She had been chartered by Bulloch at Liverpool and sailed soon after the *Oreto*. Whiting immediately alerted the island's governor as to what was about to happen. This came hard on the heels of a report from the commander of the *Greyhound* that some of the *Oreto*'s British crew had been on board his ship with tales of new men joining her without so much as a mention of her ultimate destination. The naval commander and the governor acted with commendable vigour and had both *Oreto* and *Bahama* seized and brought back to the main harbour. At the hearing before the Vice-Admiralty Court, the case was dismissed due to insufficient evidence and both vessels were declared free.

By then Maffitt had arrived at Nassau and was able to take over the command of the *Oreto* on her release (17 June). Fearing an appeal and further detention, he had her loaded up to the gunwales with Welsh coal – much of which was taken out of the government runner *Robert E. Lee* (ex-*Giraffe*) with Lieutenant Wilkinson's blessing – and steamed out of the harbour. Rounding Hog Island, he stopped to make good the damage done by pilferers while she was in custody. He was joined there by a small blockade-running schooner, *Prince Alfred*, carrying eight cannon, munitions and provisions for his crew. These had been transferred from the *Bahama*, which was still under surveillance and marked for interception by the US consul. As Federal warships were known to be in the vicinity, Maffitt took the schooner in tow and left for a safer place.

Sixty miles on, off the deserted Green Cay at the tail of the Bahama Bank, her armaments, including four 'seven-inch' rifled cannons, were transhipped from the *Prince Albert*. Unfortunately, in her haste, the *Prince Alfred* had left Nassau without the implements (spongers and so on) needed to work heavy cannons, rendering them unusable. Undeterred, Maffitt raised the Confederate flag and renamed her the css *Florida* before setting off for Cuba, just as the dreaded yellow fever broke out among his crew.

Back in Liverpool, Bulloch was fully occupied in supervising the completion of his second cruiser, being built by Lairds of Birkenhead. While still on the stocks she was referred to as 'No. 290' in the order book. This working name was to become infamous in American naval and diplomatic dispatches and with British cartoonists. When she was launched on 15 May she was given the name *Enrica*. By this time Consul Dudley had proof that Bulloch had placed the order and that Fraser, Trenholm & Company – the recently exposed financiers of many Confederate schemes in Britain – had paid for her engines. Dudley had learned his lesson from his first brush with English law. This time he secured a written affidavit from a foreman at the yard that she had been fitted with waterproof magazines.

He rushed the evidence to London where Ambassador Adams again assailed Foreign Secretary Russell with this latest grievance. He also went armed with the opinion of the leading British expert in maritime law: namely, that this was a most flagrant breach of Article 7 of the Foreign Enlistment Act. Russell asked the Queen's Advocate, Sir John Harding, to review this evidence as a matter of great urgency. It was not known at the time that Harding was suffering from the after-effects of a mild stroke and was in no fit state to offer sound judgment. Five days passed before this was realised and Russell acted to retrieve the situation by issuing an order to detain the vessel.

Adams, fully expecting Russell to hold fast to the 'narrow' interpretation of the Foreign Enlistment Act, had already ordered Craven on the USS *Tuscarora* to steam round to the Irish Sea to intercept *Enrica*. The USS *Tuscarora* was then lying at Southampton, having just returned from blockading the CSS *Sumter* at Gibraltar. Craven's orders were to lie in wait to seize or sink the *Enrica* in British waters – if need be. Henry Sanford, co-ordinating the Federal European spy network from Belgium, had no qualms about the latter option being applied. As he put it, marine 'accidents' happened all the time in the congested waters around Britain.

Bulloch had his own informant, most likely in the Foreign Office, who warned him that he had less than forty-eight hours to get her away. A sympathiser in Southampton also sent him daily reports on the movements of the *Tuscarora*. So primed, Bulloch had his most trusted British captain, Matthew J. Butcher, take her out to sea for what was billed as final 'sea trials' (28 July). To wrongfoot the numerous watchers onshore, he had her decked out in flags and invited a party of guests for what promised to be a jolly day's outing. Receiving them on board were Bulloch, Lieutenant Low (who had just returned from Nassau on the *Bahama*) and Chief Engineer McNair (from the *Fingal*).

While McNair worked up her engines, in timed runs off the Mersey, Bulloch played host. Early in the afternoon he announced to his guests that, as the trials would continue into the night, they would be put ashore by the tug *Hercules*, which was acting as her tender, in order to catch the train. To allay suspicions, Bulloch accompanied them ashore, leaving Low and McNair on board.

First thing the following morning, Bulloch had the tug take him and additional crew out to where *Enrica* lay, some forty miles away off the Welsh coast. His latest intelligence was that Craven on the *Tuscarora* was probably now off the Tuskar Rock, seven miles off the south-east corner of Ireland, where he could watch the St George's Channel exit from the Irish Sea.

Acting on this update, Bulloch ordered Butcher to take *Enrica* through the North Channel that separates Northern Ireland from Scotland. Once clear of Rathlin Island, he had her engines stopped off the Giant's Causeway. There he hailed a passing fishing boat to come alongside, which took him and the pilot ashore, leaving Butcher and Low to take her across the Atlantic. It must have been a personal wrench for Bulloch as he had fully expected to be her captain only weeks before.

Prior to her departure it had been decided that Nassau was, after Maffitt's experience, too risky a rendezvous. Low was ordered to make instead for the isolated Angra do Heroismo Bay anchorage on the south side of the island of Terceira in the Azores. He had visited this anchorage once before, in the company of Bulloch, while on the outward passage of the *Fingal*.

The *Enrica* arrived there on 18 August, after an uneventful passage. Two days later, she met up with the *Agrippina*. This barque had been bought in London for the specific purpose of carrying out eight cannon, the largest of which was a 110-pounder rifled Blakely, and their munitions. The auxiliary steamer *Bahama* arrived soon afterwards. She had been chartered by Bulloch at Liverpool. Her covert mission was to deliver Commander Raphael Semmes and his officers, previously of the css *Sumter*.

Back in January, Semmes had left the *Sumter* at Gibraltar and made his way back to Liverpool with his men. This course of action had been forced on him when the local merchants, threatened and cajoled by the US consul, refused to sell him coal or assist in making repairs. Unable to put to sea, her fate was sealed by the arrival off the harbour entrance of the much heavier armed vessels uss *Tuscarora*, *Ino* and *Kearsarge*. Since then Bulloch had taken over her papers and arranged her sale as a commercial carrier to a Southern sympathiser.

On arriving at the Azores, Semmes took command of the *Enrica*. Raising the Confederate flag, he renamed her the css *Alabama*, to the cheers of her hundred-odd crew. He then set off on his mission of destruction that took him across 75,000 miles of ocean on a cruise that lasted almost two years.

Low returned to Liverpool on the *Bahama*. By then Bulloch was very close to repeating his success for a third time with the *Alexandra*. She was the other cruiser he had ordered from Miller & Sons. By now the political fallout of the escape of 'No. 290' was such that Russell had slapped a 'detention' order (5 April 1863) on her while Adams's latest accusations were fully investigated.

Not that this brought a halt to the Confederate building programme in Britain. Indeed, as the tortuous litigation process got going in the English Court of Exchequer, the frames of a giant Confederate ironclad ram and an ocean-going cruiser were already rising in the stocks of the Clydeside shipyard of James and George Thomson.

Bulloch was not directly responsible for these new schemes.

Secretary Mallory had decided, in typically mercurial style, to send along another agent when he dispatched Bulloch back to Britain to oversee the procurement of a Confederate Navy. The new agent was Captain James H. North CSN. Although he was a naval man of some standing, he was devoid of any flair for subterfuge.

North's primary mission was to buy or place an order for a '*La Gloire* class' warship with a French shipyard. This was not to be – the ironclad naval race between Britain and France was then at its height. North turned to British alternatives. He quickly found that few yards had the capability – or the willingness – to undertake such a task. The metallurgical science behind producing naval-rated armour was then in its infancy. Indeed, in early 1862, very few British ironmasters were able to roll and hammer flanged iron plate which came near matching the British Admiralty's '*Warrior* target' test. This required the test plate to withstand three direct hits by 68-pound round shot. Each shot was propelled by exactly sixteen pounds of gunpowder and fired from 200 yards in a close overlapping pattern. If the plate cracked or badly flaked, it was rejected without payment.

In dealing with such a small fraternity, Mallory instructed Bulloch to assist North actively in his quest. Bulloch gave him the plans of the newly launched *Enrica* and also his outlines, based on the advanced ideas of Captain Cowper Coles RN, for the two small twin-turreted armour rams for which he had already contracted with Lairds of Birkenhead.

North was, however, looking for a warship twice their size. The number of British builders able to deliver such a vessel were few – and the number willing was rapidly diminishing as the political implications became more serious. The Merseyside yards were all under the most intense scrutiny and to be avoided at all costs: such an order would call unwanted attention to Bulloch's 'Laird's rams'. On the Thames, only Dudgeon of Millwall was capable of delivery but they were overstretched with the boom in building blockade runners. The Tyneside yards also had full order books. Clydeside, on the other hand, had yards still looking for business and had the apparent advantage of lying beyond the jurisdiction of the English judicial system.

At one stage it looked as if there might have been a ram already on the stocks and awaiting a buyer. Producing armoured vessels on the Clyde was Thomas S. Begbie's other big idea to profit from the war. He had been very excited by the reports of the Federal armoured 'monsters' (monitors) designed by Erickson. He urged Scott (11 April 1862) to consider building, on speculation, a sea-going ironclad in partnership with Peter Denny:

This might suit you well to gain experience and see if you could not beat them all! As it looks like *the* thing at present would be such a vessel as to act as a ram. For against her no wooden hull is safe nor indeed do I think any iron one would be in a much better case – provided she could get a good whack at her.

Three days later, he wrote to reassure him that such a vessel could easily be sold to the Confederates under the cover of an order for 'the Russians or Italians or any other not a belligerent'. Neither Scott nor Denny chose to pursue this scheme.

This left Napier & Sons, arguably the greatest yard on the Clyde at the time. They had built HMS *Black Prince*, the sister of the *Warrior*, for the Admiralty. On this occasion, however, they were not available, perhaps so as not to compromise their position for future naval contracts.

North approached James and George Thomson of Finnieston and Govan, the builders of Cunarders and the *Fingal* and the largest yard on the upper Clyde. The wily younger brother, George Thomson, was most involved in the deal. From the outset he was fully aware of his clients' requirements and was in no doubt as to the ultimate purpose of the ram. During the preliminaries to signing a contract, he visited North in London with a scale model. Her hull design was close to that of HMS *Warrior*, with watertight compartments below decks and sides pierced for an armament of twenty cannon mounted in the traditional broadside arrangement. Thomson, warming to his task, had relocated her ram beak six feet under her waterline so that it would hit beneath the armour belt of an enemy monitor. The beak was made of solid teak sheathed in armour and rounded and tapered so as to allow the ironclad to extract itself easily from its sinking victim.

Thomson guaranteed that the ram's armour, which extended four feet below the water line, would meet the '*Warrior* target' standard. This required that her main side belt was three layers deep (4½-inch thick armoured plate, backed by eighteen inches of solid teak) and fixed to the recessed inner hull of half-inch iron plate in order to present a flush hull surface to any incoming shot.

Where she differed from the *Warrior* was in her draught and beam. As she was destined to fight in the shallower waters off the Confederate coast, Thomson reduced her draught and compensated by extending her beam to fifty feet. This increased her stability in heavy seas and when firing her broadside. Her coal bunkers were also designed to be flooded (when empty) with 400 tons of sea water as a counterbalance to the great weight of her topside armour and heavy ordnance. Manned by 500 men and encased with the latest armour, this ironclad monster of 3,200 tons was fully expected to outclass the monitors and blockaders she would meet off Charleston or Wilmington.

On 21 May 1862, North placed the order for 'No. 61' with Thomson with the builder's assurance that she would be delivered by 1 June the following year. It was a massively expensive project (£164,000 without armaments) and one which was undertaken in the belief that, if finance was not forthcoming from Richmond, cotton bonds could be sold in Britain to fund it.

For his part, the canny Thomson was taking few risks – there were eleven milestone cash payments to reduce his financial exposure to a minimum. Ownership did not pass to his client until he had received final payment. Thomson was also cushioned by the knowledge that North had not thought to insist on penalty clauses for late delivery. North also failed to include a retractable propeller – essential for long-range cruising and speed under sail – as part of the deal.

Notwithstanding these omissions, North remained impressed by Thomson's diligence, discretion and financial accommodation. He recommended him to the latest agent to arrive in Glasgow from Richmond that October, Lieutenant George T. Sinclair CSN (ex-master of the *Fingal*). Sinclair had been sent by Mallory, armed with cotton bonds, to procure another cruiser – larger and more powerful than the *Alabama*. He was ordered to take command of her on completion and raid the commerce off New England or to support the rams in destroying the blockade.

He seems to have arrived with a plan in hand as he immediately contracted a well-known blockade-running owner and sympathiser, Edward Pembroke of Austin Friars, London, to fund the deal. The arrangement was that Pembroke would pay Thomson the £46,000 in cash to build her. On delivery from her sea trials, Pembroke would relinquish ownership to Sinclair for 245 cotton bonds, approved by Commissioner Mason and worth £51,250, redeemable at a Confederate port.

This was too large a liability for one blockade-running operator to handle. Pembroke was acting for a pro-South consortium. The London-Scottish partners were Smith, Fleming & Company; Robert Simpson; and Edgar Pinchback String. The Clyde partners were Alexander Collie (described as of 'Glasgow and Manchester'); James Galbraith of Glasgow; and his close associate Peter Denny of Dumbarton. To complete the subterfuge the order was placed via the office of the highly respectable

Glasgow shipbrokers, Patrick Henderson & Company. The deal was struck with Thomson on 10 October 1862 for a cruiser, 'No. 63', under the cover name *Canton*. Delivery was set for 1 July the following year.

Sinclair took up residence with North in the safe house at Bridge of Allan in Stirlingshire, where they were within easy reach of Thomson's yard in Govan and their respective projects. During that summer and autumn they had the company of the legendary blockade-running captains Lieutenant John Wilkinson and Thomas E. Taylor. Wilkinson and Taylor were in Britain to take back blockade runners for the government. When Wilkinson sailed on the *Giraffe*, he took with him a model of North's armoured ram for Mallory.

That November, matters were further complicated with the arrival of Commander Matthew Fontaine Maury CSN and his thirteen-year-old son at the doorstep of Bulloch's small office at the rear of Fraser, Trenholm & Company's premises. Yet again, Mallory had decided to send another independent agent with his own finance.

Maury was a world-famous oceanographer who had published a highly acclaimed treatise on navigation. He was also a highly vocal exponent of electrically triggered 'torpedoes' (submerged mines) and submarines. Openly critical of Mallory's leadership of the Navy Department, he had made himself a target for banishment by writing scurrilous articles under the *nom de plume* 'Ben Bow'. These had been highly instrumental in causing a Congressional select committee investigation into Mallory's leadership of his department. In retaliation, Mallory dispatched him on a 'special mission' to Britain. Coxetter on the runner *Herald* was given the job of carrying Maury's party past the blockaders, along with $1,500,000 in cotton bonds with which to purchase a new raider.

Bulloch was instructed to co-operate with Maury during his short stay at the Adelphi Hotel in Liverpool. Maury appears to have had little to do with Bulloch and soon removed himself to rented accommodation in London. There he renewed his acquaintance with the Dutch naval officer Captain Martin N. Jansen. Jansen, even though he was on active service for his country, volunteered for 'the dangerous part' as Maury's procurement agent.

It was during Jansen's tour of the British shipyards that he spotted a fast brig-rigged composite screw steamer (760 tons) nearing completion on the slip at Denny's yard at Dumbarton. She had provisionally been named the *Japan*, as she was intended for the China trade. This was changed to the *Virginian* when Miss Annie North performed the launching ceremony. It was somewhat ironic that the *Dumbarton*

Herald reported the event (10 January 1863) alongside a lengthy sermon on Christian duty and the evils of slave owning in South Carolina and Georgia.

On 28 February, Maury's cousin, Thomas Bold (a partner in Jones & Company of Liverpool), personally purchased the *Virginian* for £20,000 and changed her name, yet again, to the *Georgia*. Once the deal was struck, Denny was contracted to strengthen her main deck and fit a secure munitions room below for her new role as a commerce raider. During this time Commander Maury never made an appearance in Scotland. He relied instead on a cousin, Captain William Lewis Maury, to assist Jansen. To carry out his mission William Maury rented accommodation close to the yard, posing as a 'gentleman on holiday'. In the meantime, Commander Maury pulled rank to acquire the Confederate officers Bulloch had hand-picked for the *Alexandra*, on the grounds of 'immediate need'.

These 'passengers' arrived as the *Georgia* was being delivered to Greenock after her conversion. They were joined by a crew of some fifty men, including four quartermasters from the *Great Eastern*, sent up by train from Liverpool by Bold. These men had been paid a signing-on bounty of between £5 and £50 depending upon their skills, and promised that half-pay would be made over to their dependants during their absence. They were led to believe that they were on a two-year contract to sail to Shanghai and Hong Kong.

By now Consul Dudley in Liverpool had received information from one of the quartermasters. He promptly informed Adams and Warner L. Underwood, Prettyman's replacement as US consul in Glasgow. Underwood's detectives soon secured details of her conversion from Denny workmen. As she was not rigged for long-distance sailing, he concluded that the *Georgia* was intended as a munitions tender to the *Alabama* – not as a new ocean-going raider. Commander Maury was tipped off, probably by the same informant that Bulloch relied upon, and ordered his cousin to clear her from the Clyde at the first opportunity. She sailed with forty carpenters on board still working on the munitions magazines. These men were taken off by a tug in mid-channel.

Sailing under a Scottish captain, the *Georgia* made straight for the English Channel, where she touched at Plymouth (11 April), before heading for St Malo. In a creek in one of the Ushant Islands she met up with the small Channel Islands ferry *Alar* out from Newhaven. Commander Maury and his party of officers were on board the *Alar*, along with her heavy armaments, which consisted of Whitworth cannons (two of which were 100-pounders on pivots) and a large rifled Blakely.

It took three days to make the difficult transfer at sea, during which time there was a serious accident in the boiler room which left two men severely scalded. One was named as Alex McDuff of Edinburgh, which would indicate that William Maury had managed to recruit her engineers at Greenock. While the two injured men were being transferred to the *Alar* for their move to a Plymouth hospital, fifteen other crewmen took the opportunity to renege on their contracts and jump ship. Consequently, Maury was left with only thirteen men from the original muster roll. He managed, however, to sign on a number of men from the *Alar* for her cruise of the Atlantic and Indian Oceans.

In yet another coincidence, the issue of the *Dumbarton Herald* which carried the reports of the *Alar* and the accident also reported the seizure of the *Alexandra* while fitting out in Toxteth Dock under the title 'The Alleged Confederate Gunboats':

> Customs authorities at this port, late yesterday afternoon, [were ordered] to stop the workmen and allow nothing to be removed from the vessel . . . no person to be allowed on board until the result of the inquiry, which we understand will be proceeded with immediately, is made known.

It was the beginning of the end for Bulloch's carefully laid plans to build new cruisers and warships for the Confederacy in Britain. The same article announced that

> The Government during the present week have also been in communication with Messrs Laird Brothers of Birkenhead, relative to the two gunboats [they are] said to [be] building for the Confederate Government. Messrs Laird, in reply, formally assured the Government that they were being built for the Emperor of China.

The two gunboats were his twin-turreted rams by which Mallory was setting so much store to change the course of the war. As Bulloch pointed out, once the Merseyside yard gates were opened and the hulls investigated, it was simply impossible to explain their shape and armour as that of innocent merchantmen. In London, Adams made sure that 'Laird's rams' became the centre of the greatest diplomatic storm of the war, which raged for almost a year.

The world was captivated by the exploits of the three British-built Confederate raiders, *Florida*, *Alabama* and *Georgia*, already at sea. They were an acute embarrassment to Lord Russell and his cabinet. The *Georgia*'s exploits were particularly damning, as her crew had

been recruited in the United Kingdom and her British-made armaments delivered while still in the approaches to the English Channel. In
a belated attempt to close the stable door, Russell ordered the lord
provost of Glasgow to report immediately any suspicious purchases
on the Clyde. It also sparked the first great up-swell of local indignation. Three and a half thousand people attended a rally in Glasgow
to denounce the clandestine support of the war effort of the slave-
owning secessionists.

For his part, Adams had his agents track down the men who had
deserted the *Georgia* off Ushant and visit the wives of those still serving
to obtain depositions. These clearly showed the role Jones & Company
of Liverpool had played in recruiting the crew. On 7 December Adams
had enough evidence to lodge a strong formal protest with Russell.

Forced to act, Russell handed the file on the *Georgia* over to the courts.
Two partners from the Liverpool company which provided the crew,
Jones and Highet, were eventually charged under Section 7 of the Foreign
Enlistment Act for aiding and abetting the enlistment of British nationals
for a Confederate warship. Their defence was that they had recruited the
crew for a voyage to China in good faith. This, they claimed, was self-
evident from the fact that most had broken their contract and left the ship
when they found out the true nature of her cruise. This plea in mitigation
was accepted and they were fined £50 each.

The *Georgia* was the last newly launched cruiser acquired from a
British shipyard to make an impact on the war. Public sentiment in
Scotland had changed dramatically since the early days. From the start
the popular press had portrayed the struggle as between the cavalier
gentlemen of the South defending their independence and agrarian way
of life against their arrogant overbearing neighbours in the North.

For many Scots, the Confederate defeat at Antietam shattered the
illusion of Southern invincibility, while Lincoln's Emancipation of
Slavery Proclamation (both September 1862) had turned the war into
a moral crusade at a single stroke. Throughout 1863, the Clydeside
and Glasgow Emancipation Societies mobilised their combined ranks
to support Lincoln's war aims vigorously. This took the form of public
meetings, petitions and memorials. Old disputes between rival societies were laid aside to focus on a common cause – to expose the
Confederate warships being covertly built on the Clyde.

Begbie chose to believe that Federal-funded agitators were behind
most of it. In February 1863 he wrote to Scott: 'The Northerners are
spending a lot of money to stir up the country – abolitionist meetings
and all – but it does not suit.' There was an element of truth in his

observation. The US consuls around Britain and Ireland were then appealing to Adams for additional funds to hire detectives and bribe local informers.

The evidence presented to Seward in Washington was greatly strengthened by the seizure of a mailbag on board the Thomson-built runner *Adela*. This large steamer, once owned by the Earl of Eglinton, had been intercepted off the Bahamas, back in July 1862, by USS *Quaker City* and *Huntsville*. In the weighted satchel was correspondence between Commissioner Mason in London and Secretaries Benjamin and Memminger in Richmond, which openly referred to the Confederate shipbuilding programme in Britain.

Federal intelligence gathering received a further shot in the arm that Christmas when the Confederate safe house at Bridge of Allan was reported to the US consul at Dundee. It was immediately placed under surveillance. Reports of an increase in the 'comings and goings' there that spring brought Consul Dudley up from Liverpool to tour the Scottish shipyards. He was on the lookout for likely vessels that could readily be converted into Confederate cruisers.

He had returned to the Govan area of Glasgow again in August 1863. This time he had firm intelligence regarding Thomson's yard and Sinclair's *Canton*. While he was there, he managed to recruit an unlikely expert observer. John Comb was a local shipowner who had ready access to Thomson's yard, as he was having his own steamer built there. He passed on details of the *Canton*'s construction, which closely followed that of the *Alabama*. The plans of the latter, he claimed, were in the hands of Sinclair and the builder.

Commander North, supervising the building of the armoured ram, also soon felt the pinch of the mounting surveillance campaign. He wrote from Glasgow to Secretary Mallory, in Richmond:

> I can see no prospect of recognition from this country [Great Britain] . . . If they will let us get our ships out when they are ready, we shall feel ourselves most fortunate. It is now almost impossible to make the slightest move or do the smallest thing, that the Lincoln spies do not know of it.

That summer, as his ram was standing 'half in frame' at the Govan yard, the first rumour of a second '*Merrimac*' (as the workers referred to her) leaked out to Prettyman, the US consul in Glasgow. He immediately made a personal visit to view the 'ironclad steam frigate' and returned deeply troubled by what he saw. He wrote to his consular colleagues and Seward: 'She will be a formidable vessel, equal in her protection against shot to anything yet afloat.'

After his visit, security at the yard was tightened and the workforce muzzled by threats of instant dismissal. It was highly effective. Prettyman reported that one of his regular informers, a yard foreman, had clammed up and refused to divulge any further information. He would only say that she was not ordered by the British or French or Spanish government.

It took a few weeks for the news of Gettysburg and Vicksburg to reach Britain (22 July 1863) and for Palmerston's government to reassess their pro-South position. There were also new external pressures that made the avoidance of a war with America over the 'Laird rams' a diplomatic imperative. War was looming between Denmark and Prussia over the Duchies of Schleswig and Holstein. Russia also remained unappeased and belligerent towards Britain and France.

Bulloch was shrewd enough to see 'the writing on the wall' and acted quickly to try and save his two Mersey-built rams from seizure. He concocted an elaborate scheme to transfer their ownership to the Bravary Company of Paris. He also switched his quest for new armoured warships to the French shipyards. He believed that the more pro-Confederate and autocratic government of Napoleon III would take a more benevolent view of his activities. He left Liverpool on the assumption that his recommendation that North's Clyde ram should be sold to finance his French schemes would be accepted. Bulloch had long held the view that the ram was a great waste of scarce funds, was too large to operate close to the Confederate ports, and would, in all probability, be impounded by the British government before it could put to sea. On his departure, the next most senior Confederate officer in Liverpool, Flag Officer Samuel Barron, took over the legal fight to release 'Laird's rams' and the *Alexandra*.

Given the change in circumstances on Merseyside, Bulloch believed that the Clyde cruiser *Canton* was now the Confederates' best hope. Mallory had urged both North and Sinclair to take the greatest care in concealing the warlike nature of their two vessels under construction at Thomson's yard. He desperately needed the first to be completed – the *Canton* – out at sea but accepted that delays were now inevitable while the telltale fixtures (gun ports and ring bolts) were hidden or removed. That May, a meeting was scheduled in Paris where North and Sinclair intended to meet with Commissioners Slidell and Mason to discuss following Bulloch's lead and transfer the ownership of their respective charges to a French company. This meeting never took place, as it was agreed that it would call attention to Confederate schemes in France.

As it happened, the situation seemed to resolve itself the following month. The Court of Exchequer ruled that the *Alexandra* had been unjustly detained and found against the Crown. In the light of this favourable turn of events it was decided, without consulting Bulloch, that work in the Clyde on North's ram and Sinclair's cruiser should continue.

The Crown lodged an appeal against the judgment and continued to detain the *Alexandra*. All eyes now turned to the two small rams rapidly approaching completion at Laird's Birkenhead yard. On 5 September, Adams sent his famous note to Russell declaring that if they were allowed to leave, 'it would be superfluous in me to point out to your Lordship that this is war'. Ironically, Russell had already made up his mind only two days earlier to seize the rams in Liverpool and sidestep this highly dangerous confrontation with America. He had, however, yet to convince Palmerston and his fellow cabinet members.

Russell's initial response to Adams's apparent threat of a 'declaration of war' was to defend robustly his government's performance in policing its strict neutrality policy. Selling unarmed vessels to either belligerent did not, in his view, constitute a breach of neutrality. As he liked to put it, a sold British-made musket was 'neutral' until someone put it in the hands of a soldier. He did, however, concede that by separating the terms 'intent' from 'equip' (as used by the exponents of the 'narrow' interpretation of the Foreign Enlistment Act) created a legal loophole. This loophole allowed adapted hulls capable of instant conversion to cruisers to slip out in the guise of merchantmen. To close this option, he declared he was prepared to seek new legislation through Parliament. As for the steam rams, he now held the opinion that, as they were *de facto* warships at the moment of their launch, their warlike 'intent' and 'equip' were indistinguishable. They were clearly in breach of British neutrality.

During the following weeks Russell outlined his shift in policy in two speeches delivered at Dundee and Blairgowrie while on a visit to Scotland. Adams saw these declarations as the turning point in his great struggle to cut off the prime source of armed vessels to the Confederates: 'This is, at last, the true tone. I confess that I have more hopes of our prospect of being able to preserve friendly relations than at any moment since my arrival in England.' Pushing forward, he reminded Russell that 'There is, however, still one very large and formidable steam ram on the stocks at Glasgow, which I believe is intended for the Rebels.' He also took the opportunity to identify Sinclair's *Canton* as a likely Confederate cruiser in the making.

By late autumn, the Glasgow consulate had a team of watchers deployed along the length of the River Clyde and two local detectives, John McQueen Bar and James Ross, dedicated to shadowing North and Sinclair to and from their safe house. Prettyman was quietly confident that his surveillance operation would produce results when he wrote to Seward in October: 'No further information has yet been procured, but the train is laid that will explode the secret.'

Prettyman was also working diligently to stop the *Canton* from slipping away after her launch. While he struggled to amass sufficient hard evidence, Adams took his allegations of this latest outrage before Russell on 19 October. Russell, by now committed to appeasing America over this issue, promised an immediate investigation. The following day he asked the Admiralty to send their most senior officer on the Clyde, Captain Farquhar, to inspect the *Canton*. The Treasury and Home Office were also asked to make urgent enquiries into any signs of a breach of the Foreign Enlistment Act.

The next day, the Home Office reported the matter to the Sheriff of Lanarkshire, Sir Archibald Alison. He allocated two of his Crown agents, the Procurators Fiscal, Hart and Gemmell, to make the necessary enquiries. Hart immediately interviewed George Thomson, who blatantly lied, stating that he had no knowledge of any warlike intentions for the vessel that he was on the verge of completing.

Captain Farquhar inspected the *Canton* a few days later, just before she was due to be launched. He was quite assertive in his verdict: 'She is evidently built for aggressive purposes and from her fine lines will probably have great speed.' His inspection was reported in the local press and did much to raise local public awareness of her true identity when she was slipped into the Clyde on a spring tide on 29 October 1863.

At the ceremony, Mrs Galbraith (the wife of the principal in Pembroke's funding consortium) renamed her the *Pampero*. She was immediately towed to the Finnieston Quay where the great crane lowered in her engines and boilers. She was then towed to Lancefield Quay where teams of workmen swarmed over her in the rush to complete her outfit, prior to sea trials.

In the days that followed, the net closed on the Confederate schemes on both the Mersey and the Clyde. Bulloch, a closely marked man, wrote to North in early November:

Heretofore, I have been sanguine about getting the first of my ships to sea, but something of vital importance to us is brewing at the Foreign Office, and I fear the English ministry are about to forbid any shipment of supplies or the sailing of vessels for the service of either belligerent, and they will, I fear, issue restrictions in such a form as will prevent any British subject aiding us.

The campaign to impound the *Pampero* was now taken up by Warner L. Underwood, who had recently replaced Prettyman as US consul in Glasgow. Underwood was a protégé of Dudley, and as determined as his superior to prevent *Pampero* sailing. Despite his personal dynamism, he too found a problem in gathering hard evidence on what was an open secret. He confided to Adams on 15 October:

I have no power to compel anyone to give me his testimony; and such is the terror that the associated [ship]building and money power of this community inspire, led on no less with the spirit of secession than with the profits of blockade running and pro-Confederate shipbuilding, that it is next to impossible to find a man who will nobly bear the dangers of making a voluntary affidavit of facts which are known to all.

He did, however, point out a solution to the impasse. Unlike English law, Scots law allowed for a preliminary investigation of the parties under oath. At such a hearing Thomson, his workers and the owners could be interrogated under oath.

The day before her launch, Underwood sought legal advice from a leading Glasgow solicitor, Adam Paterson, on instigating this course of action. Paterson recommended that the American ambassador in London was the best person to press for this form of inquiry. No time was lost. The day after the launch a suitably spurred Home Office instructed Lord Moncrieff, the Lord Advocate of Scotland, to take up the matter.

At the same time, many of the resources of the embryonic Federal intelligence network were diverted to finding evidence that would stop the *Pampero* sailing. One early success was the illegal interception of a letter for Slidell in Paris to Sinclair which specifically mentioned her. More promising was an approach to Thomson's head draughtsman, Benjamin Haynes, with a large bribe of £500 for his affidavit on her warlike construction and fittings. To put pressure on him, his brother was traced to Cadiz, where the resident American consul paid for him to return to Glasgow to persuade Haynes to testify. At first Haynes agreed but later retracted his statement after he had considered the consequences of his actions – instant dismissal followed by black-listing for life by the shipbuilders the length of the Clyde. Then there was his family to consider. Most employees then lived in 'tied' housing close to the yards. Dismissal on such terms raised the spectre of homelessness and destitution after the bribe money had gone. He did, however, agree to make an informal statement to one of the Procurators Fiscal.

Without a conclusive and binding affidavit to sustain the charge, the Lord Advocate's report (6 November) concerned itself mainly with the judicial questions raised by the Solicitor-General. These centred on the pitfalls of attempting to enforce a flawed section of the Foreign Enlistment Act which was drawn up to suit English procedures. He also thought that Consul Underwood was labouring under a great misunderstanding. Interrogation of witnesses under oath – prior to trial – was only allowed under the most exceptional circumstances.

It was at this point that the mobilised wrath of the Glasgow Emancipation Society came to Adams's rescue. Their memorial, drafted by their leaders William Smeal and Andrew Paton, was received by the Foreign Office on 4 November. Adams's formal petition was delivered five days later.

The memorialists also took care to inform the press of their petition. Most of the local newspapers ran the story. Typical of the coverage was the article published in the *Greenock Telegraph* (13 November) under the headline 'Alleged Steamer for the Confederates':

The 'Glasgow Emancipation Society' lately sent a memorial to Earl Russell, Secretary of State for Foreign Affairs, regarding an iron steamer at one time named the *Canton*, but now named the *Pampero*. The memorial stated that vessel had lately been launched from the building yard of Messrs James & George Thomson there, and was rapidly fitting out in Glasgow harbour, that she was currently, and the memorialists believed truly, reported to have been constructed for the Confederate Government; that she was of a similar construction to the *Alabama*, and like her, intended to prey on the merchant ships of the Northern states; that she has been fitted with gun ports, ring bolts for guns &c., although the gun ports have since been filled up, and the fittings removed, and these things disguised as much as possible; and that the society therefore requested his lordship would cause a satisfactory investigation to be made into the character, ownership, and destination of this vessel, with the view that, if found to be of the description and for the purpose they supposed her to be, she might be prevented from leaving Britain.

Not to be outdone, their rival, the Glasgow branch of the Union and Emancipation Society, also submitted a petition which gave further details as to her gun-deck arrangements. Clearly both societies had their anonymous informers within the yard. A mass rally was also held in Edinburgh (18 November) to set up a branch of the Society in the city with the express purpose of exposing the Confederate schemes on the Clyde.

During the intervening weeks there had been a frenzy of official activity. Underwood's claim (10 November) to the Collector of Customs for Glasgow and Greenock, Frederick W. Trevor, that the renowned Captain John N. Maffitt CSN was in Glasgow was designed to raise the level of paranoia. The previous summer Maffitt had run the CSS S *Florida* into Mobile through a hail of shells. Soon afterwards, he had been laid low by yellow fever and given up her command. On his recovery, he returned to blockade running for the government.

Underwood's source was John Murray, 'who was a private on the *Florida*' and claimed to have seen his old captain in George Square, central Glasgow. Murray was then staying in lodgings at 120 Broomielaw while he worked on the newly launched runner *Will o' the Wisp*, then being outfitted at the Mavisbank Quay for the Anglo-Confederate Trading Company.

In the same correspondence, Underwood informed Collector Trevor that he also had a letter from Liverpool, stating that a number of crewmen from the *Florida* had congregated there. It was obvious to Underwood that these men were awaiting the call to join up with their old captain and take over the *Pampero* at some, as yet unknown, opportune moment.

His most damning claim was that Maffitt, passing himself off as 'Major Bissett', had also been seen inside Thomson's yard in Govan. He was observed supervising the fitting of watercocks so that parts of her hull could be flooded. This would reduce her profile to cannon fire in a sea fight. Underwood claimed this was clear evidence – along with the building of bunks and lockers for 150 men – of her warlike purpose. For good measure, he added that, mounted in front of her scroll head bow, was 'a figure of the Goddess of Liberty with Palmetto branches [the symbol of South Carolina] under her feet'.

Unfortunately for Underwood, Murray (the source of the sighting of Maffitt) skipped the country before Crown agents could interrogate him. He had left on the poorly put together blockade runner on which he had been working and sailed under the command of Captain James F. Taylor. Underwood did, however, have a replacement star witness, one Robert Mitchell, who claimed to have spoken with Murray.

Mitchell was a Glasgow-based shipping agent who had twice visited New York on business. He testified that he first met Murray only the month before, at a Masonic Lodge meeting in Glasgow. Murray identified himself as a member of a New York lodge and approached Mitchell for advice on how best to collect the $200 back pay owed to him from his short service on the css *Florida*. Mitchell obliged and arranged for its collection via Thomas Lynch, a Liverpool agent with connections to the local Confederate paymasters.

In a subsequent conversation, Murray told him of his sighting of Maffitt in George Square. Mitchell repeated what had transpired in his sworn deposition (16 November):

Murray described Captain Maffitt as a young man, rather lower in stature than myself [Mitchell was 5 foot 6] middling stout and dressed in a blue Yankee overcoat, reaching down past his knees, with a velvet collar, and was wearing a glazed cap with a large scoop in front, and having large black whiskers and moustache, and his hair, which is of the same colour, inclined to curl, and Murray mentioned that he had been drinking very hard.

Mitchell said that he had pushed Murray to reveal if Maffitt was in Glasgow to take command of the *Pampero* – but Murray declined to say. In further dramatic revelations, Mitchell claimed that he had later spotted a man, exactly matching Murray's description of Maffitt, standing on a quay close to the *Pampero*:

I immediately concluded, in my own mind, that he was Maffitt. I went up to him and addressed him as 'Captain Maffitt' and he shook hands with me. He did not deny that that was his name and asked how I knew him. I told him I thought I had seen him in Virginia, but he told me I was wrong . . . after we had talked together for a time, he said, 'I am not Captain Maffitt but a son of his.'

Mitchell volunteered the information that he was not the only one who had seen him. He claimed that a Louisianan paroled rebel army captain he knew, George J. Make, had mentioned meeting Maffitt in the Queen's Hotel on 40 George Square. He also added that several of the *Florida*'s crew were currently in lodgings in the Broomielaw – but for what purpose he did not know.

How much validity can be put on Mitchell's testimony is open to question, as it is almost certain he was paid for his information. His sources were certainly of dubious character. On the day he signed his deposition, Murray had already fled and the rebel captain George Make had just been sentenced to thirty days at the Gorbals Police Court for the theft of a watch. Whatever is the truth of these assertions, coming on top of similar claims by the memorialists they had the desired effect. The Lord Advocate ordered an immediate inquiry to ascertain if the famous Maffitt was, indeed, in Glasgow.

Make was interviewed in his cell by a Procurator Fiscal, where he admitted having met Maffitt at Nassau and said had since seen him in the company of two blockade-running captains in the Queen's Hotel. But he refused to divulge any further information, as he remained a committed supporter of the South and would not say anything that was 'injurious to the Confederate cause'. He only said that he did 'not believe he is in Glasgow at the present moment'.

This was an ingenious piece of disinformation. Maffitt was, in all probability, only a few miles down the River Clyde at Wingate & Company's Whiteinch yard. There he was overseeing the outfitting of his new runner for the Importing & Exporting Company of Georgia. She was named *Florie* after Mrs Wright of Wilmington, 'his beautiful daughter', according to the Glaswegian-born commentator James Sprunt.

The diligent Procurator Fiscal Hart also visited the Queen's Hotel, the gathering place of blockade-running captains. He reported that the porter had no recollection of a 'Captain Maffitt' but remembered the visits of a 'Captain North' along with his associate 'St Clair'. This speaks volumes as to the lack of care these two Confederate agents took to conceal their identities on their numerous visits to Glasgow.

With the *Pampero* only days away from her sea trials, the Lord Advocate ordered his court agents to inspect her personally (16 and 17 November). Rumours were already flying that she was about to be spirited away by a group of determined men lurking in and around Glasgow. There was a real chance that this might happen. The *Pampero*'s draught, when light, was such that she could run the River Clyde without a spring tide and with little warning.

Collector Trevor seems to have quickly grasped the gravity of the situation. He had her detained on a holding charge brought under sections of the Merchant Shipping Act (1854) which stipulated that every new vessel required a Certificate of Registry and a Declaration of Nationality before she could sail. He approached the Glasgow Police Commissioners for a twenty-four-hour guard but this request was refused. As a stopgap measure he set a double watch of his own Customs officers while he travelled to Greenock to confer with the Admiralty representative Captain Farquhar.

Farquhar agreed that the best course of action was to dispatch one of his small gunboats with a party of marines. On receiving the Lord Advocate's approval of this action, Trevor telegraphed Farquhar who immediately came upriver from Greenock on HMS *Goldfinch* under the command of Lieutenant Gregory. The *Goldfinch* arrived at half-past eight in the evening of 20 November and moored to buoys opposite *Pampero*'s berth at the Lancefield Quay.

Sheriff Alison's Crown agents had already ordered that the telegraph lines between Glasgow and Greenock Customs offices were to be manned twenty-four hours a day. In this way Farquhar had direct access to his principal command, the elderly screw block ship HMS *Hogue*, at all times. She was then riding to her anchors on the 'Tail o' the Bank' off Gourock, guarding the exit from the Clyde estuary. As all this was happening, the Foreign Office stepped in to ensure that there could be no repeat of the escape of 'No. 290' from the Mersey by interdepartmental delays or misunderstandings.

With the *Pampero* detained and under close guard, the Lord Advocate and the Solicitor-General for Scotland went about making their preliminary inquiries with the view of bringing a case to trial. The charge would be that the *Pampero*'s construction and concealment of fittings constituted a breach of Section 7 of the Foreign Enlistment Act. The principal owner, James Galbraith, presented himself to the Collector as the spokesman for his consortium to contest the seizure on the same day as the arrival of the *Goldfinch*.

With time of the essence, Consul Underwood stepped up his use of bribery and coercion to find damning and conclusive evidence for the forthcoming hearing. At the same time Barron (Bulloch's replacement) advised Sinclair to leave Scotland immediately to avoid being called as a witness. So warned, Sinclair took the train for London and on to Paris.

His departure left North behind to attend to the half-built armoured ram, which had the names *Santa Maria* and *Glasgow* at various times, at Thomson's yard. North wrote to Commissioner Mason in London

(21 November) that he was now under virtual siege: 'The plot thickens every day . . . spies are dodging round in every direction.' He complained that even his landlady had been summoned by Sheriff Alison for questioning. Days later, with his position untenable, he followed Sinclair to Paris. He later moaned to Mallory that he 'was forced to leave Glasgow in consequence of the system of espionage carried on there both by the authorities and agents employed by the Yankee consul'. Once in Paris he attended a meeting chaired by Slidell to decide the fate of his project. The ram was a lost cause and to be sold, with the monies diverted to Bulloch's French schemes.

Back in Glasgow, Underwood, unable to lay hands on his principal adversaries, unleashed his detectives on Thomson's key workers. Learning from the mistakes made in handling the draughtsman Haynes, he authorised them to offer free passage and a lifetime job in America – as an alternative to a large bribe – in return for written testimony. Even so, such was the grip of the shipbuilders over their men and boys, they only managed to net five willing witnesses.

The US consul's clandestine activities were seized on by the more pro-Confederate newspapers as prime examples of crude American coercion and carried out with little regard for British sovereignty or legalities. The *Glasgow Herald* published (1 December) a list of another five workmen who claimed to have been approached in pubs, and even in their own homes, by Federal agents.

The following day an equally disquieting report appeared in the *North British Daily Mail* (one of the most pro-South papers circulating in Scotland) and reprinted in the *Scotsman*. It claimed that skilled workmen were regularly being harassed:

> Not a day passes but half-a-dozen of them are cited to the County Court. They are detained for hours and, as they are chiefly the foremen on shift work, their several departments are much hindered. The nuisance has not ended there for, now and again, several Yankee agents forced themselves into Messrs. Thomsons' counting house, occupying valuable time by their mendacious and libellous tale-bearing . . . How all this hubbub has arisen; we cannot understand.

In this counter-offensive, statements were gathered from the victims and passed on to the Procurator Fiscal.

The propaganda war moved into top gear in the press, assembly halls and pulpits across Scotland, just as the Lord Advocate concluded his preliminary investigation. He informed the Home Office Secretary Sir George Grey that he considered the testimony he had heard from the handful of workmen and the two detectives detailed to follow North and Sinclair sufficient to warrant a trial. Russell agreed and on 9 December 1863 the Lord Advocate of Scotland instructed Collector Trevor to detain the *Pampero* formally for breaching the Foreign Enlistment Act. This order was implemented the following day. Trevor also set in motion arrangements to have her removed from the busy Lancefield Quay to the safety of the Bowling Dock further down river. This transfer was not made until early January due to a mechanical problem.

Her arrival there sparked a number of scares that she would be snatched. On 28 January Adams sent an urgent note to Russell that he had intelligence of a party of eleven or twelve men recently arrived at Liverpool from America. Their intention was to link up with Sinclair or Maury to make up a party to take her by guile or force. The fact that Galbraith had offered to sell the *Pampero* only weeks before on the open market and been refused permission, lends support to this conspiracy theory. The canny Collector Trevor certainly took the threat seriously. He had parts of her steering gear removed and taken ashore as a precaution.

The refusal of permission to sell was on the grounds that she would find her way into the hands of Southern sympathisers. Galbraith now sought to forestall the trial by a very clever disclosure. This was in the form of six letters which he claimed he had received from Sinclair back in October. They related how, with some realistic acrimonious details added, Sinclair had, indeed, wanted to secure the *Pampero* for the Confederacy – but the deal had since fallen through. On relinquishing his claim on her, Sinclair had demanded and received his cotton bonds back, ending the association. She had, Galbraith claimed, ceased to be of any interest to the so called 'Confederate States of America' a full month prior to the preliminary investigation by Sheriff Alison. At the time of her seizure she was an ordinary merchant ship – unless, of course, the British navy offered to buy her. It was a novel defence, that (as intended) raised a number of vexing 'points-in-law'.

There was, however, the matter of boxes containing rolls of highly incriminating military grey cloth that had been seized on board the vessel. These had been taken away by the Sheriff's zealous agents when they first inspected her. The Glasgow ship chandlers James McFarlane & Company strenuously claimed that they were the rightful owners and demanded their return.

Early in the proceedings before the Barons of the Scottish Court of Exchequer, the Lord Advocate recommended that there should be a deferment pending the outcome of the *Alexandra* case, which was expected daily. This was agreed as the authority of the Scottish Court of Exchequer dated from the Act of Union (1707) and hence acknowledged case precedent heard in England. Only days later, however, news arrived in Edinburgh that judgment on the *Alexandra* case had been deferred until the next session. The Crown officers in Edinburgh considered this delay prejudicial to their case and immediately resurrected the *Pampero* action.

The legal debate as to the relevance of the testimonies was heard by the Court of Session sitting in Parliament House, Edinburgh on 16 January 1864. Ninety-eight counts, almost all identical in nature, were laid before their Lordships for appraisal. The defence had since split into two interest groups: the owners (led by Galbraith) and the builder, Thomson, both claimed all or part ownership. The debate, predictably, turned on whether the 'narrow' or 'broad' interpretation of the Act should apply. As the Scottish court's ruling would now precede that on the *Alexandra*, the team hired by Bulloch and Barron to defend their case for the latter's release arrived from London. They were led by Sir Hugh Cairns, the Belfast advocate, Member of Parliament and staunch Confederate supporter.

By a majority of three to one, the Scottish judges accepted the Crown's 'broad' definition of the Foreign Enlistment Act. The accumulated testimony that claimed to prove the 'intent' to 'equip' an armed Confederate cruiser, was deemed both admissible and relevant. It is a defining moment in British foreign policy and maritime law that is rarely acknowledged in history books.

Lord Ardmillan's analogy in his summing up must have been music to Adams's ears:

Suppose a man walks into a druggist's shop and proposes to purchase a poison to destroy a person he names. The druggist, whose poverty and will alike consent, afraid of selling the poison, sells him two separate ingredients, neither of which itself is a poison, but informs the purchaser that, by a further process in combination of these ingredients, he will obtain the poison for his purpose. If the intent to use for murder of a particular person and a sale with that view be proved, can there be doubt that the druggist would be guilty of murder?

In concluding, he applied this principle to the *Pampero*:

> How can that case be disposed of, except by referring to the intent?
> The 'intent' explains the 'equipment' . . . pointing to the proposed
> wrong and coming danger.

It would now seem perfectly clear, at least in Scotland, that building a
modified hull (one ingredient) capable of mounting armaments (the
other ingredient) to form a cruiser of war was to be considered a
breach of the Foreign Enlistment Act.

The owners did not give up easily. From February 1864, the debate
switched to the House of Commons. There the pro-Confederate
lobby, led by Cairns, fired up the Tories to attack Russell for giving
in to Washington on this issue. Even Begbie did his bit for the Cause.
On 27 April he whinged to Scott that he had spent the previous
evening lobbying an honourable member of the House of Lords over
dinner. It was apparently hard work: 'priming a noble swell for the
debate but its dreich work loading them efficiently – almost impossible'.

In the meantime, the Crown officers in Edinburgh moved to secure a
'diligence' to secure all records, plans and models relating to the
Pampero. The purpose was to move forward with a criminal prosecution against the owners that, if successful, would lead to the condemnation of the cruiser. The trial was scheduled for 5 May, by which
time a compromise solution had presented itself that appeased all
interested parties.

It was, ironically, North's ram that provided the way out. To
extract their investment the Confederate camp decided, after heated
exchanges between North and Slidell, to let her builder Thomson sell
her to the highest bidder when she was launched at the end of
February. Their only stipulation was that she would not be sold to
the US Federal government.

Thomson had little difficulty in finding other potential buyers, as
both Prussian and Danish naval officers were touring British shipyards
in the hope of buying such an ironclad. The Danes made an offer, even
though the ram was not yet ready for sea, on condition that she would
not be seized by the British government. Britain was a declared neutral
in this short-lived conflict over the Duchies of Schleswig and Holstein.
Thomson pleaded with the Foreign Office that he would have to lay
off his workforce if the sale was blocked. Russell relented when the
Danish ambassador offered his guarantee, as a diplomat representing

his country, that she would not leave the Clyde until the war was over. This compromise was accepted by Russell.

This begged the question: could this approach be taken for the cruiser? The owners of the detained *Pampero* primed the MP for Kilmarnock and Renfrew, E.P. Bouverie, to broker a similar deal with the government. But first a legal compromise had to be reached to deal with the charges for breaching the Foreign Enlistment Act. The deal struck was that the Crown would accept the owners' plea of guilty on only one count (No. 37) when the case was called on 5 May. On that day, a plea in mitigation – that it was the absent Lieutenant George T. Sinclair who was behind the 'intent' to 'equip' her as a cruiser – would also be accepted. The owners were reassured that they would incur neither penalties nor costs by this 'compromise'. For their part they had to give an undertaking that she would not be sold for two years.

It would seem certain that Galbraith and his partners would have sold on the *Pampero* to the Confederates had the way been clear. After the court settlement she was towed down to Dumbarton on Galbraith's and Denny's guarantees that she would not 'slip' into the hands of the Rebels.

The mysterious Scots engineer 'Mack' mentions in his rambling and deeply masked memoirs (he used the cover name *Orento* for the *Pampero*) that he was involved in a belated plot to snatch her. He claims he was lured to the Queen's Hotel, where he was introduced to a cigar-smoking Yankee gentleman calling himself 'John Fraksey'. Shown upstairs to a drawing room, he was left alone with a hand-case containing £2,000 in gold guineas. They were his for the taking, as part payment, if he agreed to assist in the snatch.

His hosts' plan was to board her with a crew of chosen men on the night of a grand municipal dinner in Greenock. The local Customs officers could be relied upon to attend the dinner, leaving only an old watchman on board. The role of 'Mack' was to slip her cables and let the tide carry her out into the Firth before he started her engines. Beyond the three-mile limit, two tugs and a collier would be waiting. In his dramatic reconstruction, he refused point-blank and gave his hosts an ultimatum to quit Glasgow in twenty-four hours, after which he would inform the Collector of Customs at Greenock.

The fact that 'Mack' insists that his hosts that night at the Queen's Hotel were 'Yankees', not 'Southerners', is intriguing. It would suggest that it was either a Federal covert operation to flush out conspirators or a piece of opportunism by some unemployed blockade runners – a number of whom were from the North. This great yarn, unfortunately, cannot be substantiated.

A more likely explanation for the abandonment of the *Pampero* is that Galbraith and Denny were too involved in other schemes (Carlin's runners for the 'Bee Company' of Charleston and two tug-gunboats ordered by Bulloch – *Ajax* and *Hercules*) to risk compromising themselves in such a desperate gamble.

What is certain is that the *Pampero* lay at Dumbarton, under the watchful eye of the Clyde Port Authorities, until the end of the war. Indeed, she was not released from her detaining order until May 1865. This excessive delay was due to an oversight by the Foreign Office. North's ram finally sailed from the Clyde – as HDMS *Danmark* – in late August of that year.

All the other Confederate ram and cruiser schemes in Britain after the *Pampero* – bar one – were caught up in the tangle of legal and bureaucratic obstructions that stopped them either sailing or reaching the Confederacy in time. The *Alexandra* was released after the English Court of Exchequer upheld the 'narrow' interpretation on appeal. She was returned to her owner, Harry Lafone, who acted as an agent for Fraser, Trenholm & Company – on condition that she was converted back to a merchantman. She did not reach Nassau until late November 1864, when she was again seized by Crown agents.

The exception was Bulloch's purchase of the composite full-rigged auxiliary screw, *Sea King*, built on the Clyde by Alexander Stephen & Sons. He had spotted her back in the summer of 1863 just after she had completed her sea trials while he was inspecting a blockade runner in the company of Lieutenant Robert E. Carter CSN. Around the same time Consul Dudley also saw her and noted that she would make an ideal cruiser. He took no further interest as she was not for sale and was about to sail on her ten-month maiden voyage to Bombay. By early September 1864 she was back in the Clyde. During her absence Carter had returned to Richmond as a staff officer to Mallory's office.

Much happened to the cruiser programme during Carter's tour of duty. Three of the four British-built Confederate cruisers at sea had been decommissioned, detained or sunk. Commander Maury on the CSS *Georgia* had cruised the South Atlantic for over six months after her escape from Greenock. He made a great mistake in not inspecting her prior to purchase. While she was a fine steamer, she was very lightly rigged. Unable to pursue and catch his prey under sail, Maury spent most of his time at sea making slow progress under sail but with his furnaces banked ready for chase under steam. As all the neutral ports in his chosen hunting ground would only allow him to re-coal once every ninety days, his only hope was that his next prize was an American steamer which he could loot for coal. Of the nine prizes he took, only one had bunkered coal and this took over two weeks to transfer to the *Georgia* by bucket. There was also the problem of her iron plate hull which fouled badly during long periods at sea.

Having taken fewer prizes than the diminutive css *Sumter*, Maury aborted his cruise and put into Cherbourg. At a conference with Flag Officer Barron in Paris, he relinquished his command to one of his officers, Lieutenant Evans. This was so that he might concentrate on his next project – the ill-fated css *Rappahannock*. She was a recently decommissioned coastal gunboat, hms *Victor*. Her hull was rotten and her boilers unreliable, and so the Admiralty, unaware of the identity of the real buyers, readily parted with her.

Her refit at Sheerness attracted the notice of the US consul-general in London, Freeman H. Morse. In the absence of Adams, Morse raised the matter with the Admiralty. They ordered a Customs inspection but the local Customs surveyor took a bribe to give her clearance. At midnight of the same day, Maury ordered his officer-in-charge, Lieutenant William F. Campbell CSN, to take her to sea with a skeleton crew and the workmen still on board. In mid-channel, Campbell took command, renaming her css *Rappahannock*. The plan was that he should rendezvous with the *Georgia* off Cherbourg and there transfer her main armaments to his new charge.

To his dismay, he found the gunboat 'unseaworthy' and put into Calais, where he telegraphed Maury a damning report. While he quarrelled with his superiors he refused to put to sea. In this way he lost the last five days in which she could have left Calais unopposed by the French government. In the interim, the United States brought diplomatic pressure to bear on the French Foreign Minister, Drouyn de L'Huys, to detain the Confederate cruisers in his ports. Matters were complicated when the *Rappahannock* was involved in a collision with a French vessel in Calais' inner harbour. The subsequent wrangling was so protracted that she was abandoned where she lay.

With the prospect of a rendezvous gone, Evans on the *Georgia* left Cherbourg and sailed to Liverpool, where he had her armaments dismantled (2 May 1864). He handed her papers over to Bulloch, who arranged a cover sale to a group of sympathisers for £15,000. She never managed to slip back into Confederate service as she was seized by uss *Niagara* on her first voyage to Lisbon as a merchantman (15 August).

By then the most famous of the raiders, css *Alabama*, had been sunk in an epic battle off the Cherbourg breakwater with the uss *Kearsarge* (19 June) watched by thousands on shore. This left only css *Florida* still at large off Brazil under the command of Captain Charles Morris, Maffitt's replacement.

The loss of the *Alabama* was a propaganda disaster for the South. Mallory immediately ordered his staff officer Carter back to Liverpool with a direct order to Bulloch to acquire two cruisers of similar range and power. The world needed proof that the Confederacy still had an offensive capacity at sea. Carter arrived in late September, by which time Bulloch had already bought the *Sea King*. Reverting to his tried and tested methods, Bulloch kept away from Glasgow while the Liverpool merchant Richard Wright fronted the purchase. Bulloch had his friend and veteran blockade runner, Peter Corbett (who held a British Board of Trade master's ticket), sail her round from the Clyde to London. In his customary methodical way, he had everything needed ordered from different suppliers. The crew, including a number from the *Alabama*, were told to lie low and await the call.

In the meantime he had the Liverpool agent, Harry Lafone, purchase the Clyde-built fast screw steamer *Laurel* as her tender. In a characteristically well-oiled operation, he imposed a communications blackout on the two crews as they mustered at their respective locations. This kept him one step ahead of the Federal agents. On 7 October the *Sea King* cleared the Thames under Captain Corbett for a passage to Havana. The following day, the *Laurel* sailed from Liverpool laden with heavy ordnance and carrying the officers for this, the last Confederate raider. The rendezvous was off the uninhabited island of Deserta off Madeira. The *Laurel* arrived first and in the short time she spent at Funchal the local fruitsellers guessed her mission, reportedly shouting 'Otro Alabama!' in the streets.

Once the transfer of armaments was completed, the *Laurel* headed for Charleston while the *Sea King* (now renamed the css *Shenandoah*) departed south under her resolute captain Lieutenant-Commander James I. Waddell. Her voyage was of truly epic proportions as she circumnavigated the world in her mission to take the war into the Pacific. After a refit at Melbourne, Waddell skirted the northern shores of New Zealand in search of the American whalers before heading north to the ice-bound Sea of Okhotsk off Siberia. The US navy was caught completely off-guard. On hearing of her visit to Australia, Secretary Welles had little choice but to revoke the recent order recalling the USS *Wyoming* from Batavia and send her in a forlorn search for Waddell in the vast expanse of the Pacific.

Waddell found his prey – the great North Pacific whaling fleet. On boarding one of his first victims, his prize crew found an old newspaper announcing the surrender of General Robert E. Lee and the army of North Virginia. The same paper stated the intent of the Richmond government to fight on. So informed, Waddell chose to continue on his mission and went on to destroy virtually the entire whaling fleet. Tragically, this was six months after the American Civil War had ended – earning him the title 'Captain Rip Van Winkle' with the satirical cartoonists.

It was not until 2 August that Waddell found out that the Confederacy had fallen, when his boarding party brought back a pile of more recent newspapers from the British bark *Barracouta*, intercepted fifteen days out from San Francisco. Despite much dissent among his own officers and men, Waddell decided to decommission the *Shenandoah* as a warship at sea and sail back to Britain. On the morning of 6 November 1865 she steamed up the Mersey after a continuous passage of 122 days and 23,000 miles from the Aleutian Islands. Waddell surrendered the last vestige of the Confederate navy to Captain Paynter of HMS *Donegal*.

No review of the Clyde-built contribution to the Confederate war effort would be complete without concluding the story of the ironclad CSS *Atlanta*, previously the runner *Fingal*. After Bulloch had taken *Fingal* into the Savannah River with the largest arms cargo of the war, in November 1861, she had been blockaded by Federal warships. Bulloch failed in his attempt to run her out and left her there when he returned to Liverpool.

In February, the decision was taken by the Confederate navy to convert her into an ironclad. This crude and heavy conversion was undertaken by N. and T. Tilt of Savannah. She was cleared of all deck housing and the main deck was covered by heavy wooden planking to take the weight of cannon. This extended six feet out from her original deck to form an apron that would stop a ram reaching her thin iron hull. Over this decking was raised an armoured casement of eighteen inches of solid wood sheathed with strips of four-inch iron railway track that were nailed on. An armoured wheelhouse was built on top of this. She was armed with seven-inch rifled cannon at the bow and the stern. Her broadside was made up of slightly smaller six- and four-inch cannons. Protruding from the bow was a spar 'torpedo'.

She was now quite unrecognisable from the elegant Clyde ferry that had once run the Stornoway route. The weight of iron and armaments had increased her draught by over three feet, which dramatically altered her response to her helm. Living conditions for her 145-man crew were described as appalling by those who served on her. Renamed the css *Atlanta*, she was launched in July 1862 to wild claims from the Southern press that she would sweep away the blockaders. After that it was claimed that she would sail north to bombard New York and then round Cape Horn to terrorise the Californian Coast.

The blockaders got their first glimpse of the Confederate 'monster' on her trials downriver in late July 1862. It was soon realised that she now needed a spring tide to scrape over the obstacles in the Savannah River. There followed numerous delays and technical failures before Secretary Mallory lost patience and ordered her commander, Captain Webb, to 'do something!'

It took weeks to get her downriver and through the channels to the Wassaw Sound, during which she grounded when she failed to answer her helm. During this time the Federal authorities were kept well informed as to her whereabouts and state of preparation by runaway slaves who had worked on her.

On 17 June 1863, almost a year since her trials, she steamed out to do battle with the two blockading monitors uss *Weehawken* and *Nahant*. In her wake was a flotilla of sightseers out to enjoy the spectacle of a certain Confederate victory. It turned out to be a fiasco. Within a quarter of an hour after the first shot was fired Webb had surrendered. This was not due to lack of bravery on his part. In his zeal to close with the enemy, he ran the *Atlanta* aground. Captain John Rodgers on the turreted *Weehawken* soon found the blind spot in the *Atlanta*'s box design where none of her cannon could be brought to bear. Closing to within 300 yards he unleashed his twin battery of cannon, each twice the calibre of Webb's largest. After only five shots, the primitive armour of the *Atlanta* was pierced, killing one of the gun crew inside and totally wrecking the wheelhouse. With his position untenable, Webb raised the white flag to save his men from further needless slaughter.

It was a great propaganda victory for the North. The captured ironclad was towed to Port Royal where she was repaired and renamed uss *Atlanta* and sent back to blockade Savannah. Later that year, she was opened to the public in Philadelphia. The visitors' pamphlet described her Thomson-built engines as 'models for their beauty and action'. After the war she was sold to Haiti and renamed the *Triumph* but was lost at sea off Cape Hatteras during the transfer (December 1869).

Chapter 7

The Legacy

Early in April 1865, the *Scotsman* reported the exodus from the blockade-running business:

> Among the passengers who arrived on Thursday in the West Indies mail packet *Atrato*, were several captains of blockade runners from Havana. They were smart young men, and were chiefly mates of ships previous to commanding blockade runners. They have all made about ten or a dozen trips during the last eighteen months, netting themselves about £1,000 a trip, so that each has made a handsome fortune. They left their ships at Havana. Their occupation is gone, in the consequence of the capture of Wilmington and Charleston. The only place left for blockade running is Galveston, but vessels of lighter draught of water are required for that port than for the captured ports.

The Scots returning home, unlike their swashbuckling English naval colleagues, did not seek to call attention to their recent money-making activities. This means that only a few have since been identified from the hundreds, possibly thousands, involved.

Only one Scots captain wrote his memoirs as a blockade runner, the Ayrshire-born William Watson. Watson left Havana for home after his last run into Galveston on the *Jeanette* (ex-*Eagle*). He claims, in the conclusion to his memoirs, that his dealings in 'run' cotton had gone the same way as Begbie's last scheme – unwanted on delivery in Liverpool and eventually sold at a giveaway price. He did, however, come away with what was left of his wages and bonuses as a captain. This must have been a considerable amount, as he set himself up in business as a builder of small steamers when he returned, and eventually took over the Ladyburn Boiler Works at Port Glasgow. He also speculated in property, building three villas in his home village of Skelmorlie. He named two of them Oakhill and Pea Ridge after battles in which he had fought while serving as a sergeant in the Baton Rouge Volunteers. When he retired, he owned a house in a fashionable part of Glasgow and a villa in Skelmorlie. He died in 1906 aged eighty.

More is known of Begbie's crack captain, the Dundee-born David Leslie, due to the diligence of his descendants. He returned to Scotland via Halifax in May 1865. The previous year he had been home for a short period and took the opportunity to move his wife Ann and his family from Glasgow to the seaside resort of Dunoon on the Cowal peninsula. There, as part of his retirement plan, he was investing his profits from blockade running in building large residential villas. The first of these was occupied by his rapidly expanding family (he was home for the birth of his sixth child in November 1864).

His time as a blockade runner had certainly made an impression as he named this house Wilmington. The second was built in the adjacent plot five years later and called Bermuda. On the lawn he laid out in large pebbles the outline of his favourite blockade-running paddle steamer. Family tradition has it that it was his last charge, the magnificent steel-hulled *Banshee II*. She was built by Aitken & Mansell of Kelvinhaugh late in the war for Thomas Taylor's An-glo-Confederate Trading Company. If this is indeed the case, then Leslie (who is known to have returned to Nassau after laying up Begbie's *Helen*) was one of two diehard masters who made the last runs out of the doomed Wilmington in December 1864. On his return to Nassau, Leslie must have handed her over to Thomas Taylor, who is known to have run her into Galveston the following March.

The scale of the rewards that Leslie made from his last runs can be surmised from his actions on retiring from the sea in 1868 at the early age of thirty-eight. Elected the local Police Commissioner of Dunoon that year, he built a further three villas, Nassau, Dixie and Diego. He died in his villa Bermuda a comfortably well-off family man in 1905.

The number of local men who failed to return during or after the war will never be known. Those who were married often left their dependants destitute and thrown on the charity of relatives and neighbours. The most desperate were forced to ask for a pittance from the parish. Among the lowland working classes of the time, this was a pitiable and stigmatising final resort that the vast majority of the 'able-bodied' unemployed shunned. Those who did take this path have the dubious honour of having their fleeting lives recorded in a brief inspector's report on the Poor Relief registers of Glasgow.

One heart-breaking case is that of Mary Duffy, a 29-year-old 'rag picker', who applied for 'relief'. The 'poor inspector' visited her, in early March 1864, in her lodgings in 42 Old Wynd. This alley was in the midst of the worst slums in Glasgow. She shared rooms with her three-year-old daughter and ten-year-old son. At the time of the visit she was bed-ridden, having just given birth to her second son three days earlier. The father, her Glaswegian husband James Duffy, was reported as having 'deserted' her. The inspector noted 'her husband has been at sea for the last twenty years – never being at home more than three weeks or a month at a time'.

He had gone to Liverpool where he signed on as a stoker aboard the new paddle steamer *Deer* bound for the blockade. No doubt he had been lured there by the stories of the fortunes still to be made in this business. Duffy's service on the *Deer* was short-lived. On her first run into Charleston (18 February 1865) under the command of Joannes Wyllie, she ran aground off Fort Moultrie. Wyllie was unaware that, just the night before, the town had been evacuated and the harbour forts were in the hands of the Federal forces. Stranded without any hope of rescue, Captain Wyllie and his crew, including stoker Duffy, were taken prisoner. In November 1870, five years after all prisoners in the conflict had been released, the Poor Relief inspector noted that James Duffy had returned to his wife and family. Unlike his captains, he had made no money while in America and he immediately applied for Poor Relief for himself and his family. Six years later, after further lengthy absences at sea and four more children, he asked to enter the poorhouse as he was 'wholly' disabled by rheumatics. He was forty-five years old. His wife was certified as 'deserted' and living in 'privation' by a visiting physician and her family were granted 'outdoor relief'.

During the war, the squalor of the Glasgow slums was witnessed by the 'Southern gentlemen' who passed through the dock areas on their way to collect a new runner. In his memoirs, the Virginian-born Lieutenant John Wilkinson CSN was appalled by the pollution of Glasgow and the poverty he witnessed:

> The city was enveloped in a fog during the whole time; its normal atmospheric condition, I presume . . . We were painfully struck by the number of paupers and intoxicated females in the street; and some of our party saw, for the first time in their lives, white women shoeless, and shivering in rags, which scarcely concealed their nakedness, with the thermometer at the freezing point.

One year into the conflict, in late August 1862, as the pre-war stockpile of cotton ran out, the Glasgow employers held a specially convened meeting. There it was reported that around 5,000 workers were already unemployed and a further 9,000 part-time in the local cotton mills and related industries. The local Poor Relief system was already overwhelmed. Their fear was that, without direct intervention, this war-induced depression would lead to starvation and a return to the civil unrest of the previous decades. As the monies available to the local authorities for Poor Relief were pre-set by the Poor Law of 1845, it was decided that a petition should sent to London to seek permission to borrow funds in advance of taxes to meet the emergency.

While the textile industry owners fretted over the impending social disorder in mill towns such as Paisley, the shipbuilders were ever-vigilant for signs of an upsurge in militant trade unionism. The fear was that their workforce, most of whom were 'hired and fired' as suited, would be infected with the radical politics that flourished in the local Emancipation Societies. The comparison between the enslaved black and the exploited white workers was all too evident in their 'brotherhood of man' rhetoric.

The likes of Scott, Denny and Begbie shared, along with most of the middle classes, a revulsion to American republicanism and the deep-seated belief that the experiment in democracy had gone too far in the US. They believed that, by extending the vote to the urban mob, politics would fall into the hands of unscrupulous politicians who, with the help of the unprincipled American press, readily manipulated elections.

To ram home the message, the assumed-to-be more reputable British press gave full coverage of the draft riots and race lynchings in New York during the war. At the same time, the virtues of the British voting model (extended to the property-owning and educated middle classes by the Great Reform Bill of 1834) were extolled.

Support of the cultured elite who governed the agrarian-based Confederacy fitted well with this view. They were perceived to be gentlemen, inclined to patronage and with a high sense of honour. These characteristics, it was thought, would safeguard the long-term interests of all – black and white. They were seen as resisting the social chaos and brutal economic exploitation by the barbarians from the industrial North. Then there was the South's resolute stand against the Federal dictat on imposing a protectionist tariff barrier on imports, a tariff which threatened British trade and, inevitably, British jobs.

Some Scottish labour leaders were swayed by the 'Free Trade versus Protectionist' argument and accepted that the lesser of the two evils was to recognise the Confederacy and break the blockade. Incredibly,

Alexander Macadam (the miners' leader), and Alexander Campbell (a leading figure in the Co-operative movement) both pushed for this solution.

On the other hand, the local Anti-Slavery and Emancipation Societies were unshakeable in their insistence that the conflict was a moral crusade. The suffering of the textile workers in Lancashire and the west coast of Scotland was an unavoidable price that had to be paid to secure the freedom of slaves held in bondage in the South.

Throughout the war there was a grass-roots struggle against the combined power of the majority of the Establishment, the mercantilist interest and the press. The Emancipation Societies' support of Lincoln and his war aims was ridiculed. Newspaper reports of their meetings invariably played down the numbers attending and mocked their speakers for their moral pretensions. Even where the turn-out was undeniably large – as with the packed meeting called in the Free Church Assembly Hall, Edinburgh on 15 October 1863 to hear the Reverend Henry W. Beecher speak on the 'America Crisis' – the report in the *Scotsman* focused on the hecklers and rabble-rousers in the debate.

Unfortunately, very little documentation has survived to illuminate the inner workings of the local societies that bloomed across the industrial belt of Scotland during the war. The few minute books available are usually in a formal short-note format. What is clear is that while there was a pecking order within the Emancipation movement (led by London), smaller local groups were capable of independent action, depending on the charisma and power of their leaders.

One 'small sister' society, saved from obscurity by the survival of a few letters in the US National Archives, was the Newmilns Anti-Slavery Society. Its membership was drawn from a cross-section of this small close-knit community of (mainly) weavers and was open to both sexes. Their meetings were held on Friday evenings in a back room of the Black Bull Inn on the main street of their Ayrshire village.

Their chairman was Matthew Pollock, but their driving force was John Donald, a local man (born in 1802) and a veteran campaigner for social reform. As a young man, Donald was an ardent supporter of Wilberforce's anti-slavery movement which finally secured the freedom of slaves in the British West Indies in 1834. He later took up the Chartist cause and stood by his humanitarian principles to denounce the Crimean War as a 'crime'. He was fifty-seven years old when the American Civil War broke out and he took up the struggle for the emancipation of all black Americans.

Under his energetic leadership, the Newmilns Anti-Slavery Society passed resolutions and wrote letters of the highest biblical rhetoric in support of President Lincoln and his administration throughout the war. These were delivered to the US Legation in London. Adams duly passed them on to Seward in Washington. Seward was under a direct instruction from Lincoln to have all such letters of support from working-class associations copied and presented to Congress.

At the height of the '*Pampero* affair' (late 1864) the Newmilns Anti-Slavery Society's unflinching support was recognised by the outgoing US consul in Glasgow, Warner L. Underwood. He sent his envoy John Brooks, a black American, to present his nation's flag to the committee, along with two bound volumes of the correspondence between the Federal government and other nations.

That December the lead article in the *Glasgow Herald* sneered at this mark of favour:

The Newmilns Anti-Slavery Society had a great gala day a few months ago, on the occasion of being presented with an American Flag; and when the 'stars and stripes' were unfurled, the flow of oratory and the shouts of enthusiasm would have done Mr Lincoln's heart good to be heard. The Society rose up as one man, or perhaps as half-a-dozen altogether, and planted the Yankee banner either on the church steeple or on the lock-up house – we forget which – where it fluttered in the breeze for a few hours, and might well have given rise to the supposition that the village had sworn allegiance to the Federal President, and the Federal Constitution.

The assassination of Lincoln and the grievous wounding of Seward was a bitter blow to the Newmilns Anti-Slavery Society. At a public meeting held in early May 1865, they voted unanimously to write to the new president, Andrew Johnson, to offer their condolences:

and while we mourn, along with every true friend of humanity, the unparalleled event that has befallen your country, and although the horizon seemed dark for a time after such a calamity, we are again hopeful when we see the sun emerging from behind the cloud in your own likeness, supported by General Grant and the gallant army – Farragut and the navy – the patriotic people of America, and all who stood forward so nobly in the time of need in defence of those institutions for the good of mankind contained in the glorious republic of America, all deserving and receiving our best thanks.

Undeterred by their critics, they wheeled out the 'Lincoln flag' at every local civic occasion thereafter. It was carried, with pride, alongside the 'blue blanket'. This was the banner flown by the Covenanters at the battle of Drumclog (1679) against the King's dragoons in order to preserve their Presbyterian religion. In 1884, twenty years after the presentation of the American flag, both were carried at the head of the 600-strong Newmilns contingent at a great demonstration held in Kilmarnock to demand the franchise for the working classes.

It is not known if John Donald, who was by then eighty-two years old, marched with his townsmen. What is certain is that their banner – 'Reform, Good Laws, Cheap Government' – would have met with his approval. He died seven years later.

The economic legacy of the blockade was profound and its impact was felt for decades. Unlike Lancashire, the Clydeside cotton industry never recovered from the 'famine'. In 1861, there were over a hundred firms involved in cotton spinning within a twenty-five-mile radius of Glasgow. By 1910, there were only nine. The rising woollen industry did little to compensate as it was located mostly in the borders.

During the war, emigration was actively promoted in the press as a safety valve to avert urban unrest. The *Caledonia Mercury* ran a plea from the governor of New Zealand's southern province of Otago to send out more settlers. The Free Church of Scotland had founded a 'Scots colony' there in 1850. The first settlers were carried directly by vessels belonging to Patrick Henderson & Company of Glasgow.

The Henderson brothers were active members of this church – as was Peter Denny. During the Civil War they formed a close relationship, speculating in Confederate bonds, investing in Begbie's blockade-running firms, and building runners. When the Hendersons were approached to form the Otago Shipping Company in 1863, they naturally turned to Denny to build the vessels for the new line. He not only obliged, but also heavily invested some £25,000 of his war profits in the company and became its chairman in 1864.

On 26 May 1864, the *Dumbarton Herald* announced the departure of the first batch of immigrants under this new company. The sailing ship *Sevilla* under Captain Kerr left from Greenock with upwards of 250 emigrants on board. Most of the passengers were, however, not unemployed Glasgow mill workers but young men from the rural town of Girvan, much further down the coast. The following month, a second batch left on the clipper *Arima*. She had been launched by Alexander Stephen's yard the previous year at the same time as their latest vessel *Sea King* (later CSS *Shenandoah*) was undergoing her sea trials under the watchful eye of James Bulloch.

In that same year (1864), Denny purchased a new site on the banks of the River Leven in Dumbarton to meet the seemingly insatiable demand for his steamers. Carlin's blockade runner *Ella* was launched from there – on the same day as the *Sevilla* sailed for New Zealand.

By then the intimate circle of Denny, James Galbraith and the Henderson brothers were planning for the post-war market. In the last months of the war they were left holding, or had bought back, most of the vessels which were launched on the Clyde but failed to reach the Confederacy. These included Sinclair's *Pampero* (renamed *Tornado*); Bulloch's two gunboat tugs *Ajax* and *Hercules*; Carlin's two cruisers *Enterprise* (cover name *Yangtze*) and the *Adventure* (cover name *Tientsin*); and, finally, the *Wisconsin* (renamed *Cyclone*), which had been built by the partnership on speculation.

It was a shrewd move that paid handsomely. With Spanish South America and the West Indies erupting in rebellion, these hulls – all with strengthened gun decks – found ready buyers. The Brazilian navy took Carlin's cruisers (renamed *Brazil* and *Amazona*) while the Argentine navy bought Bulloch's two harbour gunboats. The Chilean navy purchased the *Tornado* and the *Cyclone*.

The departure of the latter two, in late November 1865, caused a great diplomatic stir. It was rumoured they had been armed at Dumbarton so that they might immediately serve as privateers raiding Spanish interests in European waters. In scenes reminiscent of the previous year, the Customs Collector for Glasgow and Greenock had his surveyor inspect them and set the river guard vessel, *Sylph*, to stand watch over them. Both vessels managed to slip away from the Clyde and headed north.

Their plan for their intended commissioning and passage to Chile was very elaborate and followed closely Bulloch's tried and tested template. The *Tornado* made for the isolated Danish Faroe Isles between the Shetlands and Iceland. There she met with a freighter from which she took on armaments (causing an uproar with the local governor) and re-coaled before sailing for warmer waters. Meanwhile, the *Cyclone* had turned south after passing the Orkneys and ran down the East Coast, first to the Firth of Forth and then on to Yarmouth. On arrival she was again boarded by Customs officers, who found no weaponry on board and who were informed by her captain that his ultimate destination was Rio de Janeiro.

The *Cyclone* was released and headed for her rendezvous with the

Tornado at Funchal, Madeira. Once there, their captains were ordered to re-coal and head for the desolate islands of Fernando de Noronha, an old pirate haunt off the Brazilian coast. They were to be met by a supply ship before heading for Buenos Aires and on to Valparaiso via Cape Horn.

As the diplomatic row gathered momentum in London, the Spanish government (emulating the recent behaviour of the Americans) acted unilaterally. They ordered their warship *Gerona* to lie in wait off Madeira. In a replay of the escapade of Captain Craven on the USS *Tuscarora* over three years earlier, this Spanish warship chased his prey in full sight of the Portuguese authorities in Funchal. She overhauled the *Tornado* (22 May 1866) and put on board a prize crew that carried her off to Cadiz. Undeterred by the local complaints, the captain of the *Gerona* resumed his search for the *Cyclone*, but gave up after a few days.

The *Tornado* case was heard in Madrid and dragged on for the best part of a year, during which the Scots crew were held prisoner. The *Scotsman* claimed that they had been roughly handled and kept in isolation during their captivity. At the hearing it was revealed that the owners were the London firm, Isaac, Campbell & Company, better known as staunch supporters and financiers to the, by now defunct, Confederacy. As no partner or agent of the firm appeared to contest the condemnation, the vessel was declared prize and immediately acquired by the Spanish navy. Her Scots crew were eventually released.

Sailing under the Spanish flag, the most lasting contribution made by the *Tornado* to maritime history happened seven years later in September 1870, when she intercepted the filibuster *Virginius* off Cuba. The *Virginius* was the ex-blockade runner *Virgin*, built by Aitken & Mansell and seized at the fall of Mobile (April 1864) after one run. She was subsequently sold to various private interests, ending up as a gun runner to the Cuban rebels under her old captain, Joseph Fry.

After his capture, Fry and most of his crew and passengers (numbering fifty-nine altogether) were put against a wall and shot. The few who survived owed their lives to the timely arrival of a British warship from Jamaica which threatened the Spanish commander with bombardment if he did not stop this butchery. As many of the victims were American, the incident took the USA and Spain to the very brink of war.

None of this affected the original sellers, Denny and his associates. By the end of the American Civil War, their fortunes had been further intertwined in the Irrawaddy Flotilla & Steam Navigation Company.

Only the year before the '*Virginius* incident', the Suez Canal had opened. The trade to Burma and the East was now within the reach of the new generation of 'CB' steamers – largely due to the improved coal consumption achieved (30 per cent reduction) by John Elder's compound engine and Napier's 'Scotch' boiler.

The leap in demand for their long-haul cargo carriers and specialised river craft was assured, guaranteeing the success of the yards that made up William Denny & Sons of Dumbarton. The early death of brother Archibald left Peter the undisputed owner of the business.

All the other builders of blockade runners also fared well. Primed by the 'super profits' of the war, the Clyde entered its 'golden period' as world leader in marine engineering. There were many new start-up companies during the war: five opened their yards in 1863 and five more in 1864. Around the same time, many of the established companies followed the example of Scott and Denny and expanded their premises or moved to new larger sites. The dynamic innovators, Randolph & Elder, gave up their Old Govan yard for the larger Fairfield yard, built on a green site a short distance down river in 1863.

In the immediate post-war years, their success was underpinned by local orders for steamers to replace those sold to the blockade runners. During the war years, the cull had been dramatic. At the start of the conflict (1861), forty-seven steamers were plying the Firth of Clyde and river routes. By 1864, when the running business was at its height, only twenty-eight (mostly elderly pre-war hulls) were still operating. Indeed, it was not until five years after the war that the number of steamers in the Clyde approached the pre-war level.

In the interim, the local industry had also undergone a radical restructuring. The small Clyde independent operators who had dominated the passenger market, cashed in their racers to the runners. McKellar of Largs, the largest pre-war operator with at one time seven steamers, was left running three old hulls – much to the chagrin of his customers.

The passenger market and the routes used were also changing with the arrival of the railways on the Renfrew and Ayrshire coasts. The first was the Greenock and Wemyss Bay Railway, a ten-mile spur line from the main Caledonia Line at Greenock opened in 1865. By 1870, competing railway companies had pushed lines through to the Ayrshire coast to the deep-water ports of Troon and Ardrossan. In that year, the new Princes Pier at Greenock, fully integrated with the railway system, was opened. The replacement 'channel class' steamers that ran the Firth of Clyde from the new railway quays were mostly owned by newly formed large firms in which a railway company held a share. Faced with such competition, most of the small 'river class' racers disappeared, along with their operators, from the open sea routes.

All the key local players in blockade running and Confederate shipbuilding programmes on the Clyde – with the exception of George Thomson, who died prematurely in 1866 – lived to enjoy the fruits of their labour and investments. None was prosecuted nor were their characters blemished in any way by their involvement in 'the trade'.

John Scott of Greenock was clever enough to resist Begbie's wild schemes to build armoured rams and runners to the exclusion of his core business – large ocean-going auxiliary steamers. Well before the war ended he had full order books. The 1871 Census reported the forty-year-old as living in 'Hillend House, fourteen rooms with windows' close to his yard, along with his Jamaican-born wife, their four-year-old son and three servants. He was credited with employing 825 men and 195 boys at his Cartsdyke yard. He died in 1903, aged seventy-three, having handed over his thriving business to his son Charles.

This was a modest living compared to Peter Denny's empire across the estuary at Dumbarton. By 1871, at the age of forty-nine, he was in full control of the family business, employing 1,400 men and 100 boys. He was then living in his great house of Helenslee, which he had built just before the war, along with his large family of eight children (four had previously died in infancy and three had already left home), a governess, three nurses, one wet nurse and five domestic servants. He died in 1895 exceedingly wealthy, despite being nearly bankrupted by a South American scheme. He had also been honoured by a doctorate for his work in promoting education amongst his workforce.

James Lumsden, the business partner in Begbie's blockade-running Universal Trading Company, rivalled Denny for wealth and accolades. From running his family's stationery firm, he rose to be a director of the Clydesdale Bank, the Glasgow & South Western Railway Company and the Clyde Shipping Company. Knighted for his service as lord provost of Glasgow, he died in 1871 leaving the Loch Lomondside estate of Arden and a portfolio of business assets. The latter included his shares in the Begbie's Universal blockade-running company.

Charles Randolph, the great innovator along with his brilliant partner John Elder, shared a similar destiny to Lumsden. Randolph joined Lumsden on the board of the Glasgow & South Western Railway Company and a host of shipping and explosives companies. At the height of his international fame as a marine engineer, in 1868, he retired at the age of sixty. A year later Elder died, ending the partnership; whereupon Randolph turned his attention to his two pet interests – improving Glasgow's appalling sewage system and perfecting steam road carriages. He died in 1878 leaving half his estate to Glasgow University.

Thomas S. Begbie died in Kensington at the age of seventy-eight, although in more modest accommodation and circumstances than he had enjoyed at the start of the war. In his later life, he diversified into mining.

As for the Confederates involved in the European procurement programme, most chose to remain in exile in Liverpool or Halifax at the end of the war. To return home then was to face arrest and imprisonment – as happened to George Trenholm. Eventually, as the bitterness of the war faded, most slipped back to resume their former lives. James D. Bulloch never returned to the United States, preferring to rebuild his life in relative obscurity as a cotton merchant in Liverpool. He died there in 1901, leaving his truly remarkable memoirs (published in 1883) for posterity.

The fate of the twenty 'CB' racers taken into the Federal navy is an impressive tale in its own right. Sent out as 'gamekeepers' they were responsible for the capture or destruction of forty-four 'poachers', twelve of which were stablemates built on the Clyde. At the final assault on Fort Fisher (January 1865), the key to Cape Fear River, six of the thirteen vessels which made up the Reserve Division cordon behind the main bombarding fleet under Rear Admiral Porter were captured 'CB' runners. These were USS *Fort Donelson* (formerly *Giraffe / Robert E. Lee*); *Neptune* (formerly *Lord Clyde / A.D. Vance*); *Gettysburg* (formerly *Douglas / Margaret & Jessie*); *Tristram Shandy*; *Little Ada*; and *Britannia*. The USS *Britannia*, a large iron-hulled paddle steamer, had only the year before survived an engagement with the ironclad CSS *Raleigh* off New Inlet.

The capture of Fort Fisher sounded the death knell for the Confederacy as a viable fighting unit. As Porter commented from his flagship: 'The gate through which the rebels obtained their supplies is closed for ever, and we can sit here quietly and watch the traitors starve.' On 22 March 1865, the last remnants of the defenders evacuated Wilmington. Later that summer most of the surviving 'CB' units in the Federal navy were decommissioned and sold off.

The few retained for post-war service were mostly 'channel class' ferries. One was the USS *Gettysburg*, the one-time Isle of Man ferry. She was sent out as a survey ship to the Caribbean and Mediterranean before she was finally sold at Genoa in 1879.

At least two of those sold off at the end of the war had further naval careers, but under different flags. The USS *Fort Donelson* (ex-*Giraffe*), whose deck had been strengthened to take two 30-pounders and five 12-pounders, was purchased by a private buyer from Baltimore. Renamed *Isabella*, she left the Brooklyn Naval Dockyard in December, ostensibly for Havana and Rio de Janeiro. Instead she sailed on to Valparaiso where she was acquired by the Chilean navy and renamed *Concepcion* (1869). She was shortly joined by the former Glasgow–Londonderry ferry and runner *Thistle* (latterly USS *Cherokee*). The *Cherokee* had a long naval service before being wrecked at Chiloe Island on the south-western coast of Chile in 1889. The fate of the *Giraffe* is unknown, presumably ending up in a local breakers' yard.

Of those captured but not retained by the navy, the most awe-inspiring post-war career was that of the experimental *Alliance*. She was, arguably, the most unsuited hull design for open-sea passages and the slowest runner to leave the Clyde for the blockade. After her capture in Wassaw Sound trying to get into Savannah, this twin-hulled oddity was sold at the Boston prize court to an Antipodean buyer. With some minor adaptations and rigged with a simple sail plan, she was dispatched home, as the *New Zealand*, via Melbourne.

Miraculously, she made it unscathed and served as a passenger steamer for the goldfields between Lyttleton and Dunedin. On her first voyage to Hokitita on the west of South Island she ran aground on a sand spit in the harbour and was wrecked (August 1865) – as far away from the sheltered waters of the Caledonian Canal as can be imagined.

Left behind on the shoals and beaches of the Confederate coast were the wrecks of those magnificent steamers that had been lost in the running trade. As most were iron-hulled their corpses could still be seen at low tide up until the 1920s. James Sprunt tells a good yarn that one piece of a wreck, carved with mysterious symbols, was washed up by a storm in 1878. The local Wilmington Historical and Literary Society thought that it was a relic of great antiquity – a pre-Columban metal artifact. The discovery caused great excitement until:

> a profane Scotchman . . . informed them that the piece of metal was no more than a part of the bow or stern escutcheon of the stranded blockade runner *Georgiana McCaw*, the palm tree in the center

surrounded by the motto 'Let Glasgow Flourish', being the coat of arms of Glasgow, Scotland, the home port of the said blockade runner.

The restoration of Anglo-American relations took almost as long as the sea did to give up that relic. The accusations continued to fly between the two nations five years after the end of the war. It took the shock of the Franco-Prussian War (1870–1) and the prospect of renewed hostilities with Russia (America's newest friend) over the Czar's handling of his rebellious Czech subjects, to move the British government to admit error and come to the negotiating table. The prime motivation was the prospect of a reversal of roles, where dozens of 'Alabama type' raiders were built and armed in America for the Russians. This threat came on top of American territorial claims over the Pig Islands off British Columbia and the ongoing clamour in the Senate to annex forcibly Canada, the British West Indies and Bermuda as war compensation.

Bellicose as the British press might be against American claims, the British Admiralty and Foreign Office had their backs to the wall. The superiority of American sea power was dramatically underlined by the official visit to the British naval docks of one of the advanced American twin-turreted ironclads, manned by war-hardened veterans. The British navy had yet to launch an answer to such armour and weaponry.

These factors pushed Britain into seeking a general settlement with the USA. This took the form of a Joint High Commission convened in Washington. It drew up a treaty of forty-three articles, which was ratified in May 1871 and contained a pre-emptive apology for the escape of the cruisers *Alabama*, *Florida* and *Shenandoah* from British ports. It was agreed that compensation would go to arbitration. In doing so it acknowledged the 'wide interpretation' of neutrality as defined in Britain's own Foreign Enlistment Act, namely, that a government had an obligation to exercise 'due diligence' to prevent the building, arming, equipping or acquisition of ships intended to serve in a war. America, for its part, finally signed the Declaration of Paris, which banned privateering.

The Tribunal of Arbitration consisted of five men – one member from each of America, Great Britain, Italy, the Swiss Confederation and Brazil – and met in Geneva in mid-December. It was almost derailed on the first day when US Secretary Fish resurrected and tabled an 'indirect' claim for the entire cost of the war since the battle of

Gettysburg – with 7 per cent interest. This was based on the claim that British-built blockade runners and armaments sales had prolonged the war by two years. Without this 'lifeline' the Confederate armies would have collapsed after that crushing Union victory. This was tabled in addition to the 'direct' claim for damages inflicted by the three principal Confederate cruisers on the Union's merchant marine.

Gladstone's calculation was that Britain stood to be assessed as liable for a staggering £8 billion in reparations. At Geneva, the America legation openly floated the idea that Canada should be handed over as compensation. This unacceptable demand was dismissed out of hand by the British delegation. For a while another war seemed imminent. By May 1872, the stand-off was such that Schenck, the US Minister in London, declared to his Secretary: 'Very well, Sir, we shall fight Great Britain and, thank God, we are ready for it!'

War speculation sparked a wave of selling American securities by panicking European investors. As the dollar plummeted, the daily cost to the American Treasury far outweighed any reasonable expectations of damages. Common sense had to prevail if this crisis was not to get out of hand. It was the veteran diplomat Charles F. Adams who saved the day by convincing his colleagues at Geneva to drop the 'indirect' claim. Fish, having made his gesture, withdrew his petition and the tribunal proceeded to adjudge the 'direct' claim only.

On 4 September 1872, the Tribunal ruled that Britain had violated the rules by failing in its duty to exercise 'due diligence' over its policing of its subjects. Consequently, the Americans were awarded damages of $15.5 million. Forced to eat humble pie and pay for it to avert a war, Britain received some satisfaction in that the country was later awarded $2 million for damage done to British shipping by illegal Union blockade practices. Other British claims raised this figure to close to $7.5 million. As all other American claims were disallowed, the net result was that Britain had to pay America only the outstanding $8 million. The British cabinet considered this a small price to pay to resolve all disputes, avoid a war and protect Canada from invasion. Even the normally pugnacious *Times* of London pronounced that 'we simply wanted the judgement of five men of sense and honour; we obtained it, and we cheerfully abide by it!'

After the payment was finally made (1877) the returned cancelled bank draft was framed and hung on the wall of the Foreign Office in Whitehall, as a reminder to all future ministers of the price of Russell's political folly.

Appendix 1

Jules Verne in Glasgow

Verne made good use of his visit to Scotland to describe the departure of the *Dolphin* for Charleston heavily laden with arms and munitions openly loaded from the Broomielaw Quay. He vividly describes her passage down the River Clyde to the lower Firth, through the North Channel, finally to reach the open Atlantic beyond Rathlin Island. Her master, port of registration and the flag flying from her jack were all British, guaranteeing her a safe passage from any Federal naval vessels cruising in British waters.

The historical details are in keeping, except the fact that there is no steamship called the *Dolphin* in the records of Tod & McGregor, which are complete for the period. Nor indeed did any other yard on Clydeside build a vessel of that name during the years 1861–5. Tod & McGregor launched seven vessels in 1862, of which the *Princess Royal*, being a large twin screw steamer, fits Verne's description of the *Dolphin* most closely. The *Princess Royal* was built for Henderson & Company for the Glasgow to New York route. Her history also matches as she attempted a direct run into Charleston with a massive cargo of munitions only to be captured in the final approach (29 January 1863).

In his story, he simply switched names of this powerful leviathan with that of a small old paddle steamer, *Dolphin*, built in 1844. The *Dolphin* left the Clyde around the time of the launch of her fictional namesake to join the blockade runners at Bermuda but was captured between Puerto Rico and St Thomas on her first run in March 1863.

Verne's literary deception was, however, utterly in keeping with the times. Those who were involved in blockade running during this war took great care to hide their identities (then and later) for fear of prosecution under the British Foreign Enlistment Act 1819.

The details of his storyline are, therefore, a mixture of fact and fiction. He probably did so to avoid a libel suit, such was the sensitivity of those engaged in blockade running, even though he published this tale ten years after the conclusion of the conflict.

The Black American Community in Glasgow

Glaswegians (as they refer to themselves) were no strangers to the true nature of the titanic struggle happening on the other side of the Atlantic. There had been a well-established black American community in Glasgow since the 1830s. They were actively seeking access to the higher education denied them in their home states. A few were fugitive slaves from the South but most were educated and politically active from New York (where slavery had been abolished in 1827). The most famous to reside in Glasgow (1845–7) was the runaway slave Frederick Douglass, whose book, *My Bondage and My Freedom*, was published in New York and widely circulated in Britain.

It is worth noting that the introduction to his book was written by Dr James McCune Smith. Smith was the first ever black American to graduate in medicine. He obtained his degree from Glasgow University in 1837. While studying there he was an active member of the Glasgow Emancipation Society.

In the aftermath of the victory in securing the emancipation of all slaves in the British Empire (1834), membership dropped away. The outbreak of the Civil War reignited interest and membership numbers were further stimulated by Douglass' tour of Scotland in 1860, which culminated in a passionate speech at Queen Street Hall in Edinburgh.

At the time of the war the most prominent figure in the Society was the black sculptress and abolitionist, Sarah Remond. She was an eloquent public speaker who supported Frederick Douglass' central tenet that the American Constitution and the Union could deliver emancipation. She was in full support of the Federal blockade and the military defeat of the South. Followers of William L. Garrison's rival Anti-Slavery Society, however, held the view that, as the American Constitution had perpetuated slavery, it should be discarded along with the Union.

Then there was debate as to how the emancipation of slaves in the South was to be managed. Many subscribed to the view that – in the best interests of all concerned – it should be phased to minimise the shock to the fragile agrarian economy, based as it was on plantation cotton. Garrisonites openly advocated that there should be a five- or seven-year compulsory apprenticeship for adults. Only then would former slaves be free to pursue their own interests as skilled free men and women.

Appendix 3

Letter from Blockade-running Captain W. Russell to Thomas S. Begbie

PS *Marmion*
Nassau, 17 December 1864

T.S. Begbie, Esquire

Dear Sir,
I beg to forward you a report of my first attempt to get into Charleston.

I left Nassau on Saturday Nov. 26th and at 11.30 p.m. of the 28th made Charleston bar and had passed seven of the outside blockading fleet. But as we proceeded further inshore, the water became very luminous which was the cause of our being first seen by a small vessel lying close into the beach. He immediately commenced firing rockets over us and making other signals to the fleet and in less than two minutes we were surrounded by three ships. The nearest one opened fire upon us with their muskets and the others trying to drive us onshore or to cut us off from getting to sea again.

Finding myself in this predicament, at that moment I could not see a shadow of a chance to save myself and I fully expected to have been forced to beach her or surrender. But being determined not to do either, but they cut me off in all directions. I cut my engines and let them come towards me which they did and as soon as they were nearly up to me I went astern full speed and passed between four of their ships. They all fired upon me but I am happy to say that none of their shots struck our ship and before they could get their ships heads round I was a sufficient distance from the breakers to set on a head again by this manoeuvre. I am happy to say we got our ship's head off shore and only one ship in chase of us, the others, I believe, had to look after their own safety. This vessel kept us in sight till four o'clock the next morning, at this time I was able to alter my course and by daylight I had got a good offing from the land and no ship in sight.

At noon I stood in again for the bar, engines working slow and at eight p.m. I was again at the entrance to Charleston bar. But unfortunately, for us, the weather was quite calm and we ran into a dense fog and although we were in an excellent position for going in my pilot refused to take charge on account of the weather. At this moment we were so close to a ship that we could hear them giving orders but could not see her. Finding it was impossible to get the pilot to take charge of my ship I determined to make the best of my way back to Nassau, as my coals would not hold out to risk another night, in case I might get chased off again. I then stood out again to sea and on the morning of the 1st of December we sighted to all appearance a large sailing ship. I immediately altered my course and in an hour altered the bearings of the stranger four points. At this time the wind freshened and it was then he showed his intentions, by setting a cloud of canvas and pointing his ship direct at us. I then saw we were in for a hard chase and as he had the advantage of a strong fair wind to cut me off from getting round Abaco. I determined to run for the nearest land and fortunately we did so, as he continued to chase me up till four p.m. At that time I ran between the Whale Rocks and Guano Cay. And he did not give up the chase till he saw that I had run clear of the rocks and was in safety. At this time he was not more than two miles from us. After we had anchored I went ashore and watched him till he was out of sight. At dark we came out to sea again and at daylight arrived safe at Nassau.

I trust in our next attempt we shall be more fortunate and that my endeavours to get into Charleston and my proceedings to save my ship will meet with your approval and be satisfactory to the directors. I must now beg to state that my ship and engines are in first rate condition and that it was her superior speed that saved her from adding another one to the Yankee prize list. I am now ready for sea and only await further instructions from Mr. Atkinson to proceed. You will observe that my provision bills are heavy owing to my lying in Falmouth so long, it interfered with my sea stock and everything in this port is fearfully dear. But I am in hopes in a short time to make the return of the ship satisfactory to all concerned in the interest of the *Marmion*. Captain Raison of the *Kenilworth*, I am sorry to say met with no better luck than myself on his first trip with her.

The *Beatrice*, Captain Randle, was driven onshore the night previous to my trying to get in. His ship was destroyed but he with a portion of his crew escaped in a boat. He returned here in the PS *Wild Rover* and has now got command of her.

I remain, Dear Sir
Your Obedient Servant
W. Russell

Note: Russell was the newest recruit to Begbie's Universal Trading Company. His paddle steamer *Marmion* was launched from John Scott's yard, Greenock.

Appendix 4
Sample of a Blockade Cargo Sale Notice

SOUTHERN CONFEDERACY [ATLANTA, GA],
31st of January 1863

Package Sale.
The Cargoes of the British Steamers
Calypso and *Douglas*
by R.A. Pringle,
137 Meeting Street,
Charleston, South Carolina,
James H. Taylor, Auctioneer.
On Wednesday Morning, February 11th, 1863,
commencing at 10 o'clock, will be sold,

Groceries.
193 chests Tea
50 cases Salad Oil

Medicines, Drugs, &c.
24 kegs Epsom Salts
21 gross Brown Windsor Soap
15 drums Caustic Soda
1 chest Rhubarb Root
1 case Asafoetida
20 cases English Cotton Card

Shoes and Leather &c.
10 cases Men's, Youths', Ladies', Boys' and Girls' Boots and Shoes
23 trunks Ladies', Girls' and Boys' Shoes
1 cask Shoe Findings
86½ dozen Calf Skins

Dry Goods &c.

[illegible] cases Mourning Delaines
21 cases, Fine White Shirtings
8 bales Brown Denims
4 bales Cotton Ticks
8 bales Regatta Stripes
1 case Tweed Trowsers
3 bales Crimean Shirts
5 bales Tweed and [illegible] Shirts
13 bales Printed Cotton Handkerchiefs
1 bale Fancy Colored Denims
13 cases Linen Thread
[illegible] cases Clark's Sewing Cotton – White, Black and Colors
3 bales men's Drill Pants
22 cases Men's Merino Shirts and Drawers
6 cases Men's Merino Half Hose
6 cases Men's Brown Cotton Half Hose
8 cases Ladies' Imitation Merino Hose
2 cases Children's Merino Socks
6 cases Men's Imitation Merino Half Hose
4 cases Ladies' White Merino Finished Hose
2 cases Super Merino Socks
2 cases Grey Merino Socks
14 bales Sea Island Cotton Bagging
9 bales Woollen Cassimeres
4 cases women's and Misses' Hoop Skirts
2 cases Fancy Scotch Tweeds
100 M Needles, assorted
[illegible] cases Madder Prints
2 cases Pins
6 cases Shoe Thread
1 bale Blue Grey Union
2 bales Kerseys and Plains
[illegible] cases Printed Challies
2 cases Cassimere, 'Super'
1 case French Bombazine
3 cases Colored DeLaines
1 case Gloves, assorted
2 bales Blue and Scarlet Twills
5 bales Damaged Blankets

Appendix 5
Technical Notes and Measurements

Engines

Data on engine designs for the period is very limited.

All marine steam engines of this period were reciprocating (i.e. the piston went up and down the cylinder with each stroke and in a straight line).

Most 'CB' paddle steamers and all 'CB' twin screw steamers deployed as runners had two compact engines that could drive the paddle wheels or propellers in unison or independently.

It would appear that most of the purpose-built runners launched on the Clyde during the war were driven by two single cylinder 'high-pressure', 'direct-acting' engines.

'Direct-acting' refers to the mode of transmission of the mechanical movement to the drive shaft: i.e. one stroke of the piston rod gave one revolution of the paddle wheel or screw propeller.

Most were 'oscillating' engines. This term refers to the design type where the whole cylinder rocked 'to and fro' with the turn of the crank. This was the simplest method of directly linking the piston rod and the crank on the drive shaft.

All the other engine types utilised were of fixed position cylinder design: 'vertical' (upright); 'inverted' (upright but upside down); 'diagonal' (usually angled at 45 degrees); 'inclined' (usually 15 degrees) / 'horizontal' (90 degrees). The type chosen was dictated by the internal space available.

The types of transmission to the drive shaft from the fixed position cylinders were 'beam', 'side lever' or 'steeple'. These designs allowed for a gear box to be inserted. 'Gearing' allowed the drive shaft to turn at a higher or lower rate than the rate of the piston stroke. Many of the 'channel class' ferries acquired for the blockade and cruisers had 'geared' transmission.

A few of the larger runners and cruisers were driven by the recently introduced 'compound' engine. This engine had two cylinders – one of small diameter using high-pressure steam and an adjacent large diameter cylinder using low pressure steam. The injected high-pressure steam drove up the piston in the smaller cylinder. At the top of its stroke the expended steam (now at a lower pressure, having performed duty) passed into the neighbouring water-cooled larger cylinder. On contact with the cold surface the steam condensed back to water creating a partial vacuum, whereupon the external atmospheric pressure acted to push the second piston down.

The other salient marine engine attributes listed in records are the diameter of the piston and the length of the stroke; the cubic capacity of the working area of the cylinder; the duty or power the engine delivered; and coal consumption per hour or day.

Piston diameter was always referred to in inches and its stroke in feet (e.g. 30 inches × 4 feet 6 inches). Cubic capacity of the cylinder was equated to how much water would occupy the internal space (e.g. 50 gallons).

The power of an engine was listed in two ways – Nominal Horse Power (NHP) and Indicated Horse Power (IHP).

NHP was the official measurement of an engine's 'rating'. It assumed that low-pressure steam (c. 10 lb per square inch) was the motive force. By 1861 it was already an anachronism as most 'racers' used high steam pressure above 20 lb per square inch and by the end of the war up to 60 lb per square inch was being achieved.

IHP was the recorded performance on test runs under high-pressure steam. By 1865 this could be as much as four times its official rating (NHP). For example, an engine officially listed as 150 NHP could deliver 600 IHP on trials.

Coal consumption was not noted by official inspectors and was only mentioned in the shipbuilder's or owner's test-run notes.

Boilers

By 1861 all boilers generating high-pressure steam were of multi-tubular design. Using tubes maximised the heated surface area in contact with the water in the boiler. Most runners had two or more boilers of either the 'haystack' or 'scotch' design. The former took its name from its external shape while the latter design was that attributed to the Scottish engineer, Robert Napier. All boilers had a number of furnaces or fireboxes. Any one of these could be extinguished and 'drawn' (raked and cleaned) without a major disruption to the operating of the boiler.

Hulls

By 1861 there were a number of hull descriptions and tonnage measurements – official and commercial – in simultaneous use.

All new or acquired vessels are required to be registered under the Merchant Shipping Act. The registration details for this period gave type of propulsion; type of rig; number of decks; and tonnage.

The official tonnage of a vessel was based on its internal carrying space, not its displacement or deadweight. This was ascertained from a series of internal measurements taken by the Customs 'measuring officer' in a manner prescribed by the Board of Trade (1856) known as the 'Moorson Admeasurement Rule'. The measurements were applied to a formula which gave two outcomes: 'nett registered' and 'gross registered' tonnage. The convention was to drop the 'nett' and simply refer to her official tonnages as 'registered' and 'gross registered'. The first was the internal carrying space as a steamer – the space taken up by the engine and its bunkers (coal storage) was not included. The second was the carrying space if the engines were removed and she reverted to a sailing vessel. If the vessel was condemned by a prize court (her papers were often destroyed at the moment of capture) and acquired by the US navy it was standard practice to re-measure her as part of the commissioning process.

The other tonnage measurements ascribed to a vessel were for commercial purposes. The most common and oldest concept was 'tons burthen' or 'builder's measure', which was what was assumed or known to be her actual carrying capacity in weight of cargo. By 1861 the newest concept was 'light displacement' (without cargo), which only seems to have been used consistently by William Denny & Sons and then only for their large ocean-going cargo vessels.

The overall result is a series of tonnages for the same vessel that seem to be contradictory or flawed.

The famous *Giraffe / Robert E. Lee / Fort Donelson* can serve as an example. On her official registration at Glasgow (1861) her measurements were given as: 270.2 ft × 19.1 ft × 8 ft, which equates to 360.39 gross registered tons (316.39 nett registered, i.e. without engine room).

When she was surveyed by the US navy after her capture (1864) her measurements were given as: 283 or 266 ft × 26 ft × 10 ft. She was also reported as 270.3 ft × 26.2 ft × 13 ft. Her tonnage was given as 642 tons – twice that of her gross registered. It can be presumed that the former figure was her assessed tons 'burthen'.

In Appendix 6 below, 'List of Vessels', the official hull measurement or the next closest has been selected. All versions of tonnage available have been listed.

Appendix 6

List of Vessels by Builder

Sources (numbered as follows after each entry)
1 *Register of Shipping for Glasgow and Greenock*, Mitchell Library, Glasgow
2 *Shipbuilders' List of Launching*, Glasgow University Archives, Glasgow
3 Wise, *Lifeline of the Confederacy*, Appendix 22
4 Silverstone, *Civil War Navies*, Acquired combatant vessels

Aitken & Mansell
Yard: Kelvinhaugh, Glasgow (1863–76)

Banshee (II) Steel paddle steamer, schooner-rigged, launched 1864
Dimensions: 252.6 ft × 31.7 ft × 11.2 ft
Tonnage: 627 gross registered / 438 registered
Engines: 2 × 250 NHP / 2 funnels / 15.5 knots
History: Acquired by John T. Lawrence for the Anglo-Confederate Trading Company of Liverpool. Sailed from Cork late August 1864. Made three runs into Wilmington from Bermuda and Nassau and one into Galveston from Havana September 1864 – April 1865. Survived the war and returned to Liverpool. [1, 2 & 3]

Florence Iron paddle steamer, launched 1864
Dimensions: 252 ft × 25 ft × 11 ft
Tonnage: no data
Engines: no data
History: At Bermuda January 1865, never ran the blockade. Survived the war. [2 & 3]

Susan O'Beirne Steel paddle steamer, schooner-rigged, launched 1864
Dimensions: 252.6 ft × 31.7 ft × 11.2 ft
Tonnage: 627 gross registered / 446 registered

Engines: 2 × 250 NHP

History: Acquired by Henry Lafone of Lancaster for the Importing & Exporting Company of Georgia early November 1864. Made one attempt to reach Wilmington but turned back to Bermuda with bad leak December 1864. Survived the war and sold at Buenos Aires. [1, 2 & 3]

Tristram Shandy   Iron paddle steamer, launched January 1864

Dimensions: 225.5 ft × 25.2 ft × 12.5 ft

Tonnage: 444 burthen / 344 gross registered / 211 registered

Engines: 2 inclined direct-acting condensing (46 in × 2 ft 6 in) / 12 knots

History: Acquired by Matthew I. Wilson for the Anglo-Confederate Trading Company. Made one run into Wilmington May 1864. Captured leaving Wilmington by USS *Kansas* May 1864. Acquired by US navy retaining name May 1864. [3 & 4]

Virgin   Iron paddle steamer, launched 1864

Dimensions: 216 ft × 24.5 ft × 10.9 ft

Tonnage: 442 burthen / 291 registered

Engines: 2 × 180 NHP

History: Acquired by the European Trading Company. Made one run into Mobile July 1864. Seized by Union forces at Mobile April 1865. After the war renamed *Virginius* and served as gun runner to Cuba [2, 3 & 4]

Vulture   Iron paddle steamer, launched 1864

Dimensions: 242 ft × 25.7 ft × 10.6ft

Tonnage: 482 gross registered / 335 registered

Engines: no data

History: European Trading Company of London. Made one run into Wilmington November–December 1864. Survived the war. [2 & 3]

Barclay, Curle & Company
Yards: Stobcross, Glasgow (1845–74) and Clydeholm (1855–1966)

Britannia   Iron paddle steamer, launched April 1862

Dimensions: 189 ft × 26 ft × 9 ft

Tonnage: 495 burthen / 371 gross registered / 275 registered

Engines: 2 × 112 NHP / steeple condensing (41 in × 3 ft 6 in) / 2 boilers / 12.5 knots

History: Acquired by Robert Barclay for Leech, Harrison & Forwood. Donald McGregor for Alexander Collie & Company. Made one run into Wilmington and Charleston March–June 1863. Captured off Eleuthera Island, Bahamas, returning from Charleston by uss *Santiago de Cuba* June 1863. Acquired by US navy, retained her name with the North Atlantic Blockading Squadron off Wilmington. [2, 3& 4]

Druid   Iron paddle steamer, launched April 1857
Dimensions: 160.2 ft × 20.6 ft × 9.7 ft
Tonnage: 229 gross tonnage / 125 registered
Engines: no data
History: Campbeltown & Glasgow Steam Packet Company. Acquired by Herbert C. Drinkwater of Manchester for the Druid Steamship Company of Charleston. Made four runs into Charleston March 1863 – February 1865. Survived the war. [2 & 3]

Emily (I)   Iron single screw steamer, launched at Stobcross November 1863
Dimensions: 181.1 ft × 22.4 ft × 12.1 ft
Tonnage: 355 gross registered / 253 registered
Engine: 1 × 79 NHP (34 in × 3 ft)
History: Owner Thomas S. Begbie. Acquired by Albion Trading Company. Sank off Wrightsville Beach heading for Wilmington on her first run February 1864. [2 & 3]

Emma (II)   Iron single screw steamer, launched November 1862
Dimensions: 164.4 ft × 21.2 ft × 11.1 ft
Tonnage: 345 burthen / 278 gross registered / 191 registered
Engine: 1 × 68 NHP oscillating (32 in × 3 ft) / 1 boiler built by John Scott / 12 knots
History: Owner Thomas S. Begbie. Made four runs in to Wilmington February–July 1863. Captured by uss *Arago* leaving Cape Fear River July 1863. Acquired by US navy and sent to the North Atlantic Blockading Squadron off Wilmington September 1863. [2, 3 & 4]

Gertrude   Iron single screw steamer, launched at Clydeholm November 1862
Dimensions: 164.4 ft × 21.2 ft × 11.1 ft
Tonnage: 345 burthen / 278 gross registered / 191 registered
Engine: 1 × 68 NHP oscillating (32 in × 3 ft) / 1 boiler built by John Scott / 12 knots

History: Owner Thomas S. Begbie. Made one run into Charleston
March 1863. Captured by USS *Vanderbilt* leaving the Bahamas on
second run April 1863. Acquired by US navy and sent to the
Western Gulf Squadron off Mobile June 1863. [2, 3 & 4]

Minnie   Iron single screw steamer, launched at Stobcross December
1863
Dimensions: 181.1 ft × 22.4 ft × 12.1 ft
Tonnage: 355 gross registered / 253 registered
Engine: 1 × 79 NHP (34 in × 3 ft)
History: Owner Thomas S. Begbie. Acquired by William Boyle for the
Albion Trading Company. Made two runs into Wilmington from
Bermuda March–May 1864. Captured by USS *Connecticut* leaving
Wilmington May 1864. [2 & 3]

Blackwood & Gordon
Yards: Cartvale, Paisley (1852–60) and Castle, Port Glasgow (1860–99)

Minho   Composite (wood on iron frame) paddle steamer, launched
at Paisley yard 1854
Dimensions: 175.1 ft × 22 ft × 13.5 ft
Tonnage: 400 gross registered / 253 registered
Engines: 2 × 90 NHP / 2 cylinders inverted
History: John Bibby & Sons of Liverpool. Acquired by Fraser,
Trenholm & Company April 1862 for Navigation Company. Made
two runs into Charleston April–October 1862. Ran aground en-
tering Charleston on third run and destroyed by USS *Flambeau*
October 1862. [2 & 3]

Tubal Cain   Iron single screw steamer, launched at Paisley yard 1853
Dimensions: 157.7 ft × 22 ft × 12.4 ft
Tonnage: 307 burthen / 165 gross registered / 81 registered
Engine: 1 × 100 NHP
History: Owner Amos Bigland. Acquired by G.S. Sanderson. Captured
entering Charleston on first run by USS *Octorara* July 1862. [2 & 3]

James Caird & Company
Yard: Mid Cartsdyke, Greenock (1840–67)

Alfred (Old Dominion)   Iron paddle steamer, launched 1863
Dimensions: 225 ft × 26.5 ft × 14.5 ft
Tonnage: 730 light displacement / 703 burthen / 518 registered

Engines: no data

History: Acquired for the Virginia Importing & Exporting Company. Made three runs into Wilmington June 1864–February 1865. Survived the war. [2 & 3]

City of St Petersburg   Iron paddle steamer, launched 1863
Dimensions: 223 ft × 25 ft × 13.5 ft
Tonnage: 698 burthen / 426 registered
Engines: 2 × 250 NHP
History: Owners McLeish & Watt of Glasgow sold to Thomas S. Begbie. Acquired by the Virginia Importing & Exporting Company. Made eight runs into Wilmington from Bermuda and Nassau December 1863 – February 1865. Survived the war. [2 & 3]

Fox   Steel paddle steamer, schooner-rigged, launched late 1863
Dimensions: 219 ft × 22 ft × 10.2 ft
Tonnage: 783 light displacement / 372 registered
Engines: 2 × 275 NHP
History: G. and J. Burns Ltd Glasgow. Made eight runs into Charleston from Nassau May 1864 – February 1865 and one into Galveston April 1865. Survived the war. [1, 2 & 3]

Hattie   Iron paddle steamer, launched late 1863
Dimensions: 212 ft × 20 ft × 8.4 ft
Tonnage: 203 registered
Engines: 2 × 130 NHP
History: Owner James Laing of Glasgow. Lost at sea en route from Cork to Havana, December 1864. [1, 2 & 3]

Lord Clyde / Advance   Iron paddle steamer, launched April 1862
Dimensions: 231 ft × 25.5 ft × 10 ft
Tonnage: 955 light displacement / 775 burthen / 431 registered
Engines: 2 oscillating side lever (63 in × 6 ft 6 in) / 6 boilers / 2 funnels / 12 knots
History: Dublin & Glasgow Sailing and Steam Packet Company ferry. Acquired by Thomas Crossan CSN for the State of North Carolina June 1863. Later half-share owned by Power, Low & Company December 1863. Made nine runs into Wilmington June 1863 – September 1864. Captured leaving Wilmington by USS *Santiago de Cuba* 10 September 1864. Acquired by US navy, renamed USS *Frolic* September 1864. [2, 3 & 4]

Mary & Ella   Iron paddle steamer, launched 1864
Dimensions: 220 ft × 22.5 ft × 11 ft
Tonnage: 510 light displacement / 352 gross registered / 242 registered
Engines: no data
History: Owned by James Betts. Acquired by David McNutt, arrived
  at Nassau December 1864. Did not attempt a run and returned to
  UK. [1, 2 & 3]

Nola   Iron paddle steamer, launched 1863
Dimensions: 223 ft × 25 ft × 13.5 ft
Tonnage: 760 light displacement / 695 burthen / 426 registered
Engines: 2 × 250 NHP
History: Owner Captain Fowler. Acquired by David McNutt, lost off
  Bermuda after hitting a reef late December 1864. [1,2 & 3]

Orion / Fannie   Iron paddle steamer, launched 1859
Dimensions: 220 ft × 26 ft × 13.5 ft
Tonnage: 733 burthen / 559 gross registered
Engines: no data
History: St Petersburg Steam Navigation Company. Acquired by
  Arthur B. Forwood for the Importing & Exporting Company of
  South Carolina and renamed *Fannie*. Made three runs into Char-
  leston and four into Wilmington May 1863 – January 1864.
  Survived the war. [2 & 3]

Roe / Agnes E. Fry   Iron paddle steamer, launched 1863
Dimensions: 220 ft × 26 ft × 13.5 ft
Tonnage: 780 light displacement / 599 gross registered
Engines: no data
History: G. and J. Burns of Glasgow. Acquired by Crenshaw &
  Company and renamed *Agnes E. Fry* reputedly after the wife of
  her captain, Joseph Fry. Made two runs into Wilmington Septem-
  ber–November 1864. Ran aground and destroyed off Old Inlet,
  Wilmington from Nassau December 1864. [2 & 3]

Sirius / Alice   Iron paddle steamer, launched 1859
Dimensions: 220 ft × 26 ft × 13.5 ft
Tonnage: 733 burthen
Engines: no data
History: St Petersburg Steam Navigation Company. Acquired by
  Arthur B. Forwood for the Importing & Exporting Company of

South Carolina and renamed *Alice*. Returned to the Clyde in the autumn of 1864 for repairs. Made two runs into Charleston and three into Wilmington May 1863 – March 1865. Survived the war. [2 & 3]

William Denny & Sons
Yards: Victoria (1844–65), Churchyard (1853–66), Albert (1853–66), North Yard (1859–68) and Woodyard (1849–67), Dumbarton

Adventure Iron twin screw steamer, barque-rigged, launched by Peter Denny, North Yard 1865
Dimensions: 250 ft × 30 ft × 16 ft
Tonnage: 1,600 light displacement / 776 gross registered / 459 registered
Engines: 2 × 235 NHP / inverted (36 in × 2 ft 6 in) / 6 round tubular boilers / 35 lb pressure / 14 knots
History: Owners Peter Denny and James Carlin of Carrickfergus for the Importing & Exporting Company of South Carolina, Charleston, November 1865. Sold back to Denny before she sailed. [2 & 3]

Ajax Iron twin screw steamer, brigantine-rigged, launched by Peter Denny, North Yard January 1865
Dimensions: 190.3 ft × 27.1 ft × 13.7 ft
Tonnage: 600 light displacement / 341 gross registered / 203 registered
Engines: 2 × 105 NHP (525 IHP) / horizontal back acting (28 in × 1.5 ft) / 2 round tubular boilers / 60 lb pressure / 13.1 knots
History: Owner P. Henderson for Bulloch and the Confederate government as a harbour defence and rescue tug for Wilmington. Aborted passage to Nassau and returned from Cork after dispute with crew and Customs to the Clyde. Sold back to Denny. [2 & 3]

Calypso Iron single-screw auxiliary steamer, three masts schooner-rigged, launched at Archibald Denny's Churchyard, April 1855
Dimensions: 190.3 ft × 27.1 ft × 13.7 ft
Tonnage: 630 burthen / 535 gross registered burthen / 487 registered
Engine: 1 twin cylinder geared steeple (44.5 in × 3 ft 6 in) by Tulloch & Denny / 2 boilers / 12 knots
History: Owners Bristol General Steam Navigation Company. Troop carrier in Crimean War. Acquired by Thomas S. Begbie. Chartered to agents acting for Fraser, Trenholm & Company. Sold to Steamship Calypso Company. Made three runs into Charleston from

Nassau January–June 1863. Captured trying to enter Old Inlet, Wilmington by USS *Florida* June 1863. Acquired by the US navy retaining her name October 1863. [2, 3 & 4]

Caroline   Iron paddle steamer, schooner-rigged, launched by Peter Denny, North Yard 1864
Dimensions: 225 ft × 28 ft × 13 ft
Tonnage: 1,165 light displacement / 705 deadweight / 634 gross registered / 404 registered
Engines: 2 × 200 NHP / oscillating / 40 lb pressure / built by Napier
History: James Carlin of Carrickfergus for the Importing & Exporting Company of South Carolina, Charleston July 1864. Made two runs into Wilmington and one into Charleston November 1864 – January 1865. Returned to UK March 1865. [2 & 3]

Charlotte   Iron paddle steamer, schooner-rigged, launched by Archibald Denny, Churchyard 1864
Dimensions: 226.3 ft × 28.2 ft × 13 ft
Tonnage: 1,165 light displacement / 705 deadweight / 634 gross registered / 404 registered
Engines: no data / built by R. Napier / two funnels
History: Originally ordered by James Carlin of Carrickfergus. Order taken over by P. Henderson & Company of Glasgow. Acquired by Edward Stringer and Edward Pembroke for the Mercantile Trading Company. Made one run into Wilmington December 1864. Captured by USS *Malvern* entering Old Inlet after the fall of Fort Fisher January 1865. [2 & 3]

Columbia   Iron single-screw auxiliary steamer, brig-rigged, launched by Archibald Denny for Peter Denny 1862
Dimensions: 174.4 ft × 24.1 ft × 16.5 ft
Tonnage: 503 burthen / 392 gross registered
Engines: 2 inverted (36 in × 2 ft 6 in) / 1 boiler
History: Owner Thomas S. Begbie. Chartered to agents acting for Fraser, Trenholm & Company. Captured off Florida on her first run by USS *Santago de Cuba* August 1862. Acquired by the US navy retaining her name November 1862. Burned off Masonboro Inlet to prevent capture January 1863. [2, 3 & 4]

Eagle / Jeanette   Iron screw steamer, launched 1852
Dimensions: 169.9 ft × 16.8 ft × 8.3 ft

Tonnage: 147 gross registered / 76 registered
Engines: no data
History: Acquired by George Wigg for the Navigation Company. Made three runs into Charleston from Nassau. Captured by USS *Octorara* coming out of Charleston on third run February 1863 – May 1863. Acquired by new owners at prize court and returned to running as *Jeanette*. One run into Galveston January 1865. Survived the war. [2 & 3]

Economist / Bonita   Iron single-screw auxiliary steamer, barque-rigged, launched by Archibald Denny, Churchyard 1860
Dimensions: 191 ft × 26.5 ft × 17.6 ft
Tonnage: 630 burthen / 487 gross registered
Engine: 1 experimental compound, 2 high-pressure concentric cylinders inside with 2 outer low-pressure cylinders / built by Tulloch & Denny / 1 haystack boiler
History: Owned by James Tulloch and Archibald Denny. Acquired for Fraser, Trenholm & Company. Made one run into Charleston from Bermuda March–April 1862. Redeployed as supply transport to the islands as *Bonita*. [1, 2 & 3]

Ella   Iron paddle steamer, schooner-rigged, launched by Peter Denny, North Yard 1864
Dimensions: 226.1 ft × 28.2 ft × 13 ft
Tonnage: 1,165 light displacement / 705 deadweight / 634 gross registered / 404 registered
Engines: 2 × 200 NHP / oscillating / 40 lb pressure / built by Napier
History: James Carlin of Carrickfergus for the Importing & Exporting Company of South Carolina, Charleston July 1864. Made two runs into Wilmington August–November 1864. Ran ashore while entering Old Inlet Wilmington on third run and destroyed by ex-runner USS *Emma* December 1864. [1, 2, 3 & 4]

Emily (II)   Iron paddle steamer, schooner-rigged, launched by Peter Denny, North Yard 1864
Dimensions: 255 ft × 34 ft × 16.5 ft
Tonnage: 1,690 light displacement / 865 deadweight / 1,442 burthen / 736 registered.
Engines: 2 × 300 NHP / oscillating / built by Napier
History: James Carlin of Carrickfergus for the Importing & Exporting Company of South Carolina, Charleston and James Galbraith of

Glasgow and Peter Denny of Dumbarton, January 1865. Arrived at Bermuda with two marine engines for the Confederacy, never ran the blockade. Sold back to Denny. [1, 2, 3 & 4]

Enterprise (II)   Iron twin screw steamer, barque-rigged, launched by Peter Denny, North Yard 1865
Dimensions: 250 ft × 30 ft × 16 ft
Tonnage: 1,600 light displacement / 776 gross registered / 459 registered
Engines: 2 inverted (36 in × 2 ft 6 in) / 6 round tubular boilers / 35 lb pressure / 14 knots
History: Owners Peter Denny and James Carlin of Carrickfergus, the latter acting for the Importing & Exporting Company of South Carolina (Charleston). Sold back to Denny (November 1865) before she sailed. [2 & 3]

Granite City   Iron paddle steamer, schooner-rigged, launched by Archibald Denny, Churchyard November 1862
Dimensions: 160 ft × 23 ft × 9.2 ft
Tonnage: 428 gross registered
Engines: 2 (38 in × 4 ft 6 in)
History: Acquired by Alexander Collie & Company. Two runs February–March 1863. Captured off Eleuthera Island, Bahamas returning from Wilmington by USS *Tioga* March 1863. Acquired by the US navy retaining her name. Captured by Confederate forces at Calcasieu Pass, Louisiana April 1864. Sold to Thomas W. House of Galveston. Ran aground and destroyed off Velasco, Texas by USS *Penguin* January 1865. [2, 3 & 4]

Hercules   Iron twin screw steamer, brigantine-rigged, launched by Peter Denny, North Yard February 1865
Dimensions: 190.3 ft × 27.1 ft × 13.7 ft
Tonnage: 600 light displacement / 341 gross registered / 203 registered
Engines: 2 × 105 NHP (525 IHP) horizontal back acting (28 in × 1 ft 6 in) / 2 round tubular boilers / 60 lb pressure / 13.1 knots
History: Owners Walter Powell of Monmouth and Walter Frankis of Bristol for Bulloch and the Confederate government as a harbour defence and rescue tug for Wilmington. Bought back from Bulloch by Denny. [2 & 3]

Imogene   Iron paddle steamer, schooner-rigged, launched by Peter Denny, North Yard 1864
Dimensions: 225 ft × 28 ft × 13 ft

Tonnage: 1,165 light displacement / 705 deadweight / 868 burthen / 397 registered

Engines: 2 × 200 NHP / oscillating / 42 lb pressure / built by Napier

History: Ordered by James Carlin of Carrickfergus for the Importing & Exporting Company of South Carolina, Charleston November 1864. Made one run into Galveston April 1865. Sold back to Denny and Galbraith, eventually sold at Rio de Janeiro. [1, 2, 3 & 4]

Japan / Virginian / Georgia Iron single-screw auxiliary steamer, brig-rigged, launched by Peter Denny, North Yard January 1863

Dimensions: 210 ft × 27 ft × 15 ft

Tonnage: 1,150 light displacement / 520 deadweight / 751 burthen / 648 gross registered / 427 registered

Engine: 1 × 166 NHP (900 IHP) steeple geared / surface condensing (49 in × 3 ft 9 in) / 2 tubular boilers / 13 knots

History: Built on speculation. Acquired by Thomas Bold of Liverpool for Commander Matthew F. Maury CSN February 1864. Commissioned as css *Georgia* off Ushant April 1863. After a short cruise was decommissioned and sold at Liverpool June 1863. Seized by uss *Niagara* off coast of Portugal August 1864. [2, 3 & 4]

Leopard / Stonewall Jackson Iron paddle steamer, 3 masts schooner-rigged, launched by Peter Denny, North Yard December 1857

Dimensions: 222 ft × 27 ft × 14.8 ft

Tonnage: 1,230 light displacement / 395 deadweight / 798 burthen / 691 gross registered / 437 registered

Engine: 1 × 340 NHP 2 cylinder side lever (66 in × 6 ft 3 in) / 2 boilers 14–20.5 lb pressure

History: Acquired by Fraser, Trenholm & Company May 1862 for £24,000. Renamed *Stonewall Jackson* February 1863. Made five runs into Charleston from Nassau June 1862 – February 1863. Ran aground and burned off Sullivan's Island while attempting to enter Charleston by uss *Flag* and *Huron* April 1863. [2 & 3]

Maude Campbell Iron screw steamer, launched by Archibald Denny, Churchyard 1864

Dimensions: 226.3 ft × 28.2 ft × 13 ft

Tonnage: 631 gross registered / 403 registered

Engines: no data

History: Owner P. Henderson & Company of Glasgow. Acquired by the Importing & Exporting Company of South Carolina. Arrived at Bermuda November 1864. Never ran the blockade. [2 & 3]

Memphis   Iron single-screw auxiliary steamer, brig-rigged, launched by Peter Denny, North Yard April 1862

Dimensions: 210 ft × 27 ft × 15 ft

Tonnage: 1,780 light displacement / 1,010 gross registered / 792 registered

Engine: 1 × 705 IHP 2 cylinder inverted direct-acting (46 in × 3 ft) / 2 tubular boilers / 14 knots

History: Built in partnership with Thomas S. Begbie. Chartered to Zollinger & Andreas of Manchester for munitions runs into Charleston March 1862. Captured leaving Charleston by USS *Magnolia* July 1862. Acquired by the US navy retaining her name September 1862. Dispatched to the South Atlantic Blockading Squadron off Charleston. [2, 3 & 4]

Phoebe   Iron screw steamer, launched 1851

Dimensions: 172.8 ft × 25.5 ft × 15.6 ft

Tonnage: 585 gross registered / 397 registered

Engines: no data

History: Acquired by Z.C. Pearson & Company. Arrived at Bermuda July 1862. Never ran the blockade. Sold to the Australian Steamship Company. [2 & 3]

Prince Albert   Iron paddle steamer, launched 1849

Dimensions: 138.1 ft × 16.7 ft × 7 ft

Tonnage: 132 gross registered / 94 registered

Engines: no data

History: Made one run into Charleston July 1864. Ran onto wreck of *Minho* entering Charleston harbour and destroyed by shellfire from Union shore batteries August 1864. [2 & 3]

Stag / Kate Gregg   Iron paddle passenger steamer, schooner-rigged, launched by Archibald Denny, Churchyard November 1853

Dimensions: 208 ft × 23 ft × 13.2 ft / 5 watertight bulkheads

Tonnage: 553 burthen / 548 gross registered / 351 registered

Engines: 2 × 240 NHP (57 in × 5 ft 6 in) built by J. and G. Thomson / 2 tubular boilers

History: Owners G. and J. Burns of Glasgow. Acquired by David McNutt of Glasgow for the Atlantic Steam Packet Company of Charleston. Renamed *Kate Gregg* September 1864. Made three runs into Charleston September–December 1864. Survived the war. [2, 3 & 4]

James Henderson & Company (1848–61)
Henderson & Coulborn (1861–74)
Yard: Renfrew West

Diamond   Iron paddle steamer, launched 1853
Dimensions: no data
Tonnage: 250 burthen
Engines: no data
History: Captured by USS *Stettin* off the coast of Georgia on her first
  run September 1863. Acquired by the US Quartermaster Depart-
  ment. [2 & 3]

Emily / Tartar   Iron paddle steamer, launched 1864
Dimensions: 230 ft × 25 ft × 11.5 ft
Tonnage: no data
Engines: no data
History: Left the Clyde November 1864 but was damaged in storm and
  returned to Cardiff. Registration transferred to Liverpool. Investi-
  gated on suspicion that she was being converted as a slaver. (1, 2 & 3)

Gem   Iron paddle steamer, launched 1858
Dimensions: 122 ft × 18 ft × 7.3 ft
Tonnage: 65 registered
Engines: 2 × 55 NHP
History: Owner Edward R. Coulborn of Glasgow, marine engineer.
  Registration transferred to Liverpool. Owner Otto H. Kaselack,
  chartered to Cobia Company of Charleston. Reportedly made one
  run into South. Sold to Henry R. Saunders of Nassau. Survived the
  war. [1, 2 & 3]

Hawk   Composite (wood on iron frame) screw auxiliary steamer,
  launched 1864
Dimensions: 254 ft × 28 ft × 12.5 ft
Tonnage: 530 registered
Engines: no data
History: Acquired by Thomas S. Begbie for the Virginia Volunteer
  Navy for conversion to privateer. Arrived Bermuda but the buyers
  had no funds June 1864. Returned to Liverpool. [2 & 3]

Lizzie (II)   Iron paddle steamer, launched 1864
Dimensions: 230 ft × 22 ft × 9 ft

Tonnage: no data
Engines: no data
History: At Havana October 1864 but does not appear to have attempted a run. [2 & 3]

Pearl Composite (wood on iron frame) paddle steamer, launched 1859
Dimensions: 182.2 ft × 19.5 ft × 7.6 ft
Tonnage: 168 gross registered / 72 registered
Engines: no data
History: Acquired by George Wigg for the Navigation Company. Captured off the Bahamas on first run by USS *Tioga* January 1863. [2 & 3]

Ruby (I) Iron paddle steamer, schooner-rigged, launched 1861
Dimensions: 209.2 ft × 19 ft × 8.5 ft
Tonnage: 102 registered
Engines: 2 × 120 NHP
History: Sold by owner James Henderson of Glasgow, shipbuilder and James Henderson of Glasgow, shipowner to William R. Coulborn of Liverpool, January 1862. Acquired by George Wigg for Alexander Collie & Company October 1862. Made three runs into Charleston February–June 1863. Ran ashore and destroyed off Lighthouse Inlet attempting to enter Charleston June 1863. [1, 2 & 3]

Ruby (II) Iron paddle steamer, launched 1857
Dimensions: 187 ft × 16.8 ft × 9 ft
Tonnage: 182 registered
Engines: no data
History: Captured on first run heading for St Marks, Florida by USS *Proteus* February 1864. [2 & 3]

Laurence Hill & Company
Yard: Inch, Port Glasgow (1853–70)

Thistle (I) Composite (wood on iron frame) single screw steamer, 2 decks, schooner-rigged, launched July 1859
Dimensions: 184.5 ft × 25.2 ft × 12.5 ft
Tonnage: 606 burthen / 366 gross registered / 206 registered
Engines: 2 × 150 NHP geared beam engines (44 in × 3 ft 6 in) / 1 boiler / 13 knots

History: Glasgow–Londonderry packet. Sold by John Cameron and Lewis MacLellan to George Wigg of Liverpool for the Navigation Company October 1862. Ran aground leaving Charleston on first run and captured by USS *Canandaigua* and *Flag* May 1863. Acquired by US navy January 1864, renamed USS *Cherokee*. [1, 2, 3 & 4]

Thistle (II)   Iron paddle steamer, launched 1863
Dimensions: 201.5 ft × 25.9 ft × 12.3 ft
Tonnage: 636 burthen / 305 registered
Engines: 2 oscillating side lever (57 ft × 5 ft) / 2 boilers / 10 knots
History: Glasgow & Londonderry Steam Packet Company. Made one run into Wilmington from Bermuda March 1864. Captured off North Carolina coast by USS *Fort Jackson* June 1864. Acquired by US navy July 1864, renamed USS *Dumbarton*. [2, 3 & 4]

Hoby & Son
Yard: Renfrew East (1850–61)

Coquette   Subcontracted by Henderson & Coulborn, iron twin screw steamer, 3 masts, launched 1863
Dimensions: 228 ft × 25 ft × 12.2 ft
Tonnage: 395 registered
Engines: 2 × 200 NHP / 1 funnel / built by Henderson & Coulborn / 13.5 knots
History: Acquired by James D. Bulloch for the Confederate navy September 1863. Sailed from Cork early November 1863. Sold on to J.R. Anderson & Company (Tredegar Ironworks) July 1864. Made four runs into Wilmington and two into Charleston April 1863 – February 1865. Her captain seized her at Havana and carried her off to Baltimore December 1865. [2 & 3]

Matilda   Subcontracted by Henderson & Coulborn, iron twin screw steamer, launched 1863
Dimensions: 228 ft × 25 ft × 12.2 ft
Tonnage: 395 registered
Engines: built by Henderson & Coulborn – no data
History: Acquired by the Confederate navy September 1863. Ran aground and wrecked on Lundy Island in the Bristol Channel on way out April 1864. [2 & 3]

Kirkpatrick & McIntyre
Yard: Bay, Port Glasgow (1863–7)

Greyhound Iron single screw steamer, 3 masts, launched 1863
Dimensions: 201.4 ft × 22.7 ft × 13 ft
Tonnage: 372 gross registered / 290 registered
Engines: 2 oscillating / built by Cairds of Greenock
History: Owner R. Little. Made one run into Wilmington April 1864. Captured leaving Wilmington with Belle Boyd on board by USS *Connecticut* May 1864. [3 & 4]

Let Her Rip / Wando Iron screw steamer, launched 1864
Dimensions: 225.3 ft × 26.1 ft × 11.3 ft
Tonnage: 650 burthen
Engines: no data
History: Acquired by Henry Lafone for the Chicora Importing & Exporting Company of Charleston. Renamed *Wando* on arrival in Wilmington. Made two runs into Wilmington from Nassau July–October 1864. Captured leaving Wilmington by USS *Fort Jackson* October 1864. [2 & 3]

A. and J. Inglis
Yard: Pointhouse, Glasgow (1863–1962)

Helen Denny Iron paddle steamer, schooner-rigged, launched 1864
Dimensions: 212.8 ft × 25.2 ft × 12 ft
Tonnage: 254 registered
Engines: no data
History: Acquired by John R. Young for the Importing & Exporting Company of South Carolina. At Havana August 1864 but her draught was too deep to run the Gulf ports. Returned to Britain. [2 & 3]

Laurel / Confederate States Iron single screw steamer, schooner-rigged, launched September 1863
Dimensions: 185.9 ft × 25.2 ft × 12.5 ft
Tonnage: 565 gross registered / 269 registered
Engines: 2 × 140 NHP / 13 knots
History: Glasgow & Londonderry Steam Packet Company ferry. Sold by owners John Cameron and Lewis MacLellan of Glasgow to Henry Lafone of Lancaster, acting for James Bulloch CSN, late September 1864. Tender to the CSS *Shenandoah*. At Charleston

made one run in from Nassau for the Treasury Department December 1864. Survived the war [1, 2, 3 & 4]

J.G. Lawrie & Company
Yard: Park, Whiteinch (c.1854–75)

Georgiana Iron single screw auxiliary steamer, brig-rigged, December 1862
Dimensions: 205.6 ft × 25.3 ft × 14.9 ft
Tonnage: 242 registered
Engine: 1 × 120 NHP
History: Acquired by N. Matheson for the Navigation Company for conversion to armed cruiser. Run ashore entering Charleston on first run and destroyed by USS *Wissahickon* March 1863. [2 & 3]

McNab & Company
Yard: Westburn West, Greenock

Beatrice Iron paddle steamer, schooner-rigged, launched 1863
Dimensions: 191.5 ft × 23 ft × 9.4 ft
Tonnage: 324 gross registered / 200 registered
Engines: 2 × 150 NHP
History: Sold by owners David McNutt of Glasgow and John N. Sliddon of Liverpool to Edward J. Lomnitz of Manchester August 1864. Made one run into Wilmington October–November 1864. Ran aground entering Charleston and destroyed late November 1864. [1, 2 & 3]

Robert Napier & Sons
Yard: Govan East (1850–1900)

Dolphin Iron paddle steamer, launched 1844
Dimensions: 170.2 ft × 21.2 ft × 10.5 ft
Tonnage: 129 registered
Engines: no data
History: G. and J. Burns & Company of Glasgow. Acquired by William J. Grazebrook of Liverpool. Captured between Puerto Rico and St Thomas on her first run by USS *Wachusett* March 1863. [2 & 3]

Douglas / Margaret & Jessie Composite (wood on iron frame) paddle steamer, launched May 1858

Dimensions: 205 ft × 26 ft × 14 ft

Tonnage: 1,100 light displacement / 950 burthen / 726 gross registered

Engines: 2 × 100 NHP / oscillating (54 in × 5 ft) / 15 knots

History: Isle of Man Steam Packet Company. Acquired by Melchir G. Klingender for Fraser, Trenholm & Company November 1862. Renamed *Margaret & Jessie* at Charleston February 1863. Made five runs into Charleston and four into Wilmington December 1862 – November 1863. Captured by USS *Nansemond, Keystone State* and *Howquah* heading for New Inlet, Cape Fear River November 1863. Acquired by the US navy and renamed USS *Gettysburg* November 1863. [2, 3 & 4]

Dundalk / Georgiana McCaw   Iron paddle steamer, launched 1844

Dimensions: no data

Tonnage: 373 registered

Engines: no data

History: Acquired by Melchir G. Klingender. Destroyed by USS *Victoria* entering Old Inlet, Wilmington on first run June 1864. [2 & 3]

Neptune   Iron paddle steamer, launched 1861, re-rigged schooner January 1862

Dimensions: 166.6 ft × 27.4 ft × 9.5 ft

Tonnage: 260 burthen / 125 registered

Engines: 2 × 100 NHP

History: Owned by J.S. Napier and J. McIntyre of Glasgow. Sold to James H. Wilson acting for Fraser, Trenholm & Company December 1862. Made two runs into Mobile from Havana April–June 1863. Captured by USS *Lackawanna* heading for Mobile June 1863. Acquired by the US navy and renamed USS *Clyde* August 1863. [1, 2 & 3]

Neilsen & Company

Yard: Glasgow

Antona   Iron single screw steamer, launched July 1859

Dimensions: 166.9 ft × 23.1 ft × 13.7 ft

Tonnage: 549 burthen / 352 registered

Engine: 1 × vertical direct-acting (26 in × 2 ft 6 in) / 8 knots

History: Owned by William Sloan & Company of Glasgow. Acquired for the Navigation Company. Captured off Mobile on first run by USS *Pocahontas* January 1863. Acquired by the US navy retaining her name late March 1864. [2, 3 & 4]

Randolph & Elder
Yard: Fairfield (1863–70)

Condor Iron paddle steamer, launched July 1864
Dimensions: 221 ft × 28.2 ft × 9.5 ft
Tonnage: 446 gross registered / 284 registered
Engines: 2 × 180 NHP / 3 funnels / 16 knots
History: Acquired by Donald McGregor for Alexander Collie & Company. Ran aground on wreck of *Night Hawk* on Swash Channel of New Inlet, Wilmington on first run October 1864. [1, 2 & 3]

Evelyn Iron paddle steamer, launched August 1864
Dimensions: 221 ft × 28.2 ft × 9.5 ft
Tonnage: 446 gross registered / 284 registered
Engines: 2 × 180 NHP / 3 funnels / 16 knots
History: Acquired by Donald McGregor for Alexander Collie & Company. Registration transferred to Limerick. Made two runs into Wilmington from Halifax (December 1864) and later, after returning for repairs, Galveston from Havana April 1865. Survived the war. [1, 2 & 3]

Falcon Iron paddle steamer, launched 12 May 1864
Dimensions: 221 ft × 28.2 ft × 9.5 ft
Tonnage: 446 gross registered / 284 registered
Engines: 2 × 180 NHP / 3 funnels / 16 knots
History: Acquired by Donald McGregor for Alexander Collie & Company. Made two runs into Wilmington from Halifax and Nassau August–October 1864. Survived the war. Sold at Rio de Janeiro. [1, 2 & 3]

Flamingo Iron paddle steamer, launched May 1864
Dimensions: 221 ft × 28.2 ft × 9.5 ft
Tonnage: 446 gross registered / 284 registered
Engines: 2 × 180 NHP / 3 funnels / 16 knots
History: Acquired by Donald McGregor for Alexander Collie & Company. Left Clyde for Bermuda via the Azores July 1864. Made one run into Wilmington from Bermuda August 1864. Survived the war. Sold at Rio de Janeiro. [1, 2 & 3]

Ptarmigan Iron paddle steamer, launched June 1864
Dimensions: 221 ft × 28.2 ft × 9.5 ft

Tonnage: 446 gross registered / 284 registered
Engines: 2 × 180 NHP / 3 funnels / 16 knots
History: Acquired by Donald McGregor for Alexander Collie & Company. One run into Galveston from Havana December 1865. Survived the war. Sold at Havana. [1, 2 & 3]

John Reid & Company
Yards: East (1846–63) and Glen (1863–c.1885), Port Glasgow

Herald / Antonica   Iron paddle steamer, launched 1851
Dimensions: 222 ft × 22 ft × 14.5 ft
Tonnage: 450 burthen / 283 registered
Engines: no data
History: Dublin & Glasgow Sailing and Steam Packet Company ferry. Acquired by Charles Taylor for Fraser, Trenholm & Company late 1861. Sold on to the Chicora Importing & Exporting Company of Charleston and renamed *Antonica* September 1862. Made eight runs in Charleston and four into Wilmington March 1862 – December 1863. Ran aground entering Old Inlet, Wilmington and destroyed by USS *Governor Buckingham* December 1863. [2 & 3]

John Scott & Sons
Yards: Westburn East (1811–63) and Cartsdyke East (1851–1934) Greenock

Constance Decima / Constance   Wooden paddle steamer, schooner-rigged, launched 1863
Dimensions: 201.4 ft × 20.15 ft × 9.4 ft
Tonnage: 345 burthen / 254 gross registered / 164 registered
Engines: no data
History: Acquired by Duncan McGregor for Alexander Collie & Company. Henry Lafone of Lancaster December 1863. Sold on to Edward J. Lomnitz of Manchester. Ran aground off Long Island attempting to enter Charleston on first run October 1864. [2 & 3]

Elsie   Iron paddle steamer, launched 1864
Dimensions: 201.4 ft × 20.15 ft × 9.5 ft
Tonnage: 262 gross registered / 169 registered
Engines: no data
History: Acquired by Duncan McGregor for Alexander Collie & Company. Captured by USS *Keystone* and *Quaker City* coming out of Wilmington on first run September 1864. [2 & 3]

Flora (II)   Iron paddle steamer, launched 1858
Dimensions: 215 ft × 25.7 ft × 13.5 ft
Tonnage: 571 gross registered / 359 registered
Engines: no data
History: Owners Bristol General Steam Navigation Company. Acquired by W.S. Lindsay & Company. Made four runs into Wilmington from Bermuda August–December 1863. Foundered at sea while heading for Halifax from Bermuda for repairs January 1864 [1, 2 & 3]

Ivanhoe   Iron paddle steamer, launched April 1864
Dimensions: 201.4 ft × 20.15 ft × 9.5 ft
Tonnage: 358 burthen / 266 gross registered / 173 registered
Engines: 2
History: Ordered by William Boyle for Thomas S. Begbie's Albion Trading Company. Ran ashore near Fort Morgan in Mobile Bay on first run and later destroyed by uss *Glasgow* June 1864. [2 & 3]

Kenilworth   Iron paddle steamer, launched August 1864
Dimensions: 201.4 ft × 20.15 ft × 9.5 ft
Tonnage: 358 burthen / 266 gross registered / 173 registered
Engines: 2
History: Ordered by John Ross Young for Thomas S. Begbie's Albion Trading Company. Transferred to his Universal Trading Company. Attempted one run but forced back by bad weather. Survived the war. [2 & 3]

Marmion   Iron paddle steamer, launched August 1864
Dimensions: 201.4 ft × 20.15 ft × 9.5 ft
Tonnage: 358 burthen / 266 gross registered / 173 registered
Engines: 2
History: Ordered by John Ross Young for Thomas S. Begbie's Albion Trading Company. Transferred to his Universal Trading Company. Turned back from Wilmington December 1864. Survived the war. [2 & 3]

Redgauntlet   Iron paddle steamer, launched April 1864
Dimensions: 201.4 ft × 20.15 ft × 9.5 ft
Tonnage: 358 burthen / 266 gross registered / 173 registered
Engines: 2
History: Ordered by William Boyle for Thomas S. Begbie's Albion

Trading Company. Trapped in Mobile on first run and was acquired as a transport by Confederate army commander. Captured at Gainsville April 1865. [2 & 3]

Talisman   Iron paddle steamer, launched June 1864
Dimensions: 201.4 ft × 20.15 ft × 9.5 ft
Tonnage: 358 burthen / 266 gross registered / 173 registered
Engines: 2
History: Ordered by William Boyle for Thomas S. Begbie's Albion Trading Company. Transferred to his Universal Trading Company. Made three runs into Wilmington October–December 1864. Ran onto wreck of css *Raleigh* leaving New Inlet. Repaired but broke up at sea escaping Wilmington December 1864. [2 & 3]

William Simons & Company
Yard: Renfrew East (1861–1961)

Julia   Iron paddle steamer, schooner-rigged, launched 1863
Dimensions: 209.4 ft × 23.5 ft × 9.7 ft
Tonnage: 735 burthen / 117 registered
Engines: 2 × 180 NHP
History: Acquired by Henry Lafone of Lancaster December 1863. Ran into the Santee River, South Carolina December 1864. Sold on to Edward J. Lomnitz of Manchester. Ran aground in a gale in Bull's Bay after leaving Charleston on first run. Captured by uss *Acadia* December 1864. [2 & 3]

Little Ada   Iron screw steamer, launched July 1864
Dimensions: 112 ft × 18.5 ft × 10 ft
Tonnage: 208 burthen / 94 registered
Engines: no data
History: Acquired by Henry Lafone of Lancaster for the Importing & Exporting Company of Georgia. Ran into Santee River, South Carolina from Nassau and captured by Union forces for a short time March 1864. Captured off Cape Romain, South Carolina by uss *Gettysburg* July 1864. [2 & 3]

Mary Bowers   Iron paddle steamer, launch date unknown
Dimensions: 226 ft × 25 ft × 10.5 ft
Tonnage: 750 burthen / 220 registered
Engines: no data

History: Acquired by Henry Lafone of Lancaster for the Importing &
Exporting Company of Georgia September 1864. Made one run in
Wilmington from Bermuda July 1864. Ran onto the wreck of the
Georgiana entering Charleston harbour late August 1864. [2 & 3]

Rothesay Castle Iron paddle steamer, schooner-rigged, launched
1861
Dimensions: 191.5 ft × 19 ft × 8.3 ft
Tonnage: 85 registered
Engines: 2 × 110 NHP
History: Glasgow–Rothesay ferry. Sold by owner Alexander Watson
of Partickhill to David McNutt of Glasgow late June 1863. Sold on
to Robert Adger of South Carolina late August 1863. Made one run
into Wilmington and one into Charleston from Nassau December
1863 – April 1864. Survived the war and sold at Halifax. [1, 2 & 3]

Stormy Petrel Iron paddle steamer, schooner-rigged, launched 1864
Dimensions: 222.4 ft × 25 ft × 10.2 ft
Tonnage: 221 gross registered
Engines: 2 × 180 NHP
History: Acquired by John T. Lawrence of Liverpool for the Anglo-
Confederate Trading Company. Ran aground and wrecked entering
New Inlet, Wilmington on her first run December 1864. [1, 2 & 3]

Will o' the Wisp Iron paddle steamer, schooner-rigged, launched
1864
Dimensions: 209.5 ft × 23.2 ft × 9.7 ft
Tonnage: 117 gross registered
Engines: 2 × 180 NHP
History: Acquired by John T. Lawrence of Liverpool for the Anglo-
Confederate Trading Company. Sold on to Power, Low & Com-
pany October 1864. Made six runs into Wilmington from Nassau
April–September 1864. Ran aground and destroyed entering Gal-
veston February 1865. [1,2 & 3]

Alexander Stephen & Sons
Yard: Kelvinhaugh (1851–70)

Fergus / Presto Iron paddle steamer, 2 masts schooner-rigged,
launched 1863
Dimensions: 210 ft × 23 ft × 9.5 ft

Tonnage: 552 gross registered / 164 registered
Engines: 2 × 160 NHP
History: Owner M. Mathieson. As *Presto* made one successful run into Wilmington January 1864. Ran aground off Fort Moultrie at the entrance to Charleston on second attempt at entry. Destroyed by shellfire from Union fort on Morris Island February 1864. [2 & 3]

Sea King　Composite (wood on iron frame) auxiliary screw passenger and cargo steamer, ship-rigged, launched August 1863
Dimensions: 222 ft × 32 ft × 20.5 ft
Tonnage: 1152 gross registered
Engine: 1 × 2 cylinder direct acting (33 in × 4 ft) / 2 boilers / 9 knots
History: Owner Robertson & Company, Glasgow. Carried troops to New Zealand (Maori Wars). On her return from Bombay was acquired by James Bulloch for the Confederate navy. Met with munitions carrier *Laurel* at Desserta Island (Madeira) and commissioned as css *Shenandoah* October 1864. Decommissioned and eventually turned over to the English authorities at Liverpool November 1865. Purchased by the Sultan of Zanzibar. [2, 3 & 4]

The Dare　Iron paddle steamer, schooner-rigged, launched 1863
Dimensions: 211.7 ft × 23 ft × 9.4 ft
Tonnage: 311 gross registered / 179 registered
Engines: 2 × 160 NHP
History: Acquired by David McNutt for the Richmond Importing & Exporting Company October 1863. Ran ashore on first run heading for Wilmington and destroyed off Lockwood's Folly by uss *Aries* and *Montgomery* January 1864. [1, 2 & 3]

James and George Thomson
Yard: Clyde Bank, Govan (1850–72)

Adela　Iron paddle steamer, brig-rigged, launched 1859
Dimensions: 211 ft × 23.5 ft × 12 ft
Tonnage: 585 burthen / 398 gross registered / 175 registered
Engines: 2 oscillating (52.5 in × 4 ft 6 in) / 4 boilers / 12 knots
History: Owned by the Malcolmson Brothers of the Ardrossan Steam Navigation Company. Captured off Bahamas by uss *Quaker City* and *Huntsville* on first run 7 July 1862. Acquired by US navy, retained her name 23 May 1863. [2, 3 & 4]

Canton / Pampero Iron single screw auxiliary steamer, brig-rigged, launched October 1863
Dimensions: 230 ft × 33.2 ft × 19.8 ft
Tonnage: 2,090 displacement
Engine: 1 × 330 NHP 2 cylinder horizontal backward acting (56 in × 2 ft 6 in) built by John Scott's Greenock Foundry / 4 boilers / 13 knots
History: Ordered by a consortium acting for George T. Sinclair CSN. Seized by the British government before she could sail December 1863. Sold to the Chilean navy after the war. [2, 3 & 4]

Emma Henry Iron paddle steamer, schooner-rigged, launched March 1864
Dimensions: 211 ft × 28.2 ft × 9.9 ft
Tonnage: 242 registered
Engines: 2 × 150 NHP
History: Acquired by Henry Lafone of Lancaster for the Importing & Exporting Company of Georgia September 1864. Made one run into Wilmington November 1864. Captured leaving Wilmington by USS *Cherokee* early December 1864. [1, 2 & 3]

Fairy Iron paddle steamer, launched 1861
Dimensions: 149.4 ft × 21 ft × 6.9 ft
Tonnage: 200 burthen
Engines: no data
History: Known to have operated between Havana and Matamoras. Survived the war and sold at Montevideo. [2 & 3]

Fingal Iron single screw steamer with retractable propeller, snow-rigged, launched May 1861
Dimensions: 185.5 ft × 25.4 ft × 12.9 ft
Tonnage: 352 registered
Engines: 2 × 120 NHP / direct acting (39 in × 2 ft 6 in)
History: Sold by owners David and Alexander Hutchison and David MacBrayne to John Low acting for James D. Bulloch of the Confederate navy September 1861. Made one run into Savannah November 1861. Converted to ironclad CSS *Atalanta*. Captured in Wassaw Sound by USS *Nanhant* and *Weehawken* June 1863. Acquired by US navy retaining name. [1, 2, 3 & 4]

Havelock Iron paddle steamer, launched May 1858
Dimensions: 223.2 ft × 26.2 ft × 14.3 ft

Tonnage: 629 gross registered / 339 registered
Engines: no data
History: Dublin & Glasgow Sailing and Steam Packet Company ferry. Acquired by Archibald Wilson for the Chicora Importing & Exporting Company of Charleston. Renamed *General Beauregard*. Made three runs into Charleston and five into Wilmington February–December 1863. Ran ashore in New Inlet, Cape Fear River and destroyed by USS *Howquah* December 1863. [2 & 3]

Giraffe / Robert E. Lee   Iron paddle steamer, launched May 1860
Dimensions: 270.2 ft × 26.1 ft × 13 ft
Tonnage: 900 burthen / 677 gross registered / 360 registered
Engines: 2 × 90 NHP / oscillating (56 in × 3 ft) / 6 boilers / 11 knots
History: Sold by owners John and James C. Burns and Charles McIver to John Williams of Liverpool October 1862. Sold on to Edward Pembroke of London early November 1862. Acquired by the government of the Confederacy and renamed *Robert E. Lee* on arrival late December 1862. Made seven runs into Wilmington from Bermuda and Nassau February–October 1863. Captured off North Carolina coast by USS *James Adger* November 1863. Acquired by US navy January 1864, renamed USS *Fort Donelson*. Eventually acquired by the Chilean navy. [1, 2, 3 & 4]

Iona (I)   Iron paddle steamer, launched March 1855
Dimensions: 225.2 ft × 20.4 ft × 9 ft
Tonnage: 325 gross registered / 174 registered
Engines: no data
History: Owners David Hutchison & Company of Glasgow. Acquired by George Wigg for the Navigation Company. Collided with steamer *Chanticleer* and sank while departing from the Clyde October 1862. [2 & 3]

Iona (II)   Iron paddle steamer, launched 1863
Dimensions: 249 ft × 25 ft × 9.5 ft
Tonnage: 325 gross registered / 168 registered
Engines: 2 × 180 NHP
History: Acquired by David McNutt for Charles H. Bostier of Richmond January 1864. Foundered off Lundy Island in the Bristol Channel en route to Nassau February 1864. [1, 2 & 3]

Lilian   Iron paddle steamer, schooner-rigged, launched March 1864
Dimensions: 226 ft × 26.1 ft × 10.6 ft

Tonnage: 630 burthen / 246 gross registered

Engines: 2 × 180 NHP / oscillating (50 in × 4 ft 4 in) / 4 boilers / 14 knots

History: Acquired by Henry Lafone of Lancaster for the Importing & Exporting Company of Georgia late April 1864. Made two runs into Wilmington June–July 1864. Captured leaving Wilmington by USS *Keystone State* and *Gettysburg* late August 1864. Acquired by US navy September 1864, retained her name. Eventually acquired by the Spanish navy. [1, 2, 3 & 4]

Little Hattie   Iron paddle steamer, schooner-rigged, launched March 1864

Dimensions: 226 ft × 26.1 ft × 10.6 ft

Tonnage: 246 gross registered

Engines: 2 × 180 NHP / oscillating

History: Acquired by Henry Lafone of Lancaster for the Importing & Exporting Company of Georgia May 1864. Made four runs into Wilmington from Halifax and Nassau August–December 1864. One run into Charleston January–February 1865. At Havana February 1865. Survived the war and sold at Rio de Janeiro. [1, 2 & 3]

Venus   Iron paddle steamer, launched June 1852

Dimensions: 159.2 ft × 17.1 ft × 8.7 ft

Tonnage: 178 gross registered

Engines: no data

History: Allan & Company, later Largs Steamboat Company. Acquired for Crenshaw, Collie & Company. Made three runs into Wilmington from Bermuda June–October 1863. Ran ashore entering New Inlet, Cape Fear River and destroyed by USS *Nansemond* October 1863. [2 & 3]

Wild Rover   Iron paddle steamer, schooner-rigged, launched March 1864

Dimensions: 226 ft × 26 ft × 10.5 ft

Tonnage: 246 registered

Engines: 2 × 180 NHP

History: Owner Harry Lafone of Lancaster. Acquired by John T. Lawrence for the Anglo-Confederate Trading Company July 1864. Made four runs into Wilmington from Bermuda and Nassau September 1864 – January 1865. Survived the war and sold at Rio de Janeiro. [1, 2 & 3]

Tod & McGregor
Yard: Meadowside, Partick (1847–73)

Alliance Twin-hulled iron paddle steamer, launched 1856, extensive rebuild 1863
Dimensions: 140 ft × 30 ft × 7 ft
Tonnage: 324 burthen / 85 registered
Engines: 2 × 85 NHP / geared
History: Owned by George Mills of Glasgow. Acquired by William J. Grazebrook of Liverpool December 1862. Ran aground off Daufuskie Island while heading for Savannah on first run and captured by USS *South Carolina*. Acquired by the US Quartermaster Department. [1, 2 & 3]

Blenheim Iron paddle steamer, launched 1848
Dimensions: 208 ft × 26 ft × 15.5 ft
Tonnage: 651 burthen / 320 registered
Engines: 2 × 400 NHP
History: Dublin & Belfast Steamship Company. Sold to Richard Eustice of Penryn, Cornwall. Made two runs into Wilmington October–December 1864. Captured entering Wilmington by USS *Tristram Shandy* January 1865. [1, 2 & 3]

Caledonia Iron paddle steamer, launched 1856
Dimensions: 163 ft × 18.5 ft × 19.5 ft
Tonnage: 276 burthen / 177 registered
Engines: 90 NHP / 2 geared
History: Glasgow & Stranraer Steampacket Company ferry. Made one successful run into Wilmington February 1864. Captured heading for Wilmington by USS *Keystone* and *Massachusetts* May 1864. [2 & 3]

Juno (I) / Helen Iron paddle steamer, launched July 1860
Dimensions: 189.5 ft × 19 ft × 8,25 ft
Tonnage: 341 burthen / 170 registered
Engine: 1 × 110 NHP / horizontal geared / 1 funnel
History: Glasgow–Largs ferry. Owners John Cameron, Duncan and Alexander McKellar sold to George Wigg of Nassau. Made one run into Charleston June 1863. Compulsory purchase by Confederate government, renamed *Helen* and deployed as gunboat in Charleston harbour December 1863. Lost in gale escaping from Charleston March 1864. [1, 2 & 3]

Jupiter (I) Iron paddle steamer, launched July 1856
Dimensions: 173.5 ft × 18.3 ft × 8.5 ft
Tonnage: 170 registered
Engine: 2 × 90 NHP / geared
History: Glasgow–Largs ferry. Owners J. Reid, Duncan and Alexander McKellar sold on. Captured by USS *Cimarron* in Wassaw Sound, Georgia on her first run September 1863. [2 & 3]

Kelpie Iron paddle steamer, launched 1857
Dimensions: 191 ft × 18 ft × 7.75 ft
Tonnage: 307 burthen / 165 gross registered / 81 registered
Engine: 2 × 100 NHP / steeple
History: Glasgow–Rothesay ferry. Owner Peter McGregor sold on. Sunk entering Nassau harbour December 1862. [2 & 3]

Mail / Susanna Iron paddle steamer, launched 1860
Dimensions: 180 ft × 18 ft × 7.75 ft
Tonnage: 291 burthen / 100 registered
Engines: 2 × 85 NHP / oscillating
History: Glasgow–Kilmure ferry. Sold by owners John, Alexander and Robert Campbell to Samuel H. Bigland of Essex, May 1863. Captured off Bayport, Florida on first run by USS *Honduras* October 1863. Sold as prize and returned to running early 1864 under name *Susanna*. Captured for second time by USS *Metacomet* leaving Galveston, November 1864. [1, 2 & 3]

Princess Royal Iron screw steamer, launched June 1861
Dimensions: 200 ft × 28 ft × 15 ft
Tonnage: 758 burthen / 494 registered
Engines: 2 × 170 NHP / horizontal geared steeple / 49 in × 3 ft 3 in / 2 boilers / 11 knots
History: Glasgow–Liverpool packet. Sold by owners Matthew Langland and Alexander Drysdale of Glasgow to Julius F. Sichell of Manchester, November 1862. Captured entering Charleston on her first run by USS *Unadilla* January 1863. Purchased from prize court March 1863 and taken into US navy, retained name. [1, 2 & 3]

Scotia II Iron paddle steamer, launched 1845
Dimensions: 141.3 ft × 17.5 ft × 8.7 ft
Tonnage: 165 burthen / 82 registered
Engines: 2 × 95 NHP

History: Ayr–Stranraer ferry. Acquired by Otto H. Kaselack. Made three runs into Wilmington October–March 1864. Captured leaving Wilmington by USS *Connecticut* March 1864. [2 & 3]

Spunkie   Iron paddle steamer, launched 1857
Dimensions: 191 ft × 18 ft × 7.75 ft
Tonnage: 307 burthen / 165 gross registered / 81 registered
Engines: 2 × 100 NHP / steeple Denny & Sons
History: Glasgow–Rothesay ferry. Sold by owner Peter McGregor of Glasgow to Peter Denny of Dumbarton. Sold on to Edward J. Lomnitz of Manchester. Made four runs into Wilmington September 1863 – February 1864. Sunk entering Old Inlet, Wilmington, February 1864. [1, 2 & 3]

Star   Iron paddle steamer, launched 1849
Dimensions: 150 ft × 18.5 ft × 8.5 ft
Tonnage: 185 burthen / 100 registered
Engines: 2 × 100 NHP
History: Henderson & McKellar Line, Glasgow–Millport ferry. Made one run into Wilmington December 1863. Burst boiler at Nassau December 1864 and retired from running. Spent remainder of war as inter-island ferry. [2 & 3]

T. Wingate & Company
Yard: East Whiteinch (1848–78)

Armstrong   Iron paddle steamer, launched 1864
Dimensions: 232 ft × 26 ft × 10 ft
Tonnage: 214 registered
Engines: no data
History: Sold by owner James Cameron to Crenshaw & Company August 1864. Made three runs into Wilmington October–December 1864. Captured leaving Old Inlet, Wilmington by USS *R.R. Cuyler*, *Gettysburg*, *Mackinaw* and *Montgomery* December 1864. [1, 2 & 3]

Florie   Iron paddle steamer, schooner-rigged, launched 1863
Dimensions: 222.4 ft × 23.5 ft × 9.6 ft
Tonnage: 349 gross / 215 registered
Engines: 2 × 160 NHP

History: Sold by owner Henry Lafone of Lancaster to Importing & Exporting Company of Georgia. Made three runs into Wilmington from Bermuda. Commandeered by Confederate navy for the Point Lookout Expedition August 1864. Ran aground and wrecked in Cape Fear River, Wilmington October 1864. [3]

Who's Who in Blockade Running

Confederates in America

Gorgas, Josiah: Colonel (later Brigadier-General) CSN. Head of the Ordnance Bureau

Heyliger, Louis: New Orleans businessman. Confederate agent in Nassau

Lamb, William: Colonel CSA. Commander of Fort Fisher

Lee, Robert E.: General of the Army of North Virginia

Mallory, Stephen R.: Secretary to the Navy

Memminger, Christopher: Secretary to the Treasury

Seddon, James A.: Secretary of War

Trenholm, George A.: Principal partner in Fraser & Co. of Charleston and Fraser, Trenholm & Co. of Liverpool. Later Secretary to the Treasury

Walker, Norman S.: Major CSA. Procurement agent in Bermuda

Confederates in Britain and Europe

Barron, Samuel: Flag Officer and Bulloch's replacement in Liverpool as chief procurement agent for the Navy Department

Beach, J.N.: American blockade-running speculator based in UK

Bold, Thomas: Cousin to Matthew F. Maury and partner in Jones & Company of Liverpool. Purchased *Virginian* on behalf of Maury

Bulloch, James D.: Commander CSN. One-time officer in the US navy. Commander in the CSN. Principal procurement agent in Europe for the Navy Department

Carlin, James: Northern Irish-born captain of a blockade runner. Procurement agent for Importing & Exporting Company of South Carolina

Coxetter, Louis M.: Charleston resident of Dutch extraction. Captain of blockade runners *Herald (Antonica)* and *Fannie & Jennie*

Crenshaw, William G.: Major CSA. Richmond merchant, artillery officer and procurement agent in UK for the Bureau of Commissary and Supplies

Crossan, Thomas: Procurement agent for the State of North Carolina

Ficklin, Benjamin: Major CSA. Agent for Memminger in procurement of engraving machinery, presses and engineers and their transport on the *Giraffe*

Huse, Caleb: Major CSA. Principal armaments procurement agent in Europe

Jansen, Martin N.: Dutch naval officer and Confederate sympathiser who conducted search in Clyde for a suitable 'CB' vessel for procurement by Matthew F. Maury

Low, John: Lieutenant CSN. Secretary to Bulloch in Liverpool

McRae, Colin J.: General CSA. Superintendent of Confederate Finances in Europe

Maffitt, John N.: Captain (later Commander) CSN. Master of CSS *Florida*. Later master of blockade runners *Lilian* and *Owl*

Mason, James: Commissioner to Europe. London-based and temporarily detained during the *Trent* incident

Maury, Matthew F.: Commander CSN. Oceanographer, procurer and commander of CSS *Georgia* (formerly *Virginian*)

Maury, William L.: Cousin of Matthew F. Maury, recruited by him to assist Jansen in procurement of Clyde-built CSS *Georgia*

North, James H.: Lieutenant (later Captain) CSN. Naval agent in charge of Glasgow ram project

Pegram, Robert: Captain CSN of *Nashville*

Pembroke, Edward: London-based businessman, speculator and Southern sympathiser

Prioleau, Charles K.: chairman of Trenholm & Company

Semmes, Raphael: Commander of CSS *Sumter* and CSS *Alabama*

Sinclair, George T: Lieutenant CSN. Naval agent in charge of *Pampero* cruiser project. Later blockade-running master

Slidell, John: Commissioner to Europe, Paris-based and temporarily detained during the *Trent* incident

Taylor, Thomas E.: Notable blockade-running captain known to have been in Scotland and author of memoirs

Waddell, James I.: Commander CSN. Master of CSS *Shenandoah*

White, John: Procurement agent for the State of North Carolina

Wilkinson, John: Lieutenant (later Lieutenant-Commander) CSN. Captain of the blockade-runner *Giraffe (Robert E. Lee)* and author of memoirs

Federals in America

Chase, Salmon P.: Federal Secretary of the Treasury

Du Pont, Samuel: Flag Officer (later Rear Admiral) USN. Chairman of the Strategy Planning Board

Farragut, David G.: Flag Officer (Later Rear Admiral) USN. Commander of the Gulf Blockading Squadron

Fox, Gustavus V.: Assistant Secretary to the Navy

Porter, David D.: Rear Admiral USN. Commander of North Atlantic Blockading Squadron

Seward, William H.: Secretary for Foreign Affairs

Trenchard, Stephen D.: Captain USN of USS *Rhode Island*, who caused an international incident when chasing *Margaret & Jessie* into Bermuda waters

Welles, Gideon: Secretary to the Navy

Whiting, Samuel: US consul in Nassau

Wilkes, Charles: Captain (later Commander) USN. Master of USS *San Jacinto* of 'Trent' incident' fame

Federals in Britain and Europe

Adams, Charles F.: Minister and Head of the US Legation in London

Craven, Tunis A.N.: Captain (later Commander) USN. Master of USS *Tuscarora*

Dayton, William L.: US ambassador in Paris

Dudley, Thomas H.: US consul in Liverpool

Eastman, Edward G.: US consul in Cork

Moran, Benjamin: Secretary to the US Legation in London

Morse, Freeman H,: US consul general in London

Prettyman, John S.: US consul in Glasgow, replaced by Underwood

Sanford, Henry S.: Chief of Federal Secret Service in Europe, based in Belgium

Underwood, Warner L.: US consul in Glasgow, replaced Prettyman

Clyde-connected Agents, Shipbuilders, Captains and Owners

Begbie, Thomas S.: London-based shipowner and broker. Correspondent with John Scott. Managing director of Albion Trading Company and Universal Trading Company and active in procuring Clyde steamers for the blockade

Burroughs, John: Captain of the blockade runners *Cornubia* and *North Heath*

Butcher, Matthew J.: Bulloch's most trusted British captain, captain of *Enrica* (later css *Alabama*)

Collie, Alexander: Manchester businessman and speculator. Southern sympathiser and active in procuring Clyde steamers for the blockade

Denny, Archibald: Brother to Peter Denny, Dumbarton shipbuilder and speculator

Denny, Peter: Dumbarton shipbuilder, owner and speculator

Galbraith, James: Glasgow businessman and speculator. Southern sympathiser and active in procuring Clyde steamers for the blockade

Gilpin, Thomas S.: Captain of blockade runners *Minnie* and *Talisman*

Halpin, R.C.: Captain of blockade runners *Eugenie* and *Emily*

Lafone, Henry: Lancaster businessman and speculator. Southern sympathiser and active in procuring Clyde steamers for the blockade

Leslie, David: Captain of blockade runners *Columbia*, *Helen* and *Emma*

Lomnitz, Edward J.: Manchester-based businessman and speculator, Southern sympathiser and active in procuring Clyde steamers for the blockade

Lumsden, James: Glasgow entrepreneur and speculator. Later lord provost of Glasgow

Mack: Possibly Peter McLellan, the sea-going draughtsman working for John Scott of Greenock. Author of memoirs

McNutt, David: Partner in the Glasgow firm McLeash and McNutt. Southern sympathiser and active in procuring Clyde steamers for the blockade

Roberts, A.: Real name Augustus Charles Hobart-Hampden RN, veteran blockade-running captain. Put Begbie's *Talisman* through her sea trials. Later master of blockade runner *Condor*

Scott, John: Greenock shipbuilder and speculator. Correspondent with Begbie

Sprunt, John: Glasgow-born commentator. Purser on blockade runners *North Heath*, *Lilian* and *Susan O'Beirne*

Watson, William: Scots captain of *Eagle* /*Jeanette* and author of memoirs

Wilson, William: Scots captain of blockade runner of *Emily St Pierre*, declared pirate by the North and hero of the South. Later master of runner *Margaret & Jessie*

Wigg, George: Liverpool businessman and speculator. Southern sympathiser and active in procuring Clyde steamers for the blockade. Also residing in Nassau at one stage

British Ministers and Officials

Bench, John: British consul in Charleston and Confederate sympathiser
Gladstone, William E.: Chancellor of the Exchequer
Lyon, Lord Richard: British ambassador to Washington
Palmerston, Lord Henry T.: Prime Minister
Russell, Lord John: Foreign Secretary

Appendix 8
A Guide to Sources

I have aimed to write this book in a style that would appeal to a broad spectrum of readers, many of whom may find footnotes a distraction from the narrative.

The technical data on and history of a specific 'CB' blockade-running vessel have been compiled and cross-referenced from a number of sources. Where these sources are contradictory, I have made assumptions on the most accurate source (e.g. preferring the shipyard's registers to the American prize court's data). These references are listed in the List of Vessels (Appendix 6) above.

Much of the data from the various registers and also the extracts from newspapers, memoirs and correspondence quoted in the text are now readily available on dedicated websites. In many cases these sites provide the only viable opportunity for a reader interested in referring to the original documents. The most informative websites are listed below.

Where new primary material is used which is neither available on a website nor previously published (such as Clydeside newspapers and Thomas Begbie's letters to John Scott), the date of publication or sending has been included in the text for ready identification. I have provided a guide to the archives holding these sources.

Websites

The best starting point is, arguably, the US Department of the Navy's own *Naval Historical Center* which has case files on those 'CB' runners which were acquired by the US navy. It also has links to other highly reputable and useful sites.
Website: www.history.navy.mil.com

The *HistoryCentral.Com* site has numerous relevant pages, of which the monthly report on naval activity and the blockade during the war

is a valuable source for those researching the course of war and the fate of individual runners.
Website: www.historycentral.com/Navy/cwnavalhistory

Cornell University's *Making of America* site abounds with digitised illustrations and key documents. This book has made extensive use of the entire first series of the *Official Records of the Union and Confederate Navies in the War of the Rebellion* (Washington, 1900) which contains dispatches from the blockading squadrons and diplomatic notes.
Website:
http://cdl.library.cornell.edu/moa/browse.monographs/ofre.html

Much information pertaining to marine archaeology of the war and the surveys of the wrecks of the 'CB' *Will o' the Wisp* and *Wild Rover* is available on Wideopenwest.com. It also has images of the complete printed memoirs of the running captains Taylor and Wilkinson.
Website:
http://www.wideopenwest.com/~jenkins/ironclads/ironclad.html

Scottish Newspapers

The *Scotsman* for the entire period is now available (for a small fee) online.
Website: http://www.archive.scotsman.com/

The other Edinburgh newspapers are held on microfilm by:
The Edinburgh Room
Edinburgh Central Library
King George IV Bridge
Edinburgh
EH1 1EG
Email: edinburgh.room@edinburgh.gov.uk

Glasgow newspapers are held by:
Archives and Special Collections
The Mitchell Library
North Street
Glasgow
G3 7DN
Email: archives@cls.glasgow.gov.uk

Dumbarton newspapers are held by:
West Dunbartonshire Libraries, Information Section
Dumbarton Library
Strathleven Place
Dumbarton
G82 1BD
Email: dumbarton.local.history@west-dunbarton.gov.uk

Greenock newspapers are held by:
The Watt Library
Union Street
Greenock
PA16 8JH
Email: library.watt@inverclyde.gov.uk

Clyde Shipbuilders' Records
Basic lists of vessels launched are searchable on:
Website: http//:www.clydesite.co.uk/clydebuilt

The *Clyde Shipbuilders' Business Records* are listed on:
Website: http//:www.archives.gla.ac.uk

Please note that the Thomas Begbie letters to John Scott are grouped
by year (last two digits), e.g.: GD 319/12/10/[18]63.
Email: dutyarch@archives.gla.ac.uk

Selected Bibliography

Manuscripts
Glasgow City Archives, Mitchell Library
Customs & Excise (CE 59 and 60 series)
Poor Relief (D-Hew 10/3/78 and 17/180/1)

Glasgow University Archives
Clyde Shipbuilders' Business Records (UGD series 1, 3, 4, 114, 136, 141, 239 & 319)
Lumsden of Arden Collection (DC112)

Public Record Office, London
Foreign Office (5 series)

South Carolina Historical Society
William Bee & Company (Importing & Exporting Company of Charleston) Papers

Primary Printed

Newspapers

Aberdeen Journal
Army & Navy Gazette
Caledonian Mercury
Cork Examiner
Dumbarton Herald
Dumfries & Galloway Review
Edinburgh Evening Courant
Glasgow Citizen
Glasgow Examiner
Glasgow Gazette
Glasgow Herald
Glasgow Sentinel
Greenock Advertiser

Greenock Telegraph
Harper's Weekly (American)
Illustrated London News
Irish Times
Morning Journal (Glasgow)
New York Herald
Paisley Herald & Renfrew Advertiser
Scotsman (Edinburgh)
Times (London)

Secondary Printed

Pamphlets and Articles

Anon., 'Rothesay Castle', *Clyde River Steamer Club*, 3 (1967). pp. 32–3

Bowman, I., 'Alliance', *Clyde River Steamer Club*, 21 (1985), pp. 27–35

Carnduff, J., 'The Rebel Skipper', *Scottish Memories* (May 2002)

Fraser, K.C. and F.G. MacHaffie, 'A Highland Steamer at War', *Clyde River Steamer Club*, 22 (1988), pp. 22–7

Kerr, D.C., 'McKellar's Boats', *Scottish Local History*, 53 (2001), pp. 18–24

MacHaffie, F.G., 'The Tale of the Giraffe', *Clyde River Steamer Club*, 17 (1981), pp. 12–20

Noirsain, S., *C.H.A.B. News Quarterly* (Confederate Historical Association of Belgium) (March and September 1999)

Peters, L., 'The Impact of the American Civil War upon the Scottish Borders Woollen Industry', *Scottish Local History* (Spring 2001), pp. 28–33

Price, M.W., 'Ships that Tested the Blockade of the Carolina Ports, 1861–1865', *American Neptune*, 8 (July 1948), pp. 196–237

Slaven, A. and S. Checkland (eds), *Dictionary of Scottish Business Biography*, vol. 1 (Aberdeen, 1986)

Sullivan, D., 'Phantom Fleet: The Confederacy's Unclaimed European-built Warships', *War International*, 1 (1987)

Wilbraham, K.P., 'Sir James Lumsden of Arden and the American Civil War', *Scottish Industrial History*, 16 (1993), pp. 21–30

Books

Anon., *Experiences of Mack, by Himself* (London, 1906)

Bemis, S.F., *The American Secretaries of State and their Diplomacy* (New York, 1958)

Bernath, S.L., *Squall Across the Atlantic* (Berkeley, 1970)

Bulloch, J.D., *The Secret Service of the Confederate States in Europe* (New York, 1959), vols 1 and 2

Duckworth, C.L.D. and G.E. Langmuir, *Clyde and other Coastal Steamers* 2nd edn (Prescot, 1977)

Hearn, C.G., *Gray Raiders of the Sea* (Shrewsbury, 1992)

Hobart-Hampden, A.C., *Never Caught: Personal Adventures connected with Twelve Successful Trips in Blockade-Running during the American Civil War, 1863–4 by Captain Roberts* (London, 1867)

Konstam, A., *Confederate Blockade Runner 1861–65* (Oxford, 2004)

Lyon, D.J., *The Denny Lists*, vols 1 and 2 (London, 1975–6)

McQueen, A., *Echoes of Clyde Paddle Wheels* (Glasgow, 1924)

Melti, F.J., *Great Britain and the Confederate Navy 1861–65* (Indianapolis, 1970).

Morgan, J.M., *Recollections of a Rebel Reefer* (London, 1918)

Nepveux, E.T.S., *George A. Trenholm: Financial Genius of the Confederacy* (South Carolina, 1999)

Silverstone, P.H., *Civil War Navies 1855–1883* (Annapolis, 2001)

Sprunt, J., *Derelicts* (Wilmington, 1920)

Stark, F.R., *The Abolition of Privateering and the Declaration of Paris* (New York, 1877)

Taylor, T.E., *Running the Blockade: A Personal Narrative of Adventures, Risks and Escapes during the American Civil War* (London, 1896)

Warneford, R., *Running the Blockade* (London, 1863)

Watson, W., *Adventures of a Blockade Runner* (London, 1892)

Wilkinson, J.T., *The Narrative of a Blockade Runner* (New York, 1877)

Wise, S.R., *Lifeline of the Confederacy: Blockade Running during the Civil War* (Columbia, 1988)

Vandiver, F.E., *Confederate Blockade Running through Bermuda* (Austin, 1947)

Verne, J., *The Blockade Runners* (London, 1876)

Index

Aberdeen 3, 85, 225, 226
Adair, W. F. 46–7
Adams, Charles F. 16–17, 24–6, 30–1, 37, 96, 127–30, 135–43, 149–50, 154, 163, 172, 218
Adderley & Co. 127
Adela 47, 78, 138, 208
Adelphi Hotel, Liverpool 134
Admiralty Prize Court US 26
Advance, see *Lord Clyde*
Adventure 165, 191
Agnes E. Fry 190
Agrippina 130
Aiken & Mansel 122, 159, 166, 185
Ajax 153, 165, 191
Alabama 12
Alabama 128–30, 131, 133, 135, 136, 138, 143, 155, 171, 217, 219
Alar 135–6
Albion Trading Company 5, 71, 86–97, 114, 187, 188, 205, 206, 218
Alexander Stephen & Sons 153, 164, 207
Alexandra CSS 130, 135, 136, 139, 140, 150, 153
Alfred/Old Dominion 188
Alison, Sir Archibald 141, 147, 148, 149
Alliance 121–122, 170, 212, 226
Amazona 165
Amelia 47
American flag 163–4
American Review 10
Anderson, Edward C. 32, 33, 34, 35
Anderson, John 31
Anglo-Confederate Trading Company 100, 144, 159, 184, 186, 207, 211
Annie Childs 37, 126
Antietam 77, 137
Anti-slavery societies 162–164, 174–175
Antona 47, 202
Antonica, see *Herald*
Antrim 113
Antwerp 72
Arago, USS 84, 187
Arden estate, Loch Lomond 168
Ardencaple Castle 71, 85
Ardmillan, Lord 150
Ardrossan 167, 208

Argyllshire 113
Arima 164
Armaments 16, 21, 30, 34, 42, 44, 50, 56, 74, 83, 102, 127, 128, 133, 135, 137, 151, 154, 155, 157, 165, 172, 217
Armstrong 214
Armstrong cannon 104
Army & Navy Gazette 58, 225
Arnot, Sir John 66
Arran 48, 80, 109, 119
Arthur, James 113
Ash, James & Co. 83, 86, 87, 88
Atkinson, T. 67, 68
Atlanta 64, 179
Atlanta, CSS & USS/*Fingal* 28–39, 41, 43, 45, 50, 110, 125, 126, 129, 130, 132, 133, 156, 157, 209
Atrato 49, 158
Ayrshire 158, 162, 167, 214
Azores 32, 126, 130, 203

Bahama 127–128, 129, 130,
Bahamas (see also Nassau) 1, 3, 4, 7, 12, 13, 22, 24, 26, 32, 33, 38, 41, 42, 43, 44, 46, 47, 49, 50, 53, 54, 56, 57, 58, 61, 64, 67, 74, 75, 75, 76, 78, 79, 81, 82, 84, 86, 87, 88, 96, 97, 98, 99, 100, 107, 110, 111, 112, 113, 114, 116, 120, 122, 127, 128, 129, 130, 138, 146, 153, 159, 176–178, 185, 187, 188, 189, 190, 191, 192, 193, 194, 195, 197, 198, 200, 201, 203, 206, 207, 208, 210, 211, 212, 213, 214, 216, 218, 220
Banavie, Fort William 84, 121
Banshee II 100, 159, 185
Bar, John McQ. 141
Barclay, Curle & Co. 78, 83, 87, 186
Barony, Lanark 71
Barracouta 156
Barron, Samuel 139, 147, 150, 154, 216
Batavia (Indonesia) 156
Baton Rouge Volunteers 159
Beach, J.N. 89, 216
Beatrice 116, 177, 201
Beaufort 5
Beauregard, Pierre G.T. 11, 36
Bee, William see Charleston Importing & Exporting Co.

Beecher, Henry W.   162
Begbie, Thomas S.   5, 23–25, 64, 68, 71–102,
    105, 111, 114, 116, 118–20, 123, 131, 137,
    151, 158–9, 161, 164, 168–9, 176–8, 187–9,
    191–2, 196–7, 205–6, 218–9, 221, 223
Belfast   47–9, 63, 106, 113, 150,
Belfast Steamship Co.   68, 212
Bench, John   17, 220
Bermuda   10, 25, 74–6, 127
Bermuda (also St George)   1, 3–5, 7, 10,
    12–3, 24, 26, 32, 34, 38, 42, 44–7, 53–4,
    56–7, 59, 61, 64, 70, 76–83, 86–91, 95–99,
    107, 110, 113, 115, 120, 127, 129, 159,
    171, 173, 185–6, 188–90, 193–7, 199, 203,
    205, 207, 210–1, 215–6, 218
Betts, John   190
Betts, Samuel   81
Birkenhead   119, 128, 131, 136, 140
Black Joke   124
Black Prince, HMS   102, 132
Blackburn Ironworks   74
Blackwood & Gordon   188–9
Blairgowrie   140
Blenheim   68, 212
Blockade Strategy Board   27, 218
Board of Trade   111
Bold, Thomas   135, 195, 216
Boston   24, 170
Bourne, John T.   44, 56, 90–1
Bouverie, E.P.   152
Bowling Dock   149
Boyle, John   113
Bramley Moor Docks   53
Bravary Co.   139
Brazil   100, 155, 165–6, 171
Brazil   165
Brennan, Edward   30
Brewer, H.O. & Co.   89
Bridge of Allan   50, 134, 138
Bristol   73
Bristol General Steam Navigation Co.   191,
    194, 205
Britannia   47, 169, 186
Brodick   109
Brooklyn Docks   76, 170
Brooks, John   163
Broomielaw   12, 28–9, 48, 52, 108–9, 144,
    146
Brown, Joseph   62–3
Buenos Aires   166, 186
Bulloch, James D.   19, 29–38, 41, 45, 59, 63,
    72, 92, 96, 125–36, 139–41, 147–8, 150,
    153–6, 165, 169, 191, 194, 199–200,
    208–9, 216–7, 219
Bureau of Commissary & Quartermaster
    CSA   59, 62, 88, 217
Bureau of Foreign Supplies CSA   64, 91
Bureau of Ordnance CSA   21, 43–4, 49, 59,
    83, 88, 216

Burgoyne, H.T.   67
Burroughs, John   77, 80–4, 87, 90, 95, 115,
    219
Butcher, Matthew J.   129, 219
Butler, Rhett   1, 3, 5, 36, 73

Caird & Co.   61, 87, 109, 112, 188–9, 200
Cairns, Sir Hugh   150–1
Caledonia   212
Caledonia Railway Co.   167
Caledonian Canal   121, 170
Caledonian Mercury   164
Calypso   179, 191
Campbell, Alexander   162
Campbell, William F.   154
Campbeltown   48
Campbeltown & Glasgow Steam Packet
    Co.   187
Canada   23, 171–2
Cannock & White of Dublin   66
Canton, see *Pampero*
Cape Fear River   51, 57, 61, 84, 96–7, 105,
    169, 187, 202, 210–11, 215
Cape Hatteras   58, 157
Cape Lookout   106
Cape Romain   76
Carlin, James   69, 70, 76, 100, 121, 153,
    165, 191–5, 216
Caroline   70, 100, 192
Carrickfergus   69, 191–4
Carter, Robert E.   153, 155
Cartsdyke shipyard   5, 168, 188, 204
Chancellorville   59
Chanticleer   111, 210
Charleston   3, 6, 10–12, 15, 17, 21–2, 26–7,
    36–7, 40, 42–6, 53–5, 58, 63–5, 69–70,
    74–5, 78, 81–6, 89, 95, 97–8, 105, 107,
    110, 116, 122, 125, 133, 153, 155, 158,
    160, 173, 176–7, 179, 187–208, 210–13,
    216, 220
Charleston Importing & Exporting Co.   89
Charlotte   68, 70, 192
Chase, Salmon P.   43, 218
Chattanooga   60
Chelsea, London   71
Cherbourg   123, 154–5
Cherokee, USS/*Thistle (I)*/*Concepcion*   47,
    53–4, 90, 110, 170, 198, 199, 209
Chicora Importing & Exporting Co.   46, 63,
    200, 204, 210
Chile   6, 99–100, 165, 170, 209–10
China   53, 105, 134, 136–7
City of St Petersburg
    +A510+A760+A685   87, 89, 90, 189
Cloch lighthouse   92, 108, 109
Clyde River Steamer Club   2, 226
Clydesdale Bank   49, 168
Coal   7, 11, 32, 38, 39, 43, 44, 46, 50, 52,
    53, 66, 75, 80, 94, 95, 108, 110, 111, 112,

120, 121, 123, 126, 128, 130, 132, 154, 165–167, 177, 182, 183

Colletis 30

Collie, Alexander 50–62, 65–66, 68, 70, 88, 89, 92, 99, 100, 117, 133, 187, 194, 198, 203, 204, 211, 219

Columbia 43, 75–76, 80, 192, 219

Columbiad cannon 39

Columbian 94, 96, 99

Compound engines 7, 118, 167, 181, 193

Condor 65, 66, 67, 92, 117, 203, 219

Confederate Bonds 44, 49, 60, 61, 64, 81, 84, 85, 88, 90, 91, 93, 94, 97, 99, 133, 134, 149, 164

Confederate flag 3, 5, 22, 27–28, 33, 34, 38, 51, 128, 130

Congress of Paris 13–14

Consett Ironworks 74

Constance Decima/Constance 204

Contraband 14, 18, 23–26, 43, 54, 61, 75–77, 79–81

Co-operative movement 162

Coquette 199

Corbett, Peter 72, 155

Corinth 47

Cork 10, 42, 80, 106, 111, 114, 122, 126, 185, 189, 191, 199, 218

Cork Examiner 62, 225

Cornubia/Lady Davis 47, 52, 73, 76, 77, 78, 79, 80, 81, 82, 83, 86, 100, 120, 219

Cotton trade 1, 6, 10, 11, 20, 21, 23, 36, 37, 42, 47, 51, 58, 60–65, 67, 74, 75, 77–96, 98, 117, 123, 124, 133, 158, 160, 161, 164, 169, 175, 179

Coulborn, Edward R. 197

Coulborn, William 52, 96, 197, 198, 199

Court of Exchequer, Edinburgh 6, 140, 150

Court of Exchequer, London 130, 140, 153

Cowal 159

Coxetter, Louis M. 45, 46, 50, 134, 216

Craven, Tunis A.N. 39, 53, 123, 126, 129, 166, 218

Crenshaw, William G. 59, 61, 62, 88, 89, 190, 211, 214, 216

Crimean War 13, 15, 73, 102, 105, 162, 180, 191

Crinan Canal 28

Crossan, Thomas 61, 189, 217

Cuba 41

Cuba (or Havana) 3, 12, 21, 22, 41, 47, 49, 67–70, 72, 89, 92, 93, 99, 100, 112, 128, 155, 158, 166, 170, 185, 186, 189, 198, 199, 200, 202, 203, 204, 209, 211

Culyer, Reverand 125

Cumbrae islands 48, 92, 108, 109

Cumbrae lighthouse 109

Cunningham, David 113

Currie, Donald 113

Customs 2, 5, 30, 32, 39, 68, 77, 120, 127,

136, 144, 147, 152, 154, 165, 183, 191, 225

Cyclone/Wisconsin 165–166

Dahlgren cannon 39, 105

Danmark, HDMS/North's ram 133–6, 138–41, 147–8, 151, 153

Dare 208

Davis, Jefferson 15, 17, 21, 22, 26, 63, 64, 67, 83, 124, 125,

Davis, Joseph 27

Dayton, William L. 16, 17, 218

De L'Huys, Drouyn 154

Declaration of Neutrality 17, 140

Declaration of Paris 13. 14, 16, 17, 18, 22, 171, 227

Deer 160

Delaware 124

Denbigh 89

Denny, William, Archibald and Peter 43, 47, 70, 72, 74–79, 85, 94, 96, 98, 99, 100, 117, 120, 131–135, 152, 153, 161, 164–168, 183, 191–196, 214, 219, 227

Desalination 32, 118

Deserta island 155

Diamond 197

Dickson, engineer on *Flamingo* 68

Dolphin paddle steamer 47, 173, 201

Dolphin Verne's screw steamer 9–11, 12, 19, 71, 105, 109, 123, 173

Donald, John 162, 164

Donegal 89

Donegal, HMS 156

Douglas, see USS *Gettysburg*

Douglass, Frederick 174

Druid 187

Druid Steamship Company 187

Drumclog flag 164

Du Pont, Samuel 11, 24, 25–27, 37, 40, 41, 218

Dublin 46, 61, 66, 106, 113, 114

Dublin & Belfast Steamship Co. 212

Dublin & Glasgow Sailing & Steam Packet Co. 45, 189, 204, 210

Dudgeon, John & William & Co. 122, 131

Dudley, Thomas H. 30, 126–128, 135, 138, 142, 153, 218

Duffy, James and Mary 159–60

Duguid, James A. 126–127

Dumbarton 37, 64, 72, 94, 133, 134, 152, 153, 165, 167, 168, 191, 194, 214, 219, 223

Dumbarton Herald 64, 134–135, 136, 164, 225

Dumbarton, USS/*Thistle II* 110, 199

Dumfries 113

Dumfries & Galloway Review 225

Dundalk, see *Georgiana McGaw*

Dundee 73, 138, 140, 159

Dunoon 159
Duvernet, Gertrude (Begbie) 71

Eagle/Jeanette 47, 117, 158, 192, 193, 219
Eastman, Edward G. 122, 218
Economist / Bonita 43, 193
Edinburgh 9, 18, 22, 35, 50, 79, 113, 125, 136, 144, 150, 151, 162, 174, 222, 226
Edinburgh Evening Courant 225
Edinburgh Review 35
Egremount Ferry 127
Elder, John 7, 66, 89, 117, 118, 167, 168, 169, 203
Eleuthera Islands 57, 58, 187, 194
Ella 70, 96, 100, 165, 193
Elsie 204
Emancipation societies 4, 6, 125, 137, 143–144, 161–162, 174–175
Emigration 164
Emily 87, 89–90, 102, 187, 219
Emily (II) 70, 193
Emily/Tartar 197
Emily St Pierre 58, 219
Emma (II) 187
Emma Henry 110, 209
Emma, USS/Emma 79, 80, 82, 84, 96, 120, 193, 219
Enfield rifles 3, 30, 36
Engravers 46, 49
Enrica, see CSS *Alabama*
Enterprise (II) 194
Eolus, USS 103
Erlanger Loan 85
Erlanger, Emile 89
European Trading Co. 89
Evelyn 66–7, 99, 117, 203

Fairfield shipyard 117, 203
Fairy 68, 111, 114, 209
Falcon 65, 67, 99, 117–8, 203
Faroe islands 165
Farragut, David G. 10, 12, 41, 69, 93, 163, 218
Fayal, Azores 126
Fergus/Presto 207
Ficklin, Benjamin 49–51, 88, 217
Fife 113
Fingal, see *Atlanta*
Finneston 28, 47, 59, 93, 99, 106, 111, 113, 132, 141, 208
Firth of Clyde 13, 28, 30, 52, 66, 112, 119, 121, 167–8, 208
Firth of Forth 165
Fish, US Secretary 171
Flag, USS 195, 199
Flambeau 109
Flambeau, USS 188
Flamingo 65, 67–8, 70, 89, 99, 117, 120–1, 203

Fleetwood, Lancashire 107
Fleming, Daniel 113
Flora 205
Florence 185
Florida 11, 28, 43, 75, 192, 198, 213,
Florida, CSS/*Oreto* 46, 54, 100, 128, 136, 144–6, 155, 171, 217
Florida, USS 89, 192
Florie 146, 214
Foreign Enlistment Acts (1819) 3, 7, 17, 24–5, 128–9, 137, 140–1, 143, 147, 149–52, 171, 173
Fort Beauregard 55, 57, 105, 116
Fort Caswell 57, 105, 116,
Fort Donelson, USS/*Robert E. Lee/ Giraffe* 47–53, 78, 81, 88, 109, 128, 134, 169–70, 183, 210, 217, 226
Fort Fisher 57, 63, 67–8, 96–7, 104–5, 169, 192, 216
Fort Matilda (Clyde) 48, 111
Fort Monroe 37, 43,
Fort Moultrie 160, 208
Fort Pulaski 11, 34, 36–7
Fort Strong 97
Fort Sumter 15, 21, 41, 55, 69, 105
Fox 189
Fox, Gustavus V. 19,
Fraksey, John 152
France 11, 14, 20, 23, 39, 74, 77, 131, 139–40
Fraquhar, Captain RN 141, 147
Fraser, John & Co. (Charleston) 36, 79
Fraser, Trenholm & Co. (Liverpool) 10, 26, 29, 32, 36, 43, 45, 58, 64, 72, 74, 97, 104–5, 108, 126, 128, 134, 153, 188, 191–3, 195, 202, 204, 216–7
Fry, Joseph 166, 190
Frying Pan Shoals 46, 57
Fuller, F.W. 87, 89
Funchal 50, 53, 110, 155, 166

Galbraith, James 100, 133, 141, 147, 149–50, 152–3, 165, 193, 195, 219
Galveston 3, 12, 21, 47, 64, 67, 70, 91, 98–100, 116–7, 158–9, 185, 189, 193–5, 203–4, 207, 213
Galway Steam Co. 122
Gareloch 28, 48, 74, 80, 108
Garibaldi red shirts 73
Garrison, William L. 174–5
Gayle, Richard N. 84
Gearing 119, 181
Gem 197
General Beauregard, see *Havelock*
Genoa 170
George Square, Glasgow 144–6
Georgia 10–11, 62, 121–2, 135, 146, 186, 195, 197, 206–7, 209, 211, 213, 215
Georgia, CSS 134–7, 153–4, 195, 217

Georgiana 201, 207
Georgiana McCaw/Dundalk 47, 170–1, 202
Gerona (Spanish navy) 166
Gertrude 79–80, 82, 84, 119, 187
Gettysburg 7, 60, 84, 139, 172
Gettysburg, USS/*Douglas/Margaret &
Jessie* 169–70, 202, 206, 211, 214
Giant's Causeway 129
Gibraltar 39, 126, 129–30
Gilles, Robert 113
Gilpin, Thomas S 90, 219
Giraffe, see USS *Fort Donelson*
Girvan 164
Gladiator 43, 163
Gladstone 8, 124–5, 172, 220
Glasgow 2–5, 9–10, 12–13, 27, 28–30, 42,
45–50, 60–4, 70–1, 76, 78, 83, 92–6, 105–14,
118–9, 121–3, 133–8, 140–52, 155, 158–60,
163–5, 168–74, 183, 185–220
Glasgow & Londonderry Steam Packet
Co. 53, 170, 199–200
Glasgow & South Western Railway
Co. 168–70
Glasgow Herald 18, 109–10, 148, 163
Glasgow University 169, 174
Glasgow, USS 93, 205
Goldfinch, HMS 147
Gone with the Wind 1
Gorgas, Josiah 43–4, 59, 83, 88, 117, 216
Gorgas–McRae Contract 117
Govan 28, 47, 59, 93, 99, 106, 110, 112–3,
117–8, 134, 138, 144, 167, 201, 208
Governor Buckingham, USS 47, 204
Granite City/City of Dundee 47, 194,
Grazebrook, William J. 121, 201, 212
Great Captain's Island 6
Great Eastern 10, 135
Great Reform Bill 1834 161
Greece 17
Green Cay 128
Greenhow, Rose 67
Greenock 5, 23, 25, 27, 29–32, 34, 39–40,
42, 47–8, 61, 64, 66, 66–8, 70–3, 76, 79,
83, 87, 92, 94, 96, 101, 108–19, 135–6,
143–4, 147, 152–3, 164–5, 167–8, 178,
188, 200–01, 204, 209, 219
Greenock & Weymss Bay Railway Co. 167
Greenock Advertiser 27, 42, 68, 111
Greenock Telegraph 31, 34, 66, 108, 112,
114–5, 143,
Gregory, Lieutenant RN 147
Grey, Sir George 149
Greyhound 200
Greyhound, HMS 127
Gulf Blockading Squadron 218

Haiti 157
Halifax, Nova Scotia 52, 56, 65, 67, 73, 90,
94–5, 100, 159, 169, 203, 205, 207, 211

Halpin, R.C. 89. 219
Hamilton, Laurence 113
Hampton Roads, Virginia 20
Hansa 97
Harding, Sir John 128–9
Harriet Pinckney 56, 76, 79, 81, 91
Harvey Birch, clipper 38, 123
Hattie 100, 112–3, 189,
Havana, Cuba 3, 12, 21–2, 41, 47, 49, 67–
70, 89, 92–3, 99, 112, 155, 158, 170, 185,
169, 198–200, 202–4, 209, 211
Havelock/General Beauregard 46–7, 63,
209–210
Hawk 96, 98, 187
Haynes, Benjamin 142–3, 148
Heddell, Robert 52
Helen 87, 90–3, 95, 97–9, 159, 219
Helen Denny 200
Helen gunboat 212
Helensburgh 71, 85,
Henderson & Son 52, 198
Henderson, Coulborn & Co. 96, 197, 199
Henderson, Henry 113
Henderson, Patrick & Co. 134, 164–5, 173,
191–2, 195
Herald/Antonica 45–7, 50, 79, 134–5, 204,
216
Hercules harbour defence 153, 165, 194
Hercules Liverpool tug 129
Heyliger, Louis 43–4, 127, 216
High Court of Judiciary, Edinburgh 6,
Hill, Laurence & Co. 53, 198
Hobart-Hampden, Augustus C. 66–7, 92,
219
Hoby & Son 199
Hogue, HMS 147
Hokitita 170
Holyhead (Anglesey) 31–2, 110
House of Commons 12, 16–17, 125, 151
House of Lords 151
House of Representatives (Washington) 24
Howquah, USS 63, 202, 210
Huntsville USS 138, 208
Huse, Caleb 19, 30, 32, 43–4, 49, 56, 59,
61, 63, 72, 75, 217
Hutchison, David & Co. 28, 111, 209–10

Imogene 70, 100, 120, 194
Importing & Exporting Company of
Georgia 62, 122, 186, 195, 197, 201–2,
206–7, 209, 211, 213, 215
Infanta Isabella 69
Ino, USS 130
International Tribunal of Arbitration 7,
171–2
Iona I 78, 111–2, 210
Iona II 113, 210
Irish crewmen 112
Irish Sea 12, 47, 49, 106, 129

Irish Times 54, 66, 118
Ironclads 1, 11, 1920, 70, 75, 171
Iroquois, USS 51
Irrawaddy Flotilla & Steam Navigation
   Co. 166
Isaac, Campbell & Co. 30, 59, 72, 81, 86,
   166
Isle of Man 12–3, 58, 106, 170, 202
Isle of Wight 39, 58
Ivanhoe 91–3, 95, 205

James Adger, USS 52, 84, 207, 210
Jansen, Martin N. 134–5, 217
Japan, see CSS *Georgia*
Johnson, Andrew 163
Johnston, Thomas 113
Julia 114, 206
Juno 109–10, 212
Jupiter 110, 213
Justitia 56
Kames Gunpowder Works 40
Kate 49, 78, 79,
Kearsarge, USS 130, 155
Kelpie 47, 115, 213
Kenilworth 91, 97–8, 177, 205
Kentucky 124
Key West 76, 81
Kilmarnock 113, 152, 164
King Cotton policy 21
Kirkpatrick, McIntyre & Co. 200
Knox, John 52

La Gloire 102, 131
Lady Nyassa 119
Lady Sterling 94, 103
Ladyburn Boiler Works 158
Lafitte, Jean & Co. 97
Lafone, Henry 62, 122, 153, 155, 186, 200,
   204, 206–7, 209, 211, 215, 219
Laing, John 112
Laird, John & Sons 5, 119, 128, 131, 136,
   139–40
Lairds rams 5, 131, 136, 139–50
Lake Erie 52
Lamar, Gazaway B. 62
Lamb, Andrew 89, 92
Lambert, Eugene 113
Lamlash 48, 80, 109, 118
Lancefield Foundry 9, 106, 141, 147, 149
Largs 109, 113, 167, 211–3
Laurel/Confederate States 155, 200, 208
Law of Nations 13, 16
Lawrie, J.G. & Co. 201
Lee, Admiral S.P. 62
Lee, Robert E. 7, 27, 59, 77–8, 96,156,
Leeburg 42, 47
Leith 15, 124
Leopard/Stonewall Jackson 47, 48, 79, 195
Leopard, HMS 53

Leslie, David 73, 75–6, 80, 84, 87, 90, 95,
   99, 120, 159, 219
Let Her Rip/Wando 200
Letters of marque & reprisal 14–15
Lewis, Isle of 28,
Lilian 106, 210, 217, 219
Limerick 66–7, 118, 203
Lincoln, Abraham 6, 15–9, 24, 85, 124,
   137–8, 162–4
Little Ada 6, 169, 206
Little Hattie 6, 100, 211
Liverpool 10, 13, 17, 26, 29–30, 32, 36–7, 43,
   45, 50, 52, 53, 64, 67, 74–5, 80, 86, 89, 93–6,
   98, 100, 104, 106, 110, 114, 121–2, 126–30,
   134–5, 137–40, 144–5, 149, 154–6, 158,
   160, 169, 185, 188, 195, 197–9, 201, 207–8,
   210, 212–3, 216–8, 220
Livingstone, Dr David 119
Livingstone, Hector 113
Lizzie 197
Lomnitz, Edward J. 116, 201, 204, 206,
   214, 219
London 5, 13, 16–8, 23–6, 30–2, 38–9,
   49–50, 53, 56, 59, 71–4, 77, 79, 81, 84,
   88–9, 92, 96, 101, 104, 111, 127–8, 130,
   132–4, 136, 138, 142, 147, 150, 154–5,
   161–3, 166, 170, 172, 186, 210, 217–8
London Illustrated News 39
London Legation US 7, 24, 30, 38, 59, 61,
   81, 127, 141, 163, 172, 218
Lord Clyde/Advance 61, 189
Louisiana 22, 36, 145, 194
Low, John 29, 127, 209
Lumsden, James 94, 168–9, 219
Lynch, Thomas 145
Lyon, Lord Richard 20, 43, 52, 54, 220

Macadam, Alexander 162
Macdonald, Angus 107
Mack 3, 107, 119, 152, 219
Madeira 12, 31, 45, 50, 53, 68, 90, 110,
   155, 166, 208
Madrid 166
Maffitt, John N. 35, 46, 69, 106, 122,
   127–8, 130, 144–6, 155, 21
Magnolia, USS 75, 196
Mail/Susanna 213
Make, George J. 146
Malakoff fortress 105
Mallory, Stephen R. 19, 35–7, 59, 69, 110,
   126, 131, 133–4, 136, 138–9, 148, 153,
   155, 157, 216
Malvern, USS 68, 192
Manchester 50, 52, 59, 61, 74, 89, 95, 113,
   116, 122, 133, 187, 196, 201, 204, 206,
   213–4, 219
Margaret & Jessie, see USS *Gettysburg*
Marine engines cargoes 20, 70, 194
Marmion 91, 176–8

Marshall, Beach & Co. 90
Martin, D.S. 122
Mary & Ella 190
Mary Bowers 206
Maryland 77, 124,
Mason, James 22, 24, 38, 46, 59, 88, 96, 111, 133, 138–9, 147, 217
Matamoros 68, 82
Mathieson, Matthew 208
Mathieson, Neil 110
Matilda 199
Maude Campbell 70, 195
Mauritius 73
Maury, Matthew F. 134–6, 149, 153–4, 195, 216–7
Maury, William L. 135–6, 217
Mavisbank Quay 144
Maxted, captain of the *Thistle* 53
McCallum, John 29
McDougall, Daniel 113
McDuff, Alex 136
McFarlane, James & Co. 149
McGregor, Donald 187, 203–4
McIver, William 113
McKellar, Alexander & Sons 109. 167, 212–4
McKinnon, Alexander 113
McLauchlin, H. 113
McLeash & McNutt 42, 219
McNair, engineer 33, 37, 129
McNair, John 113
McNutt, David 42, 71, 112–3, 190, 196, 201, 207–8, 210, 219
McRae, Colin 61, 63–5, 88–9, 99, 117, 217
Meadowside Dock 9, 49, 109, 212
Mediterreanean 15, 170
Melbourne 155, 170
Melita 72, 86
Melville, Alexander 113
Memminger, Christopher 49, 51, 63, 138, 216–7
Memphis 43, 47, 74–6, 196
Mercedita, USS 26, 75
Merchant Shipping Act 1854 147, 183
Merrimac, CSS 102, 138
Merrimac runner 56
Miller, William 32, 126, 130
Mills, George 121, 212
Millwall 131
Miners 162
Minho 47, 78, 188, 196
Minnie 85, 87, 90–1, 188, 219
Missouri 124
Mitchell, Margaret 1
Mitchell, Robert 145
Mobile 3
Moncreiff, Lord 142
Monitor, USS 102
Monitors 69, 96–7, 131, 132–3, 157

Montgomery, Hugh Earl of Eglinton 138
Montgomery, Matthew 113
Moorson Admeasurement Rule 183
Moran, Benjamin 23, 30–1, 38, 218
Morgan patent paddles 119
Morgan, Edward 127
Morning Journal (Glasgow) 2, 13, 108
Morrison, Malcolm 113
Morse, Freeman H. 154, 218
Mull of Kintyre 28, 48
Murray, Charles 59
Murray, John 144–6
Musson, A.J. 56

Nahant, USS 157
Nansemond, USS 62–3, 202, 211
Napier, Robert & Co. 9, 70, 102, 106, 108, 121, 132, 167, 182, 192–3, 195, 201–2
Napoleon III 11, 99, 139
Nashville, CSS 22–3, 32, 38–9, 58, 123, 126, 217
Nassau, Bahamas 1, 3, 4, 13, 22, 24, 26, 32–3, 41–4, 46–7, 49–50, 53–4, 56, 61, 64, 67, 74–83, 86–8, 96–100, 110–6, 120, 122, 127–30, 146, 153, 159, 176–7, 185, 189–93, 195, 197, 200–3, 206–7, 210–4, 216, 218, 220
Navigation Company of Liverpool 53
Neptune 108, 169, 202
Neutrality 4, 7, 17, 25, 31, 37, 82, 140, 171
New Inlet (Cape Fear River) 51, 57, 59, 62, 68, 97, 104–5, 169, 202–3, 206–7, 210–11
New Orleans 6, 10, 40, 43, 216
New Plan 63, 76, 89–90, 94
New York 10, 26, 28, 38, 43, 47, 51, 72, 76, 81–2, 85, 125, 145, 157, 161, 173–4
New York Herald 10, 56
New York Tribune 10, 62
New Zealand 6, 155, 164–5, 170, 208
New Zealand 170, 208
Newhaven 135
Newmilns Anti-slavery Society 162–4
Niagara, USS 154, 195
Night Hawk 67
Niphon, USS 84
Nola 190
Norfolk Dockyards 105
North Atlantic Blockading Squadron 187, 218
North Carolina 11, 16, 52, 61, 114, 189, 199, 210, 217
North Heath 87, 90, 93, 95, 97, 114–6, 219
North Pacific whalers 155–6
North, James H. 131–4, 138–41, 146–53, 217

Oakhill 158
Octorara, USS 43, 47, 188, 193
Old Inlet (Cape Fear River) 46, 68, 70, 116, 190, 192–3, 202, 204, 214

Oreto, see CSS *Florida*
Orion/Fanny 190
Orkney 165
Osborne House 39
Oscillating engines 48, 70, 78, 106, 181, 187, 189, 192–3, 195, 199–200, 202, 208, 210–11, 213
Otago Shipping Co. 164–5
Ouachita 74, 76, 78
Owl 69, 116, 122, 217

P&O Shipping Co. 94, 99
Paddon, E.S. 73, 80, 101
Paisley 123, 161, 188
Palmerston, Lord Henry T. 7, 11, 17, 23, 37, 125, 139,40, 220
Pamlico Sound 11
Pampero/Canton/Tornado 134, 138–53, 163, 165, 209, 217
Paris 16–7, 81, 86–7, 89, 94, 139, 142, 147–8, 154, 217–8
Parrott cannon 105–6
Partick, Glasgow 109, 207, 212
Paterson, Adam 142
Paton, Andrew 143
Pea Ridge 158
Pearl 47, 111, 198
Pegram, Robert 32, 38–9, 123, 126, 217
Pembroke, Edward 50, 133, 141, 192, 210, 217
Penno, A.W. 56
Pensacola 11
Perkins, George 113
Peterhoff 82
Phaeton, HMS 39
Pheobe 196
Philadelphia 19, 58, 124, 157
Pig Islands, British Columbia 171
Pinchon, W.O. 63
Playfair, James 9–12, 73
Playfair, Vincent 9–12, 71,
Pollaky, Ignatius 30
Pollock, Matthew 162
Poor Relief 159–60
Port Glasgow 45, 53, 64, 158, 198, 200, 204
Port Royal Sound 11
Porter, David D. 97, 169, 218
Portugal 195
Postage stamps 26
Power, Low & Co. 189, 207
Powhatten, USS 55
Prettyman, John S. 29–30, 42, 50, 76, 135, 138–9, 141–2, 218
Prince Albert 23
Prince Albert schooner 128
Prince Albert steamer 196
Princes Pier, Greenock 167
Princess Royal 47, 55, 105, 173, 213
Prioleau, Charles K. 45, 72, 104, 126, 217

Privateers 14–17, 22–3, 32, 38, 96, 123, 165, 171, 197
Procurator Fiscals 141, 143, 146, 148
Ptarmigan 67, 99, 117, 203
Puerto Rico 50, 173, 201
Punch 38

Quaker City, USS 55, 138, 204, 208
Queen of the Wave 47
Queen's Hotel, Glasgow 146, 152, 174
Queenstown (Cork) 10, 42, 114

Raison, Captain of *Gertrude* 80, 84, 89, 177
Raleigh, CSS 97, 169, 206
Ram see *Danmark*
Randolph, Elder & Co. 7, 66, 89, 117, 118, 167, 168, 169, 203
Ranger 47
Rappahannock, CSS 154
Rathlin island 129
Reed, George 113
Reid, John & Co. 204
Renfrew 6, 52, 64, 96, 101–2, 112, 113, 152, 167, 197, 199, 206
Reparations 7, 172
Rhode Island, USS 57, 218
Riach, John 113
Richards, Thomas 113
Richmond 17, 20, 35–6, 44, 50, 59, 64, 113, 133, 138, 153, 156, 208, 210, 216
Richmond Inquirer 10
Rio de Janerio 100, 165, 170, 195, 203, 211
Rio Grande, Texas 20, 82
River Clyde 9, 13, 27, 107, 141, 146, 173
Robert E. Lee, see USS *Fort Donelson*
Roberts, A., see Hobart-Hampden
Robson, William 113
Rodgers, John 157
Rodman cannon 105
Roe/Agnes E. Fry 190
Rooney, James 113
Rosin 36–7, 42, 126
Ross, James 141
Rothesay 52, 108, 115, 117, 213–4
Rothesay Castle 100, 207
Ruby (I) 47, 52–3, 108, 198
Ruby (II) 198
Russell, Lord John 16–7, 20, 22, 24–5, 31, 38, 39, 56, 109, 127–30, 136–7, 140–3, 149, 151–2, 172, 220
Russell, W., captain of the *Marmion* 176–8
Russians 15, 20, 105, 132, 151, 171

Saltpetre 23, 40
San Jacinto, USS 22, 38, 46, 218
Sanford, Henry S 29, 40, 129, 218
Santiago de Cuba, USS 75, 187, 189
Savannah 10–11, 17, 26–8, 32–8, 41, 74, 97, 122, 125–6, 156–7, 170, 209, 212

Savannah, CSS 17
Schenck, US Minister in London 172
Schleswig-Holstein War 139, 151
Scotch boiler 167
Scotia 77
Scotia/Fanny & Jenny/General Banks 213
Scotsman (Edinburgh) 9, 12–3, 18, 21, 23, 39, 53–4, 56, 124–5, 148, 158, 162, 166
Scott, John 5, 23, 25, 72–98, 101–2, 109, 111, 117–20, 123, 125, 131–3, 137, 151, 161, 167–8, 178, 187, 204, 209, 218, 219, 221
Scott, Sir Walter 91
Sea King, see CSS *Shenandoah*
Seddon, James A 50–1, 59–61, 63, 83, 85, 216
Semmes, Raphael 130, 217
Sevilla 164
Seward, William H. 16, 21, 23–5, 30–1, 41–3, 50, 52, 54, 60, 118, 138–41, 163, 218
Shannon, HMS 123
Shenandoah, CSS 155–6, 165, 171–200, 208, 217
Shenandoah, USS 106
Shetland 165
Shiloh 36
Shipping Register 29, 70, 113
Siccardi 32
Simons, William & Co. 6, 101, 112, 206
Simpson, Robert 133
Sinclair, George T. 37, 133–4, 138–142, 146–9, 152, 165, 209, 217
Sirius/Alice 41, 190–191
Skelmorlie 158–9
Slaves 6, 15, 21–2, 100, 124–5, 135, 137, 157, 161–2, 174–5, 197
Slidell, John 22–4, 38, 46, 59, 94, 96, 139, 142, 148, 151, 217
Smeal, William 143
Smith, captain of the *Sue* 42
Smith, Dr James McC. 174
Smith, Fleming & Co. 133
Smithville 57
Sonoma, USS 46, 81
South Atlantic Blockading Squadron 196
South Carolina 11, 16, 21, 27, 42, 58, 62, 69, 100, 121, 135, 144, 179, 190–5, 206–7, 212, 216
South Carolina, USS 122
Southampton 22, 38–9, 58, 94, 123, 126, 129
Spain 99, 166
Springbok 26, 79, 81–2
Sprunt, James 89, 105, 114–6, 122, 146, 170, 219
Spunkie 115–6, 214
St Johns, New Brunswick 76, 113
St Petersburg 20,

St Petersburg Steam Navigation Co. 190
St George, Bermuda 1, 3, 4, 13, 32, 44–5, 56, 81, 90–1, 115, 129
St Nazare, France 82
St Thomas, West Indies 49, 53, 57, 72, 82, 132, 173, 201
Stag/Kate Gregg 48, 95, 196
Stair, Lord 14
Star 110, 214
Steel hulls 35, 122, 159, 185, 189
Stevenson, James 113
Stone fleet 21
Stormy Petrel 207
Stornoway 28–9, 112, 157
Stranraer 212, 214
Stringer, Edwin P. 192
Submarines 69
Sue 42
Suez Canal 167
Sumter, CSS 23, 39, 123, 126, 128, 130, 154, 217
Surface condensers 118–9
Susan O'Beirne 100, 122, 185, 219
Syren 89

Tait, clothier of Limerick 66
Talisman 91, 95, 97, 206
Tartar 197
Tate, Captain of *Herald* 44–45
Taylor, Thomas E. 45, 112, 134, 145, 159, 217
Terceirca (Azores) 32, 130
Texas 12, 16, 20, 41, 98, 194
Theodora, CSS 22, 43, 45
Thistle (I), see USS *Cherokee*
Thistle (II), see USS *Dumbarton*
Thomson, James & George 28, 47, 59, 93, 99, 106, 111, 113, 130, 132–4, 138–9, 141–4, 147–9, 150–1, 157, 169, 196, 208–9
Thunderbolt battery 37
Tientsin, see *Adventure*
Tilt, N & T 156
Times (London) 49, 110, 173
Tioga, USS 46, 194, 198
Tod & McGregor 9, 49, 105, 109, 115, 119, 121, 173, 187, 212–4
Tontine Coffee House, Glasgow 10
Tornado, see *Pampero*
Torpedoes (Mines) 69, 156
Toxteth Docks, Liverpool 136
Treasury Department CSA 26, 46, 49, 51, 64, 201, 216
Tredegar Ironworks 199
Trenchard, Stephen D. 10, 26, 29, 32, 36, 43, 45, 58, 64, 72, 74, 97, 104–5, 108, 126, 128, 134, 153, 188, 191, 192–4, 195, 202, 204, 216–7
Trenholm, George A. 3, 26, 169, 216

Trent Incident 22–4, 26, 38–9, 57, 73, 123–4, 217–8
Tristram Shandy 68, 169, 186, 212
Troon 167
Tubal Cain 43, 47, 188
Tuscarora, USS 19, 39, 53, 58, 123, 126, 129–30, 166, 218
Tybee island 37, 122

Underwood, Warner L 60, 65, 118, 135, 142–8, 163, 218
Universal Trading Company 5, 93–9, 168, 178, 205–6, 218
Ushant Islands 135, 137, 195

Valparaiso 166, 170
Vance, Zebulon B. 61, 63
Vanderbilt, USS 81, 84, 188
Venus 59, 62, 62–3, 211
Verne, Jules 9–11, 71, 173,
Vicksburg 60. 84, 139
Victor, HMS, see CSS *Rappahannock*
Victoria Docks, London 74, 98
Victoria harbour, Glasgow 27,
Victoria, USS 202
Virgin 166–7, 186
Virginia 7, 16, 20, 22, 35, 60, 78, 96, 134–5, 145, 156, 160, 216–7
Virginia Importing & Exporting Co. 189, 195
Virginia Volunteer Navy 96, 197
Virginian, see *Georgia*
Virginius see *Virgin*
Vulcan Foundry 106
Vulture 186

Wabash, USS 24
Waddell, James I 155–6, 217
Walker, Norman S 44, 83, 216
Wantage House, Kensington 71
War Department CSA 36, 51, 59, 83
War of 1812 15, 25
Warrior, HMS 102, 132
Warrior test 131–2
Washington 6, 15, 17, 20, 22–4, 26, 28, 31, 37, 40, 43, 58, 60, 67, 122, 124, 138, 151, 163, 171, 220
Washington (of Glasgow) 27

Wassaw Sound 33–4, 36–7, 157, 170, 209, 213
Watson, James 113
Watson, William 3, 47, 117, 158–9, 219
Wave Queen 47
Wave theory 109
Webb, captain of CSS *Atlanta* 157
Weehawken, USS 157, 209
Welles, Gideon 16, 18–19, 24, 56–7, 75–6, 155, 218
Wemyss Bay 167
West Hartlepool 10, 119
Whale House magazine 56
Wharton, Fred H. 113
White, John 61
Whiteinch 64, 146, 201, 214
Whiting, Samuel 127, 218
Whitworth cannon 26, 104–5, 135
Wigg, George 53, 110, 193, 198–9, 210, 212, 220
Wild Rover 100, 178, 211, 222
Wilkes, Charles 22–4, 38, 46, 53, 57, 124, 218
Wilkinson, John 49–52, 88, 128, 134, 160, 222
Will o' the Wisp 112, 144, 207, 222
Wilmington 3, 6, 12, 37, 40, 44, 47, 49, 51–2, 55, 57, 61–4, 67–70, 80, 82, 84–91, 93–8, 103, 105–6, 110, 114–6, 122, 133, 146, 158–9, 169–70, 185–94, 199–212, 214–5
Wilmington History & Literary Society 170–1
Wilson, Archibald 210
Wilson, William 58
Windsor Castle 108
Wingate, T. & Co. 146, 214–5
Wisconsin, see *Cyclone*
Wisemans 71, 85
Wood & Reid (J. Reid & Co.) 45, 204
Wright, Richard 155
Wrightsville Beach 89, 187
Wyllie, Joannes 160
Wyoming, USS 156

Yangtze, see *Enterprise*
Yarmouth 165
Yellow fever 69, 95, 128, 144

Zollinger, Andreas & Co. 74, 196